Comparative
Management

ADMINISTRATION SERIES

Eugene E. Jennings, *Editor*

Comparative Management

Anant R. Negandhi
Kent State University

S. Benjamin Prasad
Ohio University

Appleton-Century-Crofts

Educational Division

New York   Meredith Corporation

To Our Wives,
Erny and Rosemary

HD
70
. I 4 N43
1971

PREFACE

This book reports the findings of a comparative study of selected aspects of business management in Argentina, Brazil, India, the Philippines, and Uruguay. The depth of inquiry and the scope of analysis were greatest in the case of India.

Modern organization theory provided the broad framework within which the field study was conducted. The research design was based substantially upon a scheme developed by A. R. Negandhi. Some aspects of this model, particularly the units of comparison and measurements of the dependent variable, underwent modifications in the course of the pilot study as well as in the field work stages.

A great deal of progress has been made in the systematic study of management since the days of Frederick Taylor and Henri Fayol. The human relations, the behavioral, and the sociotechnical systemic approaches represent major milestones in this progress. Many management myths have been discarded and new insights have been incorporated into the management literature. In addition, the number of possible approaches to the study of organizations and their management, and the number of bases of observation, have been vastly increased in the last decade.

The 5 countries which we selected for the purpose of field inquiry are not very advanced industrially. Despite the limitations, we feel that there is merit, both from theoretical and practical points of view, in undertaking cross-national comparative studies of management.

From the theoretical point of view, comparative studies such as the one reported here provide empirical data and analyses based upon such data which, crude though they may be, are likely to further our understanding of the management problems of other countries. Furthermore, they are likely to provide many avenues for concept refining, hypothesis testing, and theory building.

Pragmatically speaking, adaptive approaches can be developed which will fill the vacuum created by the lack of systematic studies of the

v

relevance and applicability of modern management concepts, tools, techniques, and ideologies—which have evolved in the Western countries and contributed immensely to their economic progress—to the less developed countries. Without the adaptive application of modern management methods, productive endeavors in developing countries are likely to fall short of expectations.

The title of this volume, *Comparative Management*, is intended to be expressive of the approach we have taken and the analyses we have made. The objectives of our study are reported in this volume:

(1) to document the nature of management processes and practices in the foreign subsidiaries and the local companies;

(2) to delineate the similarities and differences between these 2 sets of companies at the intracountry and international levels;

(3) to examine the relationships between management philosophy, management processes, and management effectiveness; and

(4) to shed light on cross-national research potential in the realm of management, viewing management as an important element in the process of industrial development.

In operationalizing management philosophy, which is employed in our scheme as the independent variable, we recognize that there could be several forces responsible for creating a given management philosophy, ideology, or set of values, but historical inquiry was beyond the aim of our study. We set out to operationally classify three types of management philosophy (most progressive, somewhat progressive, and least progressive) and then proceeded to analyze the data we had obtained from the companies.

In operationalizing management effectiveness, we differentiated it from enterprise effectiveness. Enterprise effectiveness is commonly measured in economic terms, whereas we have attempted to measure management effectiveness in human resource terms. The reader should not be misled, however, into believing that one is more important than the other or that an organization can pursue one without regard to the other. In point of fact, management effectiveness and enterprise effectiveness are like two sides of a coin. Our background, training, and research interests impelled us to concentrate on one rather than the other. Thus, one of our initial premises is that organizations are technoeconomic as well as social systems; enterprise effectiveness has to do with the technoeconomic system, while management effectiveness is related to the social system of any organization.

Organization of the Book

This book is divided into four parts. In Part One, Chapters 1 and 2, we elaborate on the notion of Comparative Management as a discipline and a research method, and try to point out its usefulness in building organization theory. Citing a selected number of comparative studies, we proceed to examine briefly the pioneering international studies of Harbison and Myers, and of Farmer and Richman. A discussion of interaction between the societal environments and management follows.

In Chapter 2 we present our own revised and enlarged conceptual scheme, upon which this study was based. Here we set forth the details of our study (sample, size, type of companies, the nature of variables investigated, and their operational definitions), and its limitations.

In Part Two, we present comparative analyses of management processes and practices at two levels, namely, the intracountry and the international. We focus upon long-range planning, organization building, leadership, and control systems since these aspects of managing are crucial in organizations in general.

In Chapter 3, we touch upon the meaning and growing importance of long-range planning and comparatively analyze 4 elements of long-range planning: nature and scope, length or horizon, resulting plans, and review of plans.

Organization building is the subject matter of Chapter 4. Data pertaining to personnel policies, modes of selection and development, and reward systems are examined.

Chapter 5 combines some elements of policy making, leadership, and motivation and examines these on comparative bases.

Construing controlling as a process and control systems as the outcome of this process, we analyze a limited number of control instruments in Chapter 6.

Comparative analyses of management effectiveness at the worker level and the level of managers are undertaken in Part Three. The concept of management effectiveness is elusive. Many equate management effectiveness with organizational effectiveness. Some have employed such measures as sales, profits, stock prices, market shares, and other economic criteria. Some modern organization theorists have suggested that a firm's management effectiveness be evaluated on the basis of its effectiveness in human resource management. Suggested measures include worker morale, satisfaction, and other behavioral criteria. Some writers have combined the economic and behavioral measures.

Taking into account the economic contexts of the 5 developing countries (Argentina, Brazil, India, the Philippines, and Uruguay), we have separated management effectiveness from organizational effectiveness. To us, "management effectiveness" is a dependent variable whereas "organizational or enterprise effectiveness" is an end-result variable.

Thus, in Chapter 7, we examine management effectiveness in terms of worker morale, interpersonal relationships, turnover, and absenteeism, and in Chapter 8 we examine management effectiveness vis-a-vis the utilization of managerial resources—a scarce factor in developing nations.

In the final part, Part Four, we first summarize the main findings of this study, then outline the implications of these findings for comparative management and management discipline in general (Chapter 9). In analyzing the implications of the study, we have concentrated on two topics: (1) over-emphasis on environmental and cultural variables in cross-cultural studies, and (2) the lack of concern among management scholars with various ideas, concepts, and so-called principles as subvariables in the conceptual schemes.

In Chapter 10, as an attempt toward theory building, we set forth tentative propositions based on our findings. The findings of this study are reported in statistical frequency form in the main text. However, in Appendix A attempts have been made to analyze the relationship between major variables in a rigorous statistical manner; interested readers are urged to refer to this appendix.

Details of the measurement of management philosophy are provided in Appendix B. Statistical and economic data on the 5 countries where field studies were undertaken are given in Appendix C. Our initial thoughts on the problem of transmitting advanced management know-how to developing countries are reproduced in Appendix D.

A volume such as this is exploratory, monographic, and seldom conclusive. The sources of ideas and data are varied. Before acknowledging the help and support of other individuals, we would like to say something about the division of labor in the preparation of this book. The primary responsibility for designing the study and directing the field studies fell to A. R. Negandhi, who also holds primary responsibility for the material in Chapters 2, 7, 8, 9, and 10. In addition to making modest refinements in the scheme, S. B. Prasad was largely responsible for the material in Chapters 1, 3, 4, 5, and 6. We are jointly responsible, however, for omissions and for errors of thought.

Acknowledgments

The project on which this volume is based was initially funded by the Ford Foundation Program in International and Comparative Studies at U.C.L.A. The Chancellor's Committee on International and Comparative Studies provided a financial grant to Anant R. Negandhi without which this field work in five countries would not have been possible.

We noted earlier that the depth of inquiry in India was greater than that in Argentina, Brazil, the Philippines, and Uruguay. This was because Negandhi spent more than seven months in India during 1966–1967 and 1968, collecting the data from the 34 companies located in India. Supportive field work, under the direction of Negandhi, was done by Dr. Filmon Flores in the Philippines, by Mr. Gabriel Rozman in Argentina, Brazil, and Uruguay, and by Dr. Krishna Shetty in India. A short trip to India by S. B. Prasad in the early part of 1969, funded by a research grant from the Division of Research of the College of Business of Ohio University, provided additional insights into the management processes in the U.S. subsidiaries and in the national companies located in and around Bombay. We owe special thanks to Messrs. Flores, Rozman and Shetty for obtaining the data we needed for comparative purposes, as well as for their individual dissertation-related research.

Two former research associates of Negandhi, Drs. B. D. Estafen and A. J. Papageorge, contributed greatly in the initial phases of the research project. During the later stages, Messrs. M. L. Shardana (U.C.L.A.), W. L. Benford, and Ajit Nain (Kent State) helped us with library research. To them, we owe our gratitude. Our sincere thanks are due to Mr. Surendra Mansinker, Ph.D. candidate at U.C.L.A., for his help in computer work; and to Mr. Bernard C. Reimann, doctoral student at Kent State University, for his assistance in statistical work.

Much of the work involved in the preparation of the manuscript was supported in various ways by our present institutions, namely, the College of Business Administration at Kent State, and Ohio University. In particular, the Center for Business and Economic Research at Kent State, and the Division of Research at Ohio provided varied support.

While we, as authors, are responsible for the merits and the demerits of this book, others have indirectly enhanced the merits by means of suggestions, criticims, and clarifications. Those at Kent State to whom we are indebted include Dr. Bernard Hall, former Dean of the College of Business Administration and now Vice-President and Provost, and Dr. Gail E. Mullin, Dean of the College of Business Administration. Professors John T. Doutt, Arlyn Melcher, and the late James Young, as well as Miss Diana Phesey from the University of Aston (England) deserve special citation. We are also grateful to the following at Ohio University: Professors Richard French and Paul Hersey, and Deans Harry Evarts and William Day.

All refinements in both the organization and presentation of the contents of this book are owing to the constructive and detailed criticisms of Professors Eugene E. Jennings and Dalton McFarland, both of the Graduate School of Business, Michigan State University.

Thoughts and notes are transformed into drafts of chapters, and these, in turn, invariably undergo changes and modifications. Several people were involved in this process of converting notes to readable pages, through typing, retyping, and editing. They were Mary Bacon, Janice Baughard, Virginia Browne, Anita Bechstein, and Frances Yurgen. We are grateful to all of them. Special acknowledgement is due to Mrs. Barbara Fisher for her initial editorial help.

Another group of individuals, no less crucial to the research project but who, of obvious necessity, must remain anonymous, are the many senior executives, managers, supervisors, and workers who provided us with the information we sought. Except in a few cases, their cooperation was extensive and wholehearted. We can only thank them by saying that we are deeply indebted to them for their willingness to share their thoughts and views with us.

Last, but not least, our wives Erny and Rosemary deserve our gratitude for sharing with us our ups and downs, our moods, and our preoccupation with this volume during the past two and a half years. We express our appreciation by dedicating this book to them.

A. R. N.
S. B. P.

CONTENTS

xi

FIGURES

TABLES

xv

xviii   *Tables*

ONE

THEORETICAL AND METHODOLOGICAL DIMENSIONS

1

INTRODUCTION

The management discipline is clouded by controversies over the application of ideas and concepts as subvariables in empirical investigation. Opposing philosophies have brought to bear inconsistencies that inhibit the empirical researcher in his use of subvariables to establish the influence of socioeconomic, political, legal, and cultural factors. In addition, few systematic attempts have been made to ascertain the impact of these factors on management practices and their effectiveness in industrial firms in underdeveloped countries. Much has been said and written on the importance of management in industrial and economic development. The absence, however, of adequate empirical data becomes more evident with each passing day.

In recent years the industrialization and economic development of underdeveloped countries in Africa, Asia, and Latin America has received considerable attention from scholars and statesmen alike. The degree and intensity of developmental dialogue have increased enormously since World War II. As a result, a great deal of recognition has been given to the premise that industrialization and economic development are a function not only of capital inputs but also, more importantly, of the managerial inputs. Huge capital investments have been made in underdeveloped nations, primarily through economic aid from the United States and other Western countries. The failure of these investments to generate satisfactory industrial and economic growth lend support to this premise.

Our research took place in Argentina, Brazil, the Philippines,

3

India, and Uruguay. We studied the management practices and effectiveness of 92 industrial firms within those 5 underdeveloped countries. Of these, 47 were American subsidiaries and 45 were local firms comparable to those subsidiaries. Comparability was established on the basis of industry, technology, market conditions, and size of work force. Our goal was the specific exploration of the following questions:

(1) What is the nature of management practices of industrial firms in these countries?
(2) How, in their practices and effectiveness, do the local firms compare with the American subsidiaries in those countries?
(3) What are the specific environmental and cultural factors affecting the American subsidiaries abroad, and how do they adjust to what appear to be different environmental and cultural variables?
(4) How do the American subsidiaries establish their "superiority" over local firms in underdeveloped countries?
(5) What are the environmental and cultural factors impeding the introduction of advanced management practices and know-how into underdeveloped countries?

We do not pretend to have found complete answers to all of these questions. We did, nevertheless, make a systematic attempt to inquire into these problems, in hopes that our findings would shed some light on existing difficulties. This research was undertaken within the context of modern organization theory; as subvariables, we have utilized the functional classification of the neoprocess school as well as behavioral concepts.

Research into actual managerial practices on a cross-national basis has been identified lately as the discipline of comparative management, which brings us to these questions: *What is comparative management? Is it useful as a research method? Does it have theoretical utility? Does it have practical usefulness?*

WHAT IS COMPARATIVE MANAGEMENT?

Comparative management may best be described as the study of the management phenomenon on a comparative basis. As a discipline, albeit one of recent vintage, it can be thought of as a cross-national subject matter. As a research method, its role is to detect, identify, classify, measure, and interpret similarities and differences among the phenomena being compared. The phenomenon could be the management process, managerial thinking, managerial techniques, or, for that matter, educational institutions, value systems, or any other observable phenomenon. The purpose of undertaking comparisons of the management, as we see it, is twofold: one, to examine hypotheses in a broader international context; two, to examine the pros and cons of transmitting one or more aspects to a different cultural or national context. Both of these assume that "management," however defined—as, for example, a process, a system of authority, a set of tools and techniques, a philosophy, an allocating mechanism, or leadership—interacts organizationally, nationally, and sometimes internationally.

Is It Useful as a Research Method?

We think so. Earlier we noted that the various managerial and organizational approaches pertained either to the U.S. context or to the context of advanced countries in Western Europe. If one were to examine these approaches, one could delineate such foci as behavioral, quantitative, managerial process, ecological, and systemic. As a research method, comparative management is perhaps closer to the ecological than to any other foci; nothing, however, precludes the incorporation of the concepts which are predominant in any of the other approaches. In this study, we have employed the behavioral concepts of management, as well as some of the traditional concepts.

As a research method, comparative management entails systematic and meaningful comparisons, as well as comparisons across national boundaries. Just what is a comparison is a question which is likely to generate a variety of responses. One can simplify the variety by saying that, in the final analysis, all studies are comparative. However, comparative management, when thought of as a research method in cross-cultural situations, cannot simply be dismissed as such. Comparison is a basic methodological concept, not merely a convenient term vaguely symbolizing the focus of one's research interest.

Since comparative management is still in its infancy, one could

underscore its usefulness by drawing from other social sciences.[1]
First of all, findings emanating from comparative studies are likely
to enhance proper understanding of management elsewhere. The increasing interdependence of nations, the flow of capital, technology,
and ideas from one country to the other, and a constant search for
better methods in most productive endeavors add to the importance
of a proper understanding of management in a world context.
Speaking from a public administration point of view, Heady has remarked that "The success of Congo or Indonesia organizing for administrative action is no longer just a matter of intellectual curiosity;
it is of immense practical significance in Washington, Moscow, and
London, not to mention Manila, Cairo and Peking."[2] Writing with
particular reference to organizational structures in formal organizations, Evan has pointed to the need for cross-cultural comparative
studies in these words: "A major qualifying variable affecting the
impact of organizational hierarchy is the social and cultural structures of the society in which the organizations in question are embedded. . . . This suggests the need for cross-cultural research."[3]

The main value of the comparative approach is eloquently
underscored in a statement by Kendell, made more than 35 years
ago in reference to the value of comparative studies in education:
"The chief value of a comparative approach to such [educational]
problems lies in an analysis of ·the causes which have produced
them, in a comparison of the differences between the various systems and the reasons underlying them, and finally in a study of the
solutions attempted."[4] Thus increased understanding of different so-

---

[1] For an excellent summary of the role of the comparative studies, see
S. H. Udy, "The Comparative Analysis of Organizations," in J. G. March (ed.),
Handbook of Organizations (Chicago: Rand McNally and Co., 1965); Reinhard
Bendix, "Concepts and Generalizations in Comparative Sociological Studies,"
American Sociological Review, Vol. 28, August 4, 1963, pp. 532–539; and J.
Boddewyn, "The Comparative Approach to the Study of Business Administra-
tion," *Academy of Management Journal*, Vol. 8, No. 4 (December 1965), pp.
261–267. For a discussion of comparative method in administrative studies see
S. B. Prasad, *Directions of Research in Administrative Science* (Athens: Divi-
sion of Research, Ohio University, 1968).

[2] Farrel Heady, *Public Administration: A Comparative Perspective*
(Englewood Cliffs, N.J.: Prentice-Hall, Inc., 1966), p. 4.

[3] William M. Evan, "Indices of the Hierarchical Structures of Industrial
Organizations," *Management Science*, Vol. 9, No. 3 (April 1963).

[4] Quoted from *Comparative Education Review*, Vol. 9, No. 3 (October
1965), p. 257.

cieties, and analysis of the causes which underlie different situations therein, constitute part of the usefulness of cross-national comparative studies. In addition, one can also add the notion of concept development and refinement. As Bendix suggested, "To be analytically useful, universal concepts [in sociology] require specifications which will help us bridge the gap between concept and empirical evidence."[5] Substituting the word management in the brackets would make sense, too.

Does It Have Theoretical Utility?

More than a decade ago, Simon suggested the prerequisites for a sound approach to developing administrative theory: "Before a science can develop principles, it must possess concepts. The first task of administrative theory is to develop a set of concepts that will permit description . . . of administrative situations."[6]

By theory we mean something which is applicable to a number of contexts or situations rather than to all, or just one, of them. Thus, theories of management and theories of organization must possess concepts which have a wider applicability; this can be accomplished only by widening the context of the studies. In other words, a considerable amount of field work in various cultural and social settings needs to be undertaken before one can meaningfully refine the existing concepts.

During the last decade or so, the loose threads of theorizing about business and other formal organizations have been woven into perceptible patterns. The theorizing has also become more sophisticated and has received valuable contributions from the social and behavioral sciences. What is this logic of theorizing? We tend to believe that theorizing ought to be more than explaining and predicting. That is to say, logic lies in impelling appropriate action in the present in order to influence the future. New hypotheses emanating from comparative management studies might thus produce appropriate managerial action in managerial contexts irrespective of the country in question.

[5] Reinhard Bendix, *op. cit.*, 1963.
[6] Herbert A. Simon, *Administrative Behavior* (New York: The Macmillan Company, 1961), p. 37.

Does It Have Practical Usefulness?

The answer is definitely yes. Very briefly put, such studies are likely to minimize the impediments to the introduction of advancement management know-how in developing countries.

While the foregoing analysis may be construed as some justification for engaging in comparative cross-national management studies, one might ask: What has been done thus far? Have not there been comparative studies? Are there not comparative models?

Table 1-1   Some Comparative Management Studies

Year	Researcher(s)	Phenomenon compared
1955	F. Harbison, et al.	Management organization in 2 steel works located in the U.S. and West Germany
1956	R. Stewart & Duncan Jones	Background/career of British and American managers
1959	J. Berliner	Managerial behavior and decision-making in the U.S. and the U.S.S.R.
1960	Harbison & Myers, et al.	Management as resource, authority system, and class in twelve countries
1961	J. E. Humblot	Managers' characteristics and influence in Belgium, France, and the United Kingdom
1962	D. Granick	Management style in five European countries
1964	O. Nowotny	Management philosophy in the U.S. and W. Europe
1964	E. McCann	Management philosophy and decision-making in the U.S. and Latin American countries
1966	M. Haire, et al.	Managerial thinking and cognitive patterns in the role of managers in 14 countries
1966	J. Dunning	Managerial performance in British and American companies operating in U.K.
1967	D. Clark & T. Mosson	Characteristics of managers in Belgium, France, and U.K.
1968	James A. Lee	Value orientations of managers in Ethiopia, Pakistan, and the U.S.

See Bibliography at end of this chapter for details of sources.

There are some studies and there are two models which we consider comparative management models. In Table 1-1, we have arranged twelve comparative studies chronologically, identifying the aspects of management that were compared. This is by no means a comprehensive list, but merely an illustrative one.

An examination of Table 1-1 suggests that there have been some comparative studies in management and that comparisons have been made with respect to certain aspects such as the managers' backgrounds, definition and role of managers, managerial organization and style, management decision making, managerial performance, and managerial philosophy.

There are two models or approaches that can be regarded as comparative management models. One is the Harbison-Myers approach,[7] the other is the Farmer-Richman model.[8]

The Harbison-Myers Approach

Their purpose was to trace the logic of management development as it related to the process of industrial growth. Their concern was more with the dynamics of development and the basic trends of managerial growth than with an analysis of particular practices at any point in time. In their words, "We have concentrated on the processes of evolution of management and the forces which are likely to mold its future development."[9]

They provided a typology of management by identifying it as an economic resource, as a system of authority, and as a class or elite. Their study was an international analysis of management among 12 countries. Their approach is comparative to the extent that they do make international comparisons—of managers as well as the problems and prospects of generating them; of the management structure which manifests a particular system of authority as well as the forces which brought about such a system and those which tend to modify it; and, finally, of the nature of the managerial

[7] Frederick Harbison and Charles Myers, *Management in the Industrial World* (New York: McGraw-Hill Book Company, 1959).

[8] Richard Farmer and Barry Richman, "A Model for Research in Comparative Management," *California Management Review*, Vol. 4, No. 2 (Winter 1964), pp. 55–68.

[9] Harbison and Myers, *op. cit.*

elite and the inevitability of its becoming more professionally oriented as industrialization advances.

If we accept that management is made up of at least three components—the people (managers and others), the framework (authority structure and the organizational environment), and actions, or the things which managers have to do in executing their roles (management process)—then the Harbison-Myers international analysis deals only with the first two of these. We are not suggesting that this is a weakness of their model, but simply pointing to the focus of their model. Somewhat in contrast to the pioneering approach of Harbison and Myers is the scheme of Farmer and Richman.

The Farmer-Richman Model

As the authors expressed it, the purpose of their model was to "develop a new conceptual framework for comparative studies which will prove more useful in the analysis of critical comparative management problems."[10]

They employ four key concepts: *comparative management problems*—"the question of relative managerial efficiency among cultures"; *internal management*—coordination of human effort and material resources toward the achievement of organizational objectives; *external constraints*—the external environment, which they termed macromanagerial structure, and external constraints classified as economic, legal-political, sociological, and educational; and *managerial efficiency*—degree of efficiency with which members of productive enterprises achieve their stated goals.

The variables in this scheme are aggregate variables. The independent variables are the external constraints and they employ a numerical ranking scheme to quantify the numerous elements subsumed under each of the four classifications.

The cardinal concern of this model is perhaps twofold: one, to establish a functional relationship between aggregate managerial efficiency in a country and a set of selected numbers of aggregate variables, and two, to present this relationship in a manner which would pinpoint the problem areas for inquiry.

[10] Farmer and Richman, *op. cit.*

When one examines their model critically, one finds little that is comparative but much that is ecological.[11] Since the model has yet to reach field work stage, it is justifiable to say that it remains a skeleton of a scheme yet to be beefed up.

One of the fundamental assumptions on which that scheme rests is the notion that "environment" determines "management effectiveness." All phenomena, of course, take place within given societal contexts, and there is a constant interaction between institutions and their environment. In its substance, then, the Farmer-Richman model appears more a scheme for comparing environmental systems than for comparing management. The latter is our primary interest, but not to the exclusion of the former. Let us contrast these two models and briefly discuss the significant interrelationships between management and the socioeconomic environment.

[11] Schollhammer has classified Farmer-Richman scheme as the ecological approach to comparative management. Commenting upon this approach he had . this to say:

> The emphasis on environmental conditions has the effect that the individual enterprise is regarded as being basically a passive creature of external "constraints." As a result, there is generally an overemphasis on the necessity for environmental adaptation and not enough attention is paid to the fact that management may choose to act in defiance of certain external conditions. More often than not management uses the business organizations entrusted to them as instruments for active influence on environmental conditions in order to make them more conducive to efficient business operations. In other words, an ecological approach generally neglects to investigate management's role as a change agent. This does not mean that scholars like . . . Richman and Farmer are not aware of the active influence of management on environmental constraints, but they simply tend to discount the potentiality of management's nonconformist role, at least in the short run. Another shortcoming of the ecological approach to comparative management theory, as it has been advocated thus far, is its inability to cope with the fact that practically all environmental conditions are interrelated, yet their impact on business operations is not cumulative and not uniform. Theoretically, it is possible—and it makes an orderly, logical impression on the reader—to draw up a list of external environmental factors and separate them into black boxes with labels such as cultural-sociological constraints, etc. However, empirically it is almost impossible to appraise the precise impact of a given constraint category on internal management practices and management effectiveness. As a basis for empirical research, the ecological orientation of comparative management theory is thus operationally defective. It simply allows too much discretion in the evaluation of external environmental phenomena and their influence on management practices.

(Hans Schollhammer, "The Comparative Management Theory Jungle," *Academy of Management Journal*, Vol. 12, No. 1 (March 1969), pp. 86–87). For comprehensive critique of Farmer-Richman model also see S. B. Prasad, "Comparative Managerialism as an Approach to International Economic Growth," *Quarterly Journal of AIESEC International*, Vol. 2, August 1966, pp. 22–30.

Contrasts Between the Harbison-Myers and Farmer-Richman Approaches

There are two main contrasts between the Harbison-Myers and Farmer-Richman models: (1) the Harbison-Myers model is dynamic in the sense that it is concerned not only with those forces which have brought about one or the other type of management in a country but also with those which are likely to modify it, while the Farmer-Richman model is static in the sense that it purports to inquire as to what environmental factors have produced a given level of managerial efficiency in a country; (2) the Harbison-Myers model, from a social scientist's point of view, offers a typology of management, specific concepts, and a general logic, whereas these are notably absent from the Farmer-Richman model.

ENVIRONMENT AND MANAGEMENT

The concept of environment can be expressed in various ways. Most simply, it is a set of forces which surround either an object or a subject. The environment in which a formal organization such as a business firm operates is the set of economic, technological, social, and other forces which surround its decisions and actions.

Much has been written on the subject of environmental influences on the functioning of business organizations.[12] Yet, it is only during the last decade that writers and researchers have focused their attention on the impact of environmental forces upon the man-

---

[12] See, for example, Joseph McGuire, *Business and Society* (New York: McGraw-Hill Book Company, 1963); Keith Davis and R. L. Blomstrom, *Business and Its Environment* (New York: McGraw-Hill Book Company, 1966); Francis Aguilar, *Scanning the Business Environment* (New York: The Macmillan Company, 1967); Scott Walton, *American Business and Its Environment* (New York: The Macmillan Company, 1966); Neil Chamberlain, *Enterprise and Environment* (New York: McGraw-Hill Book Company, 1968). For the treatment of the environmental factors as variables affecting internal structure see Garlie A. Forehand and B. Von Haller Gilmer, "Environmental Variation in Studies of Organizational Behavior," *Psychological Bulletin*, Vol. 62, No. 6 (December 1964), pp. 361–382. Also see Paul R. Lawrence and Jay W. Lorsch, "Differentiation and Integration in Complex Organizations," *Administrative Science Quarterly*, June 1967, pp. 1–47.

agement of organizations. The concept of environment in such a context is that of societal environment, which differs from organizational environment (work atmosphere) and from the environment of decisions.

There is quite a diversity of views as to what constitutes the societal environment and in what ways the various factors, identified as environmental variables, exercise their impact upon the management process and management effectiveness at the micro- and the macro-levels.

Merely to assert that management is management wherever it is practiced suggests a lack of appreciation of the environmental factors. A number of writers who have observed or studied management in various countries have underscored the significance of the environmental impact on management.

Oberg, for example, argued that if the ground rules, i.e., the environmental factors, are different in different countries, then it is fruitless to search for a common set of management strategies.[13] The need to understand management in relation to the social and economic environment, and the suggestion that management principles and techniques are conditioned by the demands of the sociocultural environment, were emphasized by Chowdhry and Takezawa, two well-known management scholars from India and Japan, respectively.[14]

While it would be rather naive to suggest that the contrary is true, and while it does not take a great deal to convince readers that environmental factors are very important to the study of management, the issue of which set of environmental factors is amenable to systematic analysis, and therefore of which set one should concentrate upon, remains unsettled. In business literature one finds a treatment of a series of environmental variables. Some writers have concentrated on a small number of crucial variables, while others argue in favor of a large number of variables. Blough, for example, treats government—and its policies toward businesses—as the en-

[13] Winston Oberg, "Cross-Cultural Perspective on Management Principles," *Academy of Management Journal*, Vol. 6, No. 2 (June 1963), pp. 141–142.

[14] Kamala Chowdhry, "Social and Cultural Factors in Management Development in India and the Role of the Expert," and Shinichi Takezawa, "Sociocultural Aspects of Management in Japan," *International Labour Review*, Vol. 94, No. 2 (August 1966), pp. 132–147 and 147–174, respectively.

vironmental factor.[15] Megginson has suggested that the cultural elements which have the greatest influence on managerial effectiveness are the "spiritual values and the educational system. The former are included in the managerial philosophies and . . . the latter largely determines the knowledge and analytical processes used by executives."[16] In contrast, there are other writers, Farmer and Richman, for example, who would include a large number of economic, cultural, legal-political, and educational factors in the concept of environment.[17]

(While it may be challenging to take into account a series of variables as environmental factors, it poses serious logical as well as methodological problems when attempts are made to posit causal relationships.)This difficulty can be illustrated by the following statement by Farmer and Richman concerning centralization-decentralization:

In words, Equation 4-1 says that the degree of centralization or decentralization of authority depends significantly on literacy level, specialized vocational and technical training, secondary education, higher education, special management development programs, attitude toward education, view of industrial managers and management, view of authority and subordinates, attitude toward wealth and material gain, view of the scientific method, relevant legal rules, general economic framework, factor endowment and social overhead capital.[18]

The above statement posits a causal relationship between 20 or more independent variables and power distribution, i.e., centralization-decentralization, in a crisscross manner. Furthermore, as though to assign priorities among these variables, these authors go on to point out that some of them might be more important than others.[19] Thus, in trying to say so much about centralization-decentralization, the distinctions and measures of which are not always

[15] Roy Blough, *International Business: Environment and Adaptation* (New York: McGraw-Hill Book Company, 1966), especially Chs. IV, V, and VI.

[16] Leon Megginson, "The Interrelationship between the Cultural Environment and Managerial Effectiveness," *Management International Review*, Vol. 7, No. 6 (1967), p. 69.

[17] Richard Farmer and Barry Richman, *Comparative Management and Economic Progress* (Homewood, Ill.: Richard Irwin, 1965), especially pp. 29–30.

[18] *Ibid.*, p. 38.
[19] *Ibid.*, p. 39.

clear, they end up by saying very little about the significant relationships involved.

Recognizing such logical problems, no doubt, other writers have employed a small number of variables in their empirical work relating to management. Some good examples are to be found in the studies reported by French and Israel,[20] Harbison and Burgess,[21] Whyte,[22] Fayerweather,[23] McClelland,[24] and Dill.[25]

Assessing the Environmental Impact

In the previous section, we noted briefly the issue of which and how many variables would be crucial to examining the impact of environment upon management processes and managerial effectiveness. A related issue of significant import is that of assessing the environmental impact. In other words, the issue revolves around the question of how one goes about ascertaining the influence of environmental variables, whatever they may be. Dill's remarks seem apropos here. He observed that "Administrative science needs propositions about the way in which environmental factors constrain the structure of organization and the behavior of organization participants."[26]

Propositions which tend to posit causal relationships can be and have been formulated; but how one views the concept of environment, as a constraint or as an interacting mechanism, makes some difference in the nature of the propositions. The previous state-

[20] John R. P. French, J. Israel, *et al.*, "An Experiment on Participation in a Norwegian Factory," *Human Relations*, Vol. 8, No. 1, pp. 1–9.

[21] Frederick Harbison and E. Burgess, "Modern Management in Western Europe," *American Journal of Sociology*, Vol. 60, No. 1 (July 1954).

[22] William F. Whyte, "Framework for the Analysis of Industrial Relations: Two Views," *Industrial and Labor Relations Review*, Vol. 3, No. 3 (April 1960).

[23] John Fayerweather, *The Executive Overseas* (Syracuse: Syracuse University Press, 1959).

[24] David McClelland, *The Achieving Society* (New York: D. Von Nostrand Company, 1961), and "Business Drive and National Achievement," *Harvard Business Review*, July-August 1962.

[25] William R. Dill, "Environment as an Influence on Managerial Autonomy," *Administrative Science Quarterly*, Vol. 2, No. 4 (March 1958), pp. 409–443.

[26] *Ibid.*, p. 409.

ment by Dill contains the notion of environment as a constraint; this is similarly true throughout the theoretical treatment by Farmer and Richman. We, however, tend to subscribe to the view that environment is not always a constraint; rather, we feel, environment is most often an interacting mechanism. In other words, all organizations exist in given environments, but there is interaction between organizations and their environment. Argyris expresses the same idea: ". . . all organizations are open systems in the sense that they are influenced by and they in turn influence the environment in which they are embedded. . . ."[27]

Thus, one can suggest at least three major issues in the study of environment and management: (1) how the environment influences management; (2) how the management influences environment; and (3) how the management adapts to changes in the environment.

We have not studied any of these issues in depth, but we have paid some attention to the general issue of management and its environment in a very limited sense. In relation to the first issue, examining only two environmental constraints, one societal and the other organizational, we have argued elsewhere that the sellers' market condition and the short-run profit maximization philosophy which prevail in the contemporary context of India have impeded the adaptation of modern management methods.[28] That these two constraints overemphasize output-related activities and impel managers to become unduly technically oriented, thus creating a circular web which impedes introduction of modern management, can be seen in Figure 1-1.

We have not dealt with the issue of how management affects the environment in which its organization functions; in our field-work, however, we attempted to find out how the managers and executives of the American subsidiaries and comparable national companies perceived and adapted to environmental conditions as they viewed them. Relevant data and discussion of this point are to be found in Chapter 10.

[27] Chris Argyris, *Integrating the Individual and the Organization* (New York: John Wiley & Sons, Inc., 1964), pp. 153–154.

[28] Anant R. Negandhi and S. B. Prasad, "Transmitting Advanced Management Know-How to Underdeveloped Countries," *Management International Review*, Vol. 3, No. 6 (1967), pp. 75–81.

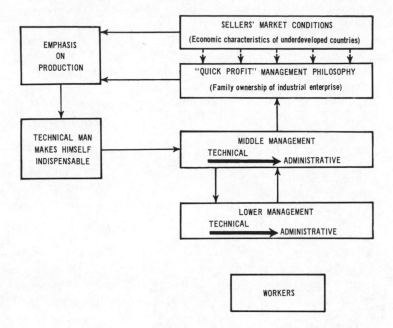

**EFFECTS OF SELLERS' MARKET POSITION ON
THE MANAGEMENT OF INDUSTRIAL ENTERPRISES**

Figure 1-1   Effect of Sellers' Market Position on the Management of Industrial
Enterprises (Dotted line indicates probable but not certain relationship)

What approach, then, did *we* follow in our study? This question leads to the design of study and method of analysis—the subject of the next chapter.

As will be evident throughout this book, a study such as the one reported here suffers from some unavoidable weaknesses. We have recognized these and have refrained from making undue generalizations. Notwithstanding these weaknesses, we have attempted to operationalize some management concepts and have examined enterprise management comparatively, although not in its entirety.

A reader interested in glancing through the major findings of the study may turn to Chapter 9, where the findings and major premises of this study are set forth.

2

DESIGN OF THE STUDY

The main purpose of this research was to compare and contrast the management of U.S. subsidiary companies with their local or national counterparts with a view toward delineating the similarities and differences within a country and in a cross-national context. In doing so, we recognized that there could be at least three segments of inquiry in which the comparative approach could prove fruitful. These areas were: (1) refinement of management concepts so as to make them relevant to cross-cultural settings and to posit their plausible relationships; (2) examination of the impact of specific environmental factors upon the management processes and effectiveness; and (3) inquiry into the real problems of transmitting modern management know-how to the developing countries.

BACKGROUND OF RESEARCH DESIGN

As we noted earlier, the Harbison-Myers approach and data were not so much concerned with enterprise management per se, as with the broad forces which brought about particular types of management systems in given countries and possible directions for their change. We also noted that the Farmer-Richman scheme focuses its attention upon a host of environmental factors and proposes to assess their impact upon management effectiveness in an aggregate economic sense. However, since our interests were directed toward the management of business organizations per se, we concentrated

FIGURE 1

Significance of Model

The model presented here will enable the ascertainment of the following:

(a) The impact of specific external environmental factor(s) on the particular function(s) of the manager.

(b) Provide an answer to our question of which elements of the American management know-how are transferable and which are nontransferable in differing culture and environment.

(c) Identify the most efficient process in a given socio-economic, legal and political environment, and suggest the means through which this process can be implemented.

(d) Identify the strategic environmental factors which do affect the management process and thereby managerial efficiency.

(e) Determine external factors which are controllable and those which are noncontrollable.

(f) Indicate the upper limit to which we might transfer American management know-how in underdeveloped areas.

THE MODEL

a) **Management Philosophy**

Elements

1. Consumer
2. Employee
3. Supplier
4. Distributor
5. Government and Community
6. Stockholders

b) **Management Process**

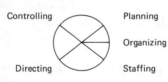

Elements

1. Planning
2. Organizing
3. Staffing
4. Directing
5. Controlling

c) **Management Effectiveness**

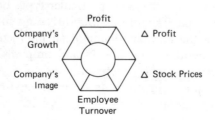

Elements

1. Gross and Net Profit
2. Growth in Profit
3. Growth in Market Share
4. Growth in Price of Stock
5. Employee Turnover
6. Consumer Ranking

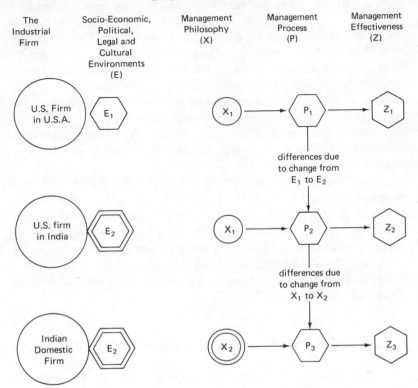

Figure 2-1 Experimental Model and Design

SOURCE: Reproduced from A. R. Negandhi "Applicability of American Management" in S. B. Prasad and A. R. Negandhi, *Managerialism for Economic Development* (The Hague: Martinus Nijhoff, 1968), pp. 76–77. Permission of the publisher is greatfully acknowledged.

on the management processes and effectiveness of industrial firms in the five underdeveloped countries.

The initial model as presented by Negandhi[1] addressed itself primarily to the question of determining the applicability of U.S.

[1] Anant R. Negandhi, "Determining Applicability of American Management Know-How in Differing Environments and Cultures," a paper presented at the annual meeting of the western division of the Academy of Management, San Diego, April 9, 1965; the published version of this paper (with B. D. Estafen) appeared in the *Academy of Management Journal*, Vol. 8, No. 4 (December 1965), pp. 319–323.

management know-how to (developing) countries with different cultural patterns. Therein, three concepts—management philosophy, management process, and management effectiveness—were employed as variables. Management philosophy was defined as the expressed and implied attitude of the managers of an organization toward its external and internal agents such as consumers, employees, suppliers and distributors, the government, the community, and the workers' organizations. Management process was identified in the generally accepted sense of managerial planning, organizing, staffing, leading, and controlling. Managerial effectiveness, however, was defined in terms of profits, market share, employee turnover, consumer ranking, price of stock, and so forth.

In utilizing these concepts, it was suggested that a three-way comparison among a set of U.S. firms operating in the United States, a set of U.S. subsidiaries operating in a developing country (India, for example), and a set of comparable local firms, made with the aid of empirical data, would provide insights into the questions of determining which aspects of advanced management know-how would be applicable. A summary expression of the initial model and its significance are shown in Figure 2-1.

MODIFICATION IN THE RESEARCH DESIGN

There are two implicit assumptions made in the research scheme presented in Figure 2-1: (1) that the American subsidiaries and their respective parent companies in the United States will pursue the same or similar management philosophy; (2) that the American subsidiaries and their local counterparts will pursue differential management philosophies.

Our pilot study in India, however, revealed that this was not necessarily the case. The management philosophy, as defined above, was neither culture- *cum* environment-bound nor ownership-bound. In other words, some American subsidiaries, parent U.S. companies, and local foreign companies were alike in their management philosophies, while others were worlds apart.

The field experience in India, therefore, alerted us to the possibility that instead of comparing the management process and ef-

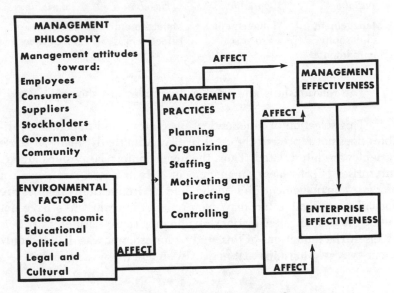

Figure 2-2 Comparative Management Construct

fectiveness of U.S. subsidiaries with those of their parent organizations in the U.S., and with those of their local counterparts, as suggested in the initial model, it would be useful to compare foreign subsidiaries and their comparable local firms on the basis of different management philosophy in order to assess the impact of this variable on management processes and effectiveness.

Our field experiences, both in India and in the U.S., also suggested that how managers or executives perceive the external environment as decision makers has a more significant bearing upon the decisions that they make than a generalized listing of environmental factors, in some rank order, might indicate.

With a view toward enlarging the scope of inquiry, i.e., to pursuing the objectives indicated above, we also modified the initial model in several ways. First, we increased the number of variables from three to five—management philosophy, environmental variables, management process, management effectiveness, and enterprise effectiveness. The specifications of these variables are:

Independent variables	Intervening variables	Dependent variable	End-result variable
Management Philosophy Environmental Factors	Management Processes	Management Effectiveness	Enterprise Effectiveness

The relationships among these variables are shown in Figure 2-2.

This selection of independent, mediating, and dependent variables does not represent the total reality. Admittedly, many of these variables are interrelated. Thus, the reverse interrelationships among enterprise effectiveness, management effectiveness, management processes, management philosophy, and environmental variables are not only conceivable but may even reflect the reality. We have not investigated such interrelationships among these variables. This is precisely the limitations of this study. Our attempt was directed only at one-way relationships that may exist among these variables.

DEFINITIONS OF VARIABLES

We retained the initial definition of management philosophy as the implied and expressed attitudes of the managers toward consumers, employees, the stockholders, suppliers, distributors, government, and community.[2] Details of the factors evaluated are provided in Appendix B.

The concept of management process also retains the initial definition of the managerial framework for functions such as planning, organizing, staffing, leading, and controlling. Of course, readers will recognize that this is one approach to the study of management—the so-called process school of thought. We preferred to make use of

---

[2] Thus defined the concept of management philosophy is quite similar to the concept of task environment as defined by Dill (William R. Dill, "Environment as an Influence on Managerial Autonomy," *Administrative Science Quarterly*, II, March, 1958, pp. 409–433); Thompson (James D. Thompson, *Organization in Action*, New York: McGraw-Hill Book Co., 1967, pp. 26–38); and Thorelli ("Organizational Theory: An Ecological View," *Academy of Management Proceedings*, 1967, pp. 68–72). These authors studied the impact of task environment on organizational functioning while we have argued that the perception of the task environment by the decision maker is more relevant to the functioning of organizations than the task environment per se.

this framework to collect data for two reasons: (1) it would best facilitate query and inquiry as well as response from practicing managers; and (2) we could use the data as the intervening variable. This usage should not be interpreted as suggesting that we have ignored the behavioral aspects of management. On the contrary, we have endeavored to incorporate many behavioral concepts both as intervening variables and, more significantly, as dependent variables.

The concept of management effectiveness that we have employed in our study provides a good indication of this if one considers how we have operationally defined it. In the initial model, it was a conglomeration of both economic and behavioral measures. We preferred to separate them and concentrate more on the behavioral measures than on the economic measures of effectiveness. Managment effectiveness in the revised version of the model takes into account the degree to which the organization was able to develop and maintain a social system. The measures are employee morale, worker turnover and absenteeism, harmony of interpersonal relationships, ability of the organization to attract and retain high-level managerial manpower, utilization of high-level manpower, and organizational ability to adapt to changing external conditions.

Although the concept of management effectiveness in the initial model included such economic measures as profit, market share, earnings-price ratios of stock, and so forth, we grouped such measures under enterprise or organizational effectiveness and have not dealt with them in this study, except in a cursory fashion. The reason was not only the extreme difficulty in procuring reliable data from the companies, but also our concern with management effectiveness defined in behavioral terms. Therefore, while we do recognize that the success and viability of organizations depend upon such effectiveness, we are eager to point out that the very nature of the economic conditions prevailing in developing countries—such as the difficulty of entry by a new company, sellers' market condition, inflation, lack of foreign exchange, and a host of other factors—somehow seem to obscure enterprise effectiveness if measured in the generally accepted economic or monetary terms. Equally important is the fact that modern organization theory tends to emphasize the interaction patterns and the effectiveness of people and their subgroups in organizations rather than profits and profitability of undertaking productive effort per se.

ON THE INDEPENDENT VARIABLE, MANAGEMENT PHILOSOPHY

Rationale of Using Management Philosophy as a Variable

As we noted in Chapter 1, many cross-cultural researchers have argued about the dominant influence of the socioeconomic, political, legal, and cultural factors upon management practices and effectiveness. In the writings of Harbison and Myers,[3] Kerr,[4] Gonzalez and McMillan,[5] Oberg,[6] and Farmer and Richman[7] particularly, one can discern an attempt to explain managerial differences on the basis of environmental and cultural variables at play in a given country. However, if the environmental and cultural factors were the sole determinants of management practices and effectiveness, as has been argued by the above mentioned authors, one would expect close similarities in the management practices—under given industry and technological conditions in a country—of two comparable industrial enterprises. Such similarity, however, is far removed from reality.[8]

Scattered evidence provided by both practitioners[9] and acade-

[3] Frederick Harbison and Charles Myers, *Management in the Industrial World* (New York: McGraw-Hill Book Company, 1959).

[4] C. Kerr, J. T. Dunlop, *et al.*, *Industrialism and Industrial Man* (Cambridge, Mass.: Harvard University Press, 1960).

[5] Richard F. Gonzalez and Claude McMillan, Jr., "The Universality of American Management Philosophy," *Academy of Management Journal*, Vol. 4, No. 1 (April 1961), pp. 33–41.

[6] Winston Oberg, "Cross-Cultural Perspectives on Management Principles," *Academy of Management Journal*, Vol. 6, No. 2 (June 1963), pp. 129–143.

[7] Richard Farmer and Barry Richman, "A Model for Research in Comparative Management," *California Management Review*, Winter 1964, pp. 55–68.

[8] Consider, for example, the two American retail chains Montgomery Ward and Sears-Roebuck, which are basically in the same business and confronted with similar market and environmental conditions. Yet, their managerial practices and effectiveness are hardly the same.

[9] For an excellent review of the various meanings assigned to the concept of management philosophy, see W. D. Litzinger and T. E. Schaefer, "Management Philosophy Enigma," *Academy of Management Journal*, Vol. 9, No. 4 (December 1966), pp. 337–343.

micians seems to pinpoint the influence of the management philosophy upon management practices and effectiveness.

Chowdhry and Pal,[10] for example, showed the relationship between some elements of management philosophy and management practices. In their experiment, conducted in two textile companies in India, they found that the company with a quick profit philosophy and a changing manufacturing policy had lower morale and efficiency than the product-conscious company with a long range profit philosophy. They argued that the differential philosophies have had considerable impact on organization structure, delegation of authority, span of control, and other structural elements.

In providing a comparative conceptual schema for organizational analysis, Pugh and his co-researchers have identified three sets of variables: structural, contextual, and performance. They have suggested that these can serve as independent-dependent variables. In their schema, the contextual variables are treated as independent variables. This set includes the origin and history of the firm, ownership and control, size, technology, location, and charter. The charter variable relates to ideology, operating procedures, and role definition of the firm.[11] We are inclined to believe that this set is more or less the same as what other writers have referred to as management philosophy or policy.

To Likert, "the causal variables are independent variables which determine the course of developments within an organization and the results achieved by the organization. These causal variables include those independent variables which can be altered or changed by the organization and its management."[12] The list of these independent variables includes management philosophy, policy, and values with respect to employees, customers, the public, unions, suppliers, and others.

On the basis of this evidence, we operationalized the concept of management philosophy and sought to ascertain its impact on the

10 Kamala Chowdhry and A. K. Pal, "Production Planning and Organizational Morale," reprinted in A. H. Robenstein and C. J. Haberstroh (eds.), *Some Theories of Organization* (Homewood, Ill.: Dorsey Press, Inc., 1960), pp. 185–196.

11 D. S. Pugh, *et al*, "A Conceptual Scheme for Organizational Analysis," *Administrative Science Quarterly*, Vol. 8, No. 3 (December 1963), pp. 289–315.

12 Rensis Likert, *Human Organization: Its Management and Value* (New York: McGraw-Hill Book Company, 1967), especially p. 212.

management practices and effectiveness of industrial firms in under-developed countries. Inference and measurement of the management philosophy of firms studied were as follows.

Inference

The management philosophy of companies in our sample was inferred from interviews with the top executives and managers of each of the companies surveyed. These interviews were nondirective in nature. The interviewers simply asked the respondents to speak about the company's policies. These were also preliminary interviews and they were, for the most part, group interviews rather than individual ones. The company personnel interviewed included company chairmen; general managers; directors of sales, production, finance, and personnel; chief accountants; controllers; and some members of the board of directors. In each of the companies, six to eight of the upper level people described company policies; we endeavored to verify these accounts as much as possible by talking to middle-level managers, supervisors, and shop-level workers. In judging the policies for purposes of classifying them, we were concerned mainly about what the executives did.

Two researchers were involved in judging the companies' policies and several factors were taken into account in order to examine specific policies toward the employees, consumers, distributors, suppliers, stockholders, government, and community. Tables B-1 through B-7 in Appendix B outline these factors.

Measurement

Our main purpose in inferring a company's management philosophy by evaluating its policies and practices was to suggest relationships between management philosophy and management processes on the one hand, and between management philosophy and management effectiveness on the other.

To establish causal relationships between these on the basis of each of the elements of the management practices appeared an impossible task of dubious value. In order to make this task manageable and meaningful, we developed an index of the overall company philosophy with respect to all of the agents. To do so we assigned numerical values, as shown in Figure 2-3.

Employee	MUCH OR VERY MUCH CONCERN	MILD CONCERN	LITTLE OR NO CONCERN
	20	10	0

Consumer	THE KING	NECESSARY AGENT	PASSIVE AGENT
	20	10	0

Community	MUCH OR VERY MUCH CONCERN	SOME CONCERN	LITTLE OR NO CONCERN
	10	5	0

Government	GOOD PARTNER	NECESSARY EVIL	GOVERNMENT BE DAMNED
	10	5	0

Supplier	GOOD RELA-TIONSHIP ABSOLUTELY NECESSARY	GOOD RE-LATIONSHIP HELPFUL	RELATIONSHIP A NECESSARY EVIL
	15	7.5	0

Distributor	GOOD RELA-TIONSHIP ABSOLUTELY NECESSARY	GOOD RE-LATIONSHIP HELPFUL	RELATIONSHIP A NECESSARY EVIL
	15	7.5	0

Stockholder	OWNERS, MASTERS, GOOD PUBLIC RELATION PERSONNEL	OWNERS, MASTERS ONLY	PROFIT-EATERS
	10	5	0

Figure 2-3 Ranking of Management Philosophy Elements

From Figure 2-3 it can be seen that two of the agents, employees and consumers, were assigned higher points than others, for we recognized the direct importance of these factors insofar as the internal working of the organization was concerned. In doing so we subscribed to the view of other researchers who hold that attitudes (values) toward these two factors are, to a large extent, responsible for the molding of management practices. As an illustration of this point, we would assume that a company's highly favorable attitude toward workers as members of the organization would be likely to have an important bearing upon such managerial processes as delegation of authority, structuring of the organization, and so forth. Similarly, a company's highly favorable attitude toward consumers, those whose needs the company's products or services must adequately satisfy, is likely to have an important bearing upon such managerial processes as product planning, distribution organization, quality control, and so forth.

The company's overall management philosophy, determined on the basis of the numerical values, represented an aggregate score for each company, the maximum possible score being 100. On the basis of this total score, we classified the 92 companies in our sample into 3 groups, as follows:

		Score
Most Sophisticated	Management Philosophy (MS)	75–100
Somewhat Progressive	Management Philosophy (SP)	40– 74
Not Progressive	Management Philosophy (NP)	0– 39

Thus categorized, firms with a score between 75 and 100 have had the most favorable attitudes toward consumers, employees, suppliers, distributors, stockholders, government, and community. Firms with a score of 40–74 showed somewhat favorable attitudes toward most of these agents and highly favorable attitudes toward employees or consumers or both. Firms with a score of 39 or less manifested unfavorable attitudes toward most of these agents.

To compare the U.S. subsidiary companies and their local (national) counterparts, data are arranged on the above basis in addition to that of ownership-nationality as such.

METHOD OF DATA COLLECTION

Our initial contacts eventually produced 63 American subsidiaries, 61 comparable local companies, and 30 U.S. parent companies willing to cooperate in the project. Background data were obtained from records and published sources. The information on management philosophies, processes, practices, and effectiveness was gathered by means of personal interviews. The total number of interviews was 570. Of these, about 440 interviewees were middle- and upper-level managers; the rest were supervisory and nonsupervisory personnel.

Structured and nonstructured interview guides were prepared; altogether, seven investigators conducted these interviews in the five countries. Some were nationals of the country in question and others were fluent in the language of the country. Some interviews were repeat interviews for purposes of clarification. The field interviews were conducted during the period from January 1966 to September 1967.

Table 2-1 Size of Companies in the International Sample, $n = 92$
(Number of Employees)

Number of Employees	Argentina		Brazil		India		Philippines		Uruguay	
	U.S. Subsidiary	Local Company	U.S. Subsidiary	Local Company	U.S. Subsidiary	Local Company	U.S. Subsidiary	Local Company	U.S. Subsidiary	Local Company
100 to 500	2	2	2	4	10	6	6	4	5	3
501 to 2,000	3	2	5	2	4	8	4	6	1	2
2,001 to 3,000	1	1	—	1	1	1	—	—	—	—
3,001 and over	—	—	1	—	2	2	—	1	—	—
Totals	6	5	8	7	17	17	10	11	6	5

Theoretical and Methodological Dimensions

Although 63 subsidiaries and 61 comparable local companies participated in the study, the gathering of relevant information was in every case a difficult task. Thus, the following analysis is based upon data from and concerning 47 subsidiaries and 45 local firms. Table 2-1 provides a breakdown of these 92 organizations in terms of size, ownership, and location.

Each of the American subsidiaries was paired with a local firm on the basis of product, technology, and sales volume in each of the five countries. The companies thus paired represented several industry categories. Table 2-2 illustrates this point.

Table 2-2 Industry Classification of the Companies in the International Sample, $n = 92$

Industry Group	Argentina U.S. Subsidiary	Argentina Local Company	Brazil U.S. Subsidiary	Brazil Local Company	India U.S. Subsidiary	India Local Company	Philippines U.S. Subsidiary	Philippines Local Company	Uruguay U.S. Subsidiary	Uruguay Local Company
Chemicals and Pharmaceutical	2	1	1	2	5	5	3	3	1	1
Petroleum	—	—	—	—	1	1	1	1	—	—
Light Engineering	—	—	1	—	2	2	—	—	—	—
Heavy Engineering	—	—	—	2	2	2	1	1	2	1
Electrical-Consumer	—	—	—	—	1	1	—	—	—	—
Rubber Tires	—	—	—	—	1	1	1	1	—	—
Soaps and Cosmetics	1	2	3	1	2	2	1	1	1	1
Soft Drinks-Canned Foods	1	1	2	2	2	2	2	2	2	2
Electrical-Industrial	2	1	1	—	1	1	1	2	· —	—
Totals	6	5	8	7	17	17	10	11	6	5

ANALYSIS OF DATA

A fairly detailed analysis of the management process was made, on an intranational basis, between U.S. subsidiaries in India and local comparable firms in India. This is due to the relatively larger size of the sample (17 U.S. subsidiaries and 17 Indian companies) and to our assumption that India exemplified the underdeveloped environment.

Because of the nature of the research involved—the small-sample study—comparative frequency statistics, rather than statistical analysis of data, are given in the various tables in Section Two.

Comparisons are made essentially at three levels: at the intranational level, just referred to; at the international level—comparing management processes and effectiveness of the U.S. subsidiaries with those of their local counterparts—among companies in Argentina, Brazil, India, the Philippines, and Uruguay; and, most importantly, on the basis of management philosophy.

TWO

COMPARATIVE ANALYSES OF MANAGEMENT PROCESSES AND PRACTICES

3

PLANNING FOR THE FUTURE

Long-range planning is a favorite contemporary theme in organizational management. It is generally agreed that those who manage should help to create the future of the organization by defining goals, by formulating strategies and plans of action, and by making commitments.

In the United States, during the early phases of its industrial growth, the idea of long-range planning would have elicited little enthusiasm from businessmen, for the U.S. was then regarded as a nation of unequaled resources and opportunities. The perspective now is quite different; competitive forces at home and abroad have changed this picture and have necessitated a shift in managerial thinking about planning for the future.

Early in the 20th century, as an alternate to the market mechanism exemplifying the U.S. economy, centralized economic planning was initiated in the Eastern European countries, particularly in Soviet Russia. Since then, many of the newly independent and developing countries of Asia and Africa have emulated centralized economic planning in one form or another. India is the largest democratic country seeking economic development and social justice via the path of centralized economic planning.[1] It is thus apparent that it is not only business and other organizations who pay heed to

[1] In December 1954, the Indian Parliament declared that the broad objective of economic planning was to achieve the *socialistic pattern of society*. This pattern, envisaged in India's plans, did not imply that all economic initiative must rest with the state. Indeed, it assigned to private enterprise an important role in national development.

37

planning for the future; nations do also. However, planning at the national level assumes various forms. It may mean centralized allocation of almost all resources, as in the Soviet Union; or plans to develop a healthy public sector to supplement a private sector, as in the case of India; or indicative planning, as the French refer to it; or simply forecasting the economic future, as in the United States. Our concern in this chapter is with long-range planning as it is practiced by the 92 business organizations in our sample. Along with a brief discussion of the meaning of long-range planning, we will present data and make comparative analyses.

WHAT PLANNING FOR THE FUTURE IS AND IS NOT

According to Drucker,[2] three things are definitely *not* long-range planning. First, it is not forecasting; since forecasting the long-range is difficult, organizations need long-range planning. Second, long-range planning does not deal with future decisions but with the futurity of present decisions. Third, long-range planning is not an attempt to eliminate risk. It is not even an attempt to minimize risk.

Then what *is* long-range planning? According to Drucker, "It is the continuous process of making present entrepreneurial (risk-taking) decisions systematically and with the best possible knowledge of futurity, organizing systematically the efforts needed to carry out these decisions and measuring the results of these decisions against the expectations through organized systematic feedback."[3]

Defining long-range planning generically, Steiner states that "The implication of long-range planning is that current decisions to do something are made in the light of their future consequences. . . . Long-range planning begins with the specifications of basic purposes and develops objectives and concrete targets and goals to form a network of aims."[4]

[2] Peter Drucker, "Long-Range Planning, Challenge to Management Science," *Management Science*, Vol. 5, No. 7 (April 1959), pp. 238–249.
[3] *Ibid.*
[4] George Steiner, "The Nature and Significance of Multinational Corporate Planning," in *Multinational Corporate Planning*, G. A. Steiner and W. M. Cannon (eds.), (New York: The Macmillan Company, 1966), p. 9.

Investigations seem to indicate that the keynote of fast-growing and successful companies in the U.S. is the great emphasis they place on long-range planning. The Stanford Research Institute inquired into the question "Why do companies grow?" One of the major conclusions of their study was that "In the cases of both high-growth and low-growth companies, those that now support planning programs have shown a superior growth rate in recent years."[5]

.   In a nutshell, long-range planning is an intellectual process which symbolizes the purposefulness of modern management, reflects the strategic approach to organizational behavior, and more importantly, in the case of developing countries, provides a sense of direction to the organizations.

The data and analyses which follow relate not so much to the specifications of basic purposes of the organizations, development of concrete goals, or making decisions with future consequences in mind, as to more fundamental questions, such as "Do these companies engage in long-range planning, and if they do, can its nature be discerned? Are these differences based on nationality-ownership or management philosophy?" Thus, the analysis is not strictly concerned with long-range planning in the U.S. subsidiaries and their local counterparts.

COMPARISONS OF PLANNING FOR THE FUTURE

In order to examine the above questions, information from the respondents was sought about: (1) the nature and scope of planning, whether planning is systematic or not, partial or comprehensive; (2) whether plans are of the long-range type; (3) how systematic and detailed the plans are; and (4) how frequently is the progress of the plans reviewed.

These questions relate to the scope of planning in the companies studied. As a background for any inference to be derived from the data, we have regarded the idealized scope as follows: that systematic long-range planning envelops all aspects of the organization's resource, not simply financial aspects, and is formu-

---

[5] Quoted from George Steiner, "Does Planning Pay Off?" *California Management Review*, Vol. 5, No. 2 (Winter 1962), p. 37.

lated with the consensus of the largest possible number of the members of the organization.[6]

Intracountry Comparisons (India)

As noted in Chapter 2, intracountry comparisons are made with a view to examining the similarities and differences when the environment is held constant. It is valid to assume that the environmental conditions in India are almost the same for both the U.S. subsidiaries and their Indian counterparts.

What differences are there, then, with reference to planning for the future, and what accounts for such differences? Data in Table 3-1 and a few personal opinions of the respondent managers provide the answer that differences in management philosophy rather than ownership status appears as an explanatory factor. Let us examine the details.

Data in Table 3-1 pertain to the four aspects of planning, referred to earlier, and are arranged for two sets of companies: (1) U.S. and Indian, and (2) Most Sophisticated (MS), Somewhat Progressive (SP) and Not Progressive (NP) companies, in columns 2 and 3, respectively.

The data in column 2 reveals that 14 out of 17 U.S. subsidiaries' planning and 9 out of 17 Indian companies' planning could be characterized as systematic and comprehensive, meaning that it touched upon all aspects of the organization. There was one U.S. subsidiary which engaged in financial planning only. Three of the Indian firms also planned in financial terms only, while there were three Indian firms which did no planning at all.

Among the 14 U.S. subsidiaries which undertook comprehensive planning, 12 of them could be characterized as focusing on the long-range. Five of these companies planned on a 10-year basis while 7 of them planned on a 5-year basis. Among the 9 Indian companies which undertook comprehensive planning, 6 of them could be characterized as focusing on the long-range, i.e., 5 and 10 years.

Among the 12 U.S. subsidiaries which undertook comprehensive long-range planning, half of them developed systematic, de-

---

[6] For the management practices of the large U.S. companies in the United States, see P. E. Holden, C. A. Pederson, G. E. Germane, *Top Management* (New York: McGraw-Hill Book Company, 1968).

Table 3-1 Comparisons of Four Aspects of Planning in U.S. Subsidiaries and Indian Companies

	Overall Comparisons		Management Philosophy					
			Most Sophisticated		Somewhat Progressive		Not Progressive	
	U.S.	Indian	U.S.	Indian	U.S.	Indian	U.S.	Indian
	$n=$ 17	$n=$ 17	$n=$ 5	$n=$ 5	$n=$ 11	$n=$ 7	$n=$ 1	$n=$ 5
Nature of planning								
Systematic								
Financial only	1	3	–	1	1	–	–	2
Comprehensive	14	9	5	3	9	6	–	–
Random	2	2	–	1	1	1	1	–
No formal planning	–	3	–	–	–	–	–	3
Planning orientation								
Short-term (1 to 2 years)	4	8	1	2	3	4	–	2*
Medium-term (5 years)	7	3	–	1	7	2	–	–
Long-term (10 years)	5	3	4	2	1	1	–	–
Indefinite period	1	3	–	–	–	–	1	–
Resulting plans								
Systematic detailed plans with the aid of computers	6	3	5	3	1	–	–	–
Systematic detailed plans without computers	2	3	–	2	2	1	–	–
Systematic but limited plans	5	6	–	–	3	2	1	2*
Limited forecasts randomly done	4	2	–	–	3	2	1	–
Frequency of review								
Quarterly	9	4	5	3	4	1	–	–
Semiannually	1	1	–	1	1	–	–	–
Quarterly and annually	5	2	–	–	5	2	–	–
As and when required	2	7	–	1	1	4	1	2*

* Remainder of NP Indian firms did no planning in a formal sense.

tailed plans with the aid of computers while two others did so without computers. The use or lack of use of computers should be taken as indicative merely of the quantity of data analyzed rather than of the superiority or inferiority of the plans themselves. Among the 6 Indian companies which undertook comprehensive long-range planning, 3 of them developed systematic, detailed plans with the aid of computers, while the other three did so without the aid of the computers.

The above comparisons, made on the basis of nationality-ownership (U.S. vs. Indian company) seem to indicate that, proportionately, many more U.S. subsidiaries than their Indian counterparts engaged in systematic, comprehensive long-range plans and thus provided a sense of direction for their organizations. Let us make comparisons on the basis of management philosophy and see if markedly different results emerge.

Column 3 in Table 3-1 refers to the three types of management philosophy which we inferred from the management philosophy score (Appendix B). If we consider the subset of Most Sophisticated companies (5 U.S. and 5 Indian), planning in all of the 5 U.S. subsidiaries could be featured as being systematic and comprehensive. Three of the 5 Indian companies could also be so characterized.

Among the above 5 U.S. subsidiaries, 4 of them engaged in long-term planning; all of the above 3 Indian companies are long-term oriented. Furthermore, these 5 U.S. subsidiaries and the 5 Indian companies develop systematic detailed plans for the future.

In order to obtain a contrasting picture, we can compare the management process of planning in the one U.S. subsidiary and the 5 Indian companies in the third subset—Not Progressive, in column 3.

The one U.S. company which is considered Not Progressive on the management philosophy count did undertake planning in an unsystematic way for indefinite periods of time, made limited forecasts, and its plan was reviewed as required. Among the 5 Indian companies in this subset, three did no planning in a formal way; those remaining did short-term financial planning and the resulting plans were reviewed as required.

Thus, although the size of the two subsets differs, there is some indication from the data that the Most Sophisticated companies, which manifest progressive management philosophy, whether U.S. subsidiaries or local firms, manifest concerted efforts to provide a sense of direction through planning for the future, in spite of the rather unstable economic environment in India.

One might, at this point, raise this question: "Why are these companies so oriented?" Again, the explanation would seem to be that organizations need a sense of direction, as borne out by the following two opinions of the executives.

The following is a statement made by an Indian national who is an executive in a U.S. subsidiary in India; this company is one of the 5 MS companies.

It's true that our forecasts and targets will never be reached . . . but if we don't plan for five or six years, our people [managers and non-managers] will lose the sense of direction. As a company we will never grow; our growth [30 per cent annual increase in sales during 1961-66] is largely due to our planning . . . It gives us a sense of direction and a preview of the problems which we will have to face.

Similar in tone was the expression of an Indian national who is an executive in an Indian company which is one of the 5 MS companies in our sample. He defended his company's planning for the future thusly:

Planning for the future is one thing which we never underemphasized. Those who don't believe will keep on arguing against it and point to the rising prices and government controls and ask "why plan?" But they never realize that the damn government itself does this and pours out a lot of figures which business houses can use to chart out their growth . . . Let me give you an example. You know . . . Company. Fifteen years ago they were one of the biggest pharmaceutical companies here. Look where they are now. We moved in late but we are going places. By their own system [referring to American management methods] we are giving them tough competition *and* winning.

To contrast the attitudes toward planning, as evident in the statements of the executives of the one U.S. subsidiary which is an NP company and one Indian company which does no formal planning at all and which is also an NP company, we may examine the following. According to an Indian executive of this U.S. subsidiary, the rationale for not doing any planning was to be found in the policies of the government of India:

The Government's policies are the main hindrance to our growth . . . we can't plan because we don't know whether the government will let us do what we plan to do or not . . . .

Similar blame for inaction was placed by an Indian national who held the job of a senior executive in one of the NP Indian companies:

How can any body plan with the changing government policies, rising prices and political upheaval . . . we have given up . . . our planning goes as far as this afternoon . . . we don't know what our product next year will be. Of course, we will manufacture our present line but it is getting tough to survive.

These four quotations illustrate both the recognition of the need for long-range planning, and the lack of it. Coupled with the data presented in Table 3-1 and our impression of the managers and executives of other companies, management philosophy rather than nationality of ownership appears to be a crucial variable accounting for the differences in planning philosophies when comparisons are made at the intranational level.

Intercountry Comparisons

The data regarding the nature and time orientation of planning as well as the nature and review of plans for the five countries —Argentina, Brazil, Uruguay, India and Philippines—are provided in Tables 3-2 through 3-5. Companies in the Latin American countries are grouped together in these tables.

The nature of planning by the companies in all five of the countries can be characterized thusly: the U.S. subsidiaries' planning is systematic, long-range, and to a large extent comprehensive, compared to that of the local companies, except in the case of those in India. It is only in India that 9 out of 17 (53 percent) local companies engaged in such planning.

Another fact which emerges from the data in the above table is that the absence of formal planning is not typical of local companies alone. There were 2 U.S. subsidiaries in the Philippines which engaged in no formal planning and were thus atypical of American business operations abroad. But these were not companies which were classified as those with Most Sophisticated management philosophy.

The time orientation of planning was found to be generally long-range in the majority of U.S. subsidiaries in all of the five countries. Table 3-3 indicates that 15 out of the 20 U.S. subsidiaries in the Argentina-Brazil-Uruguay group planned for a period of from

Table 3-2 Types of Planning in American Subsidiaries and Local Companies in Argentina-Brazil-Uruguay, India, and Philippines

Country					
	Overall Comparisons	Most Sophisticated	Somewhat Progressive	Not Progressive	
	U.S. Local Sub. Cos.	U.S. Local Sub. Cos.	U.S. Local Sub. Cos.	U.S. Local Sub. Cos.	
Argentina–Brazil–Uruguay	$n=$ $n=$ 20 17	$n=$ $n=$ 2 1	$n=$ $n=$ 18 15	$n=$ $n=$ 0 1	
Comprehensive planning*	13 3	1 –	12 3	– –	
Limited planning**	5 6	1 –	4 5	– 1	
Financial planning only	2 3	– 1	2 2	– –	
No formal planning	– 5	– –	– 5	– –	
India	$n=$ $n=$ 17 17	$n=$ $n=$ 5 5	$n=$ $n=$ 11 7	$n=$ $n=$ 1 5	
Comprehensive planning*	14 9	5 3	9 6	– –	
Limited planning**	2 2	– 1	1 1	1 –	
Financial planning only	1 3	– 1	1 –	– 2	
No formal planning	– 3	– –	– –	– 3	
Philippines	$n=$ $n=$ 10 11	$n=$ $n=$ 4 4	$n=$ $n=$ 6 7	$n=$ $n=$ 0 0	
Comprehensive planning*	6 –	4 –	2 –		
Limited planning**	1 7	– 4	1 3		
Financial planning only	1 4	– –	1 4		
No formal planning	2 –	– –	2 –		

* Systematic planning covering financial, product, manpower, market, and other aspects for the entire company.
** Not comprehensive as above, but limited either to product or plant planning.

5 to 10 years; in India the number of such companies was 12 out of 17; and in the Philippines, 6 out of 10 (Table 3-3).

The time orientation of planning by local companies in these countries was either undefined or short-term, ranging from 1 to 2 years. Column 2 in Table 3-3 indicates that local companies engaging in short-term planning numbered 7 out of 17 in the Latin American group; 8 out of 17 in India; and 4 out of 11 in the Philippines.

However, taking the management philosophy of the local companies in these countries into account, one perceives that in both India and the Philippines (there was only one MS local company in

Table 3-3   Time Orientation of Planning in American Subsidiaries and Local
Companies in Argentina-Brazil-Uruguay, India, and Philippines

Country	Overall Comparisons		Most Sophisticated		Somewhat Progressive		Not Progressive	
	U.S. Sub.	Local Cos.	U.S. Sub.	Local Cos.	U.S. Sub.	Local Cos.	U.S. Sub.	Local Cos.
Argentina–Brazil–Uruguay	$n=$ 20	$n=$ 17	$n=$ 2	$n=$ 1	$n=$ 18	$n=$ 15	$n=$ 0	$n=$ 1
Short-range (1 to 2 yrs)	3	7	–	–	3	6	–	1
Long-range (5 to 10 yrs)	15	1	2	–	13	1	–	–
Nonspecific period	2	9	–	1	2	8	–	–
India	$n=$ 17	$n=$ 17	$n=$ 5	$n=$ 5	$n=$ 11	$n=$ 7	$n=$ 1	$n=$ 5
Short-range (1 to 2 yrs)	4	8	1	2	3	4	–	2
Long-range (5 to 10 yrs)	12	6	4	3	8	3	–	–
Nonspecific period	1	3	–	–	–	–	1	3
Philippines	$n=$ 10	$n=$ 11	$n=$ 4	$n=$ 4	$n=$ 6	$n=$ 7	$n=$ 0	$n=$ 0
Short-range (1 to 2 yrs)	2	4	–	1	2	3		
Long-range (5 to 10 yrs)	6	7	4	3	2	4		
Nonspecific period	2	–	–	–	2	–		

the Latin group) 3 out of 5 and 3 out of 4 of these, respectively, engaged in long-range planning.

Thus, on the basis of these data we can say that long-range
planning as an element of the modern management process manifests itself more in the case of U.S. subsidiaries in these countries
than in the case of local companies. This, in itself, is generally
known. There is, further, a good indication that, as an exception to
the above observation which underscores nationality of ownership
of the companies, the local companies which profess and practice

sophisticated management philosophy are quite likely to employ long-range planning as an element of their management process. Further indications along these lines can be seen when we examine the nature of plans which are the outcome of the planning processes.

Data in Table 3-4 refer to the plans. Examining the data in column 2 of this table, we can say that in the Argentina-Brazil-Uruguay group, 10 out of 20 of the U.S. subsidiaries formulate systematic and detailed plans according to which they would carry on activities of the enterprise. In contrast, none of the local companies

Table 3-4 Nature of Plans* in American Subsidiaries and Local Companies in Argentina-Brazil-Uruguay, India, and Philippines

	Overall Comparisons		Most Sophisticated		Somewhat Progressive		Not Progressive	
Country	U.S. Sub.	Local Cos.	U.S. Sub.	Local Cos.	U.S. Sub.	Local Cos.	U.S. Sub.	Local Cos.
Argentina–Brazil–Uruguay	$n=$ 20	$n=$ 17	$n=$ 2	$n=$ 1	$n=$ 18	$n=$ 15	$n=$ 0	$n=$ 1
Systematic and detailed plans**	10	–	1	–	9	–	–	–
Systematic but limited	4	9	–	1	4	7	–	1
Randomly done limited forecasts	4	4	1	–	3	4	–	–
No information	2	4	–	–	2	4	–	–
India	$n=$ 17	$n=$ 17	$n=$ 5	$n=$ 5	$n=$ 11	$n=$ 7	$n=$ 1	$n=$ 5
Systematic and detailed plans**	8	6	5	5	3	1	–	–
Systematic but limited	5	6	–	–	5	4	–	2
Randomly done limited forecasts	4	2	–	–	3	2	1	–
No information	–	3	–	–	–	–	–	3
Philippines	$n=$ 10	$n=$ 11	$n=$ 4	$n=$ 4	$n=$ 6	$n=$ 7	$n=$ 0	$n=$ 0
Systematic and detailed plans**	6	5	4	2	2	3		
Systematic but limited	2	2	–	1	2	1		
Randomly done limited forecasts	1	4	–	1	1	3		
No information	1	–	–	–	1	–		

* As operational programs for company's future action—results of planning process.
** Formulated with or without the use of computers, covering almost all aspects of the company—financial, managerial and product-market line.

in this group developed similar plans; however, 9 out of 17 of them developed limited plans, limited either to the financial or product aspects.

In India, the picture appeared better than in the Latin American group so far as developing detailed plans was concerned. While there were 8 out of 17 U.S. subsidiaries which developed such plans, there were 6 out of 17 Indian companies formulating detailed plans. Of the 8 American subsidiaries, 5 were MS companies; of the 6 Indian companies, 5 were also MS companies.

In the Philippines, 6 of the 10 U.S. subsidiaries (of which 4 were MS companies) and 5 of the 11 local companies (of which 2 were MS companies) formulated systematic and detailed plans. These data can be interpreted to mean that a sense of direction through detailed plans on all phases of business activities was apparent in about half of the U.S. subsidiaries and in a small number of local companies when all of the five countries are taken into account.

The frequency and the regularity of the plans is one of the indications of how alert the management of an organization is vis-a-vis changes in the business environment in which it operates. If, for comparative purposes, quarterly reviews can be used as a norm and an indication of reasonable alertness, then the following picture emerges from the data (Table 3-5) on the five countries.

In Argentina-Brazil-Uruguay ($n=37$), 1 of the MS and 5 SP American subsidiaries follow this norm. The corresponding figures for the local companies are 2 SP companies. In India ($n=34$), 5 of the MS and 4 SP U.S. subsidiaries, as well as three MS and one SP local companies, review their plans on a quarterly basis. In the Philippines ($n=21$), two MS and one SP local companies do so.

In sum, 9 out of the 34 companies in India, 8 out of the 37 companies in the Argentina-Brazil-Uruguay group, and 3 out of the 21 companies in the Philippines undertook quarterly review of their plans. If, to these figures, the number of companies which review on a monthly basis are added, one arrives at the following picture.

The proportion of U.S. subsidiaries which are alert is: Latin America, 9 out of 20; India, 14 out of 17; Philippines, 3 out of 10. The corresponding figures for the local companies are: Latin America, 6 out of 17; India, 7 out of 17; Philippines, 4 out of 11.

Comparing the review practice on the basis of management

Table 3-5 Frequency of Review of Plans in Argentina-Brazil-Uruguay, India, and Philippines

Country	Overall Comparisons		Most Sophisticated		Somewhat Progressive		Not Progressive	
	U.S. Sub.	Local Cos.	U.S. Sub.	Local Cos.	U.S. Sub.	Local Cos.	U.S. Sub.	Local Cos.
Argentina–Brazil–Uruguay	n = 20	n = 17	n = 2	n = 1	n = 18	n = 15	n = 0	n = 1
Monthly	3	4	–	1*	3	3	–	–
Quarterly	6	2	1	–	5	2	–	–
Semiannually	4	5	–	–	4	5	–	–
Annually	2	1	–	–	2	–	–	1
As and when needed	4	3	–	–	4	3	–	–
No information	1	2	1**	–	–	2	–	–
India	n = 17	n = 17	n = 5	n = 5	n = 11	n = 7	n = 1	n = 5
Monthly								
Quarterly	14	6	5	3	9	3	–	–
Semiannually	1	1	–	1	1	–	–	–
Annually								
As and when needed	2	7	–	1	1	4	1	2
No information	–	3	–	–	–	–	–	3
Philippines	n = 10	n = 11	n = 4	n = 4	n = 6	n = 7	n = 0	n = 0
Monthly	2	1	–	–	2	1		
Quarterly	1	3	–	2	1	1		
Semiannually	2	–	1	–	1	–		
Annually	4	2	3	1	1	1		
As and when needed	1	4	–	1	1	3		
No information	–	1	–	–	–	1		

* In Argentina
** In Brazil

philosophy, we found (column 3, Table 3-5) that 5 of the American MS companies but only 3 Indian MS companies followed suit. In the Philippines, the 3 American MS companies reviewed their plans on an annual rather than a quarterly basis, but 2 of the 4 Filipino MS companies reviewed on a quarterly basis. Information was available on only one of the 2 U.S. subsidiaries in the Latin American group, and that MS company also reviewed on a quarterly basis.

Summary

Viewing long-range planning as not merely forecasting, or as planning to minimize risks entailed in the business world, we emphasized that it is an intellectual process which symbolizes the purposefulness of modern management and provides a sense of direction to organizations.

Comparative data were presented for four aspects of long-range planning, namely, its nature and scope, length of plans, inclusiveness of plans, and their review. These data suggest that, proportionately, many more U.S. subsidiaries than their Indian counterparts engage in long-range planning. However, this difference becomes insignificant when such U.S. subsidiaries are compared with Indian companies at the same management philosophy indicator.

4

BUILDING THE ORGANIZATION

The nature and scope of organizations—from the less complex to the more complex—which prevail in societies in general, vary on several dimensions. Like other formal organizations, the business firm may be best described as a social, economic, and political system.

Formal organizations can be viewed as: products of historical development, as in the writings of Beard, Gaus, Macmahon, Mansfield, Waldo, and White;[1] societal phenomena, as in the explanations of Clemmer, Mayo, Miller and Form, Selznick, Warner and Low, and Weber;[2] organic cooperative systems, as in the writings of Barnard, Follet, McCurdy, Miller, and Simon;[3] and as production systems productive of goods and services.

Viewing organizations as productive systems takes into ac-

[1] See Dwight Waldo, *Perspectives of Administration* (University: University of Alabama Press, 1956), especially pp. 50–76 for an elaboration of the works of these authors.

[2] Donald Clemmer, *The Prison Community* (Boston, 1940); Elton Mayo, *The Social Problems of Industrial Civilization* (Boston, 1945); Delbert Miller and W. H. Form, *Industrial Sociology* (New York, 1951); Philip Selznick, *Leadership in Administration* (Evanston, Ill., 1957); W. L. Warner and O. Low, *The Social System of the Modern Factory* (New Haven, 1947). For a statement of Max Weber's thesis see Robert K. Merton, *et al.*, *Reader in Bureaucracy* (Glencoe, Ill., 1952).

[3] Chester Barnard, *The Functions of the Executives* (Boston, 1938) and *Organization and Management* (Boston, 1948); Metcalf and Urwick (eds.) *Dynamic Administration, the Collected Papers of Mary Parker Follet* (New York, 1941); John McCurdy, *The Structure of Morale* (Cambridge, 1943); and Herbert A. Simon, *Administrative Behavior* (New York, 1954).

count the structuring of goals, tasks, functions, individuals, and resources into a productive relationship such that the defined goals are optimally accomplished.

Starting with the people—participants in an organization—one can examine their tasks, relationships, reward systems, and so on in terms of the goal accomplishment of the organizations. We do not claim to have data on all of the interesting aspects which can be subject to comparative analyses. However, in this chapter we will compare the policies, modes of selection and development, and reward systems of the U.S. subsidiaries and local companies. On the surface, our analysis might appear to be a comparative analysis of personnel management practices in these companies, but we view them from the point of view of building, in terms of the participants, effective and viable organizations.

Whether the companies have similar views or not is at least indicated by the manner in which they handle their human resources. Whether or not the personnel management activity is organized and carried out as a separate activity, such as production or marketing, is a good indication of the importance which, in practice, managers attach to the personnel activity.

Our data suggested that, on an overall basis, in 11 of the 17 U.S. subsidiaries and in 9 of the 17 Indian-owned companies, the activity of managing men was, in fact, organized as a separate department. In the remaining cases, this function was performed either as a part of another business functional department or as one of the responsibilities of the office of the chief executive of the company. The organizational setup of managing participants was not too different among these 34 companies, either on an ownership basis or on the basis of differences in management philosophy.

What guidelines were there for managing men? Policies are guidelines, and in order to effectively perform the task of managing and developing men it is essential that there be policies which are explicit and formally documented. The nature of the policies pertaining to management of men, and by whom they were formulated, are indicated in Table 4-1. Data in this table indicate that in 8 of the 17 U.S. subsidiaries and in 12 of the 17 Indian-owned companies, there were personnel policies which were formally stated and documented. There were 8 American companies in which the general personnel policies were neither formally stated nor documented but which were deemed adequate because it was claimed that they were generally known to the members of the organization. A similar situation prevailed in 3 Indian-owned companies. Without assessing the merits or the demerits of such practices, but still making a comparison of the 5 most sophisticated (MS) American subsidiaries and 5 MS Indian companies, we can say that companies with the MS management philosophy are likely to formalize the guidelines for the management of men in their organizations.

Table 4-1   Policy Making for Personnel Management
in American and Indian Companies

	Overall Comparisons		Management Philosophy					
			Most Sophisticated		Somewhat Progressive		Not Progressive	
	U.S.	Indian	U.S.	Indian	U.S.	Indian	U.S.	Indian
	n = 17	n = 17	n = 5	n = 5	n = 11	n = 7	n = 1	n = 5
Policies								
Most policies are formally stated and documented	8	12	5	5	3	5	–	2
Most policies are not formally stated or documented but generally known to personnel	8	3	–	–	8	2	–	1
No policies as such but expedients only in personnel matters	1	2	–	–	–	–	1	2
Policies formulated by								
Chief executive	1	2	–	–	–	–	1	2
Chief executive and a committee	9	14	–	5	9	7	–	2
Special committee	7	–	5	–	2	–	–	–
Undiscernible	–	1	–	–	–	–	–	1

One good indication of whether or not such formal guidelines are really helpful in building the organization is the question of who formulates them. Is it the chief executive? Or is it the chief executive in collaboration with others? Data in Table 4-1 indicate that in the majority of cases the chief executive formulated these guidelines in collaboration with others. In 7 of the 17 U.S. subsidiaries there were special committees entrusted with the responsibility of formulating the policies; 5 of those firms were MS companies.

While the general personnel policies spell out the company's underlying philosophy toward the members of an organization, specific policies may deal with such aspects as selection, compensation, training and development, and so forth.

PERSONNEL PRACTICES

Selection Process and Authority

In order to recruit, select, and develop people in organizations, jobs need to be analyzed, described, and specified. These tasks are commonly subsumed under the label of job evaluation. Selection of people involves matching traits and levels of ability with job specifications and requirements. While the methods of selection generally follow similar patterns, such as evaluating the background and experience of the applicant, and assessing his aptitudes and abilities on the one hand and attitudes on the other, we were more interested summarily in the process of selection rather than in the details. We identified the selection process either as formal or informal, based on what we learned from the companies. Also, we inquired into the question of who actually made the final decision in the selection process. Data on these two points are given in Table 4-2.

Data in Table 4-2 indicate the following features of selection. On the basis of overall comparisons, 8 of the 17 U.S. subsidiaries, but only 4 of the 17 Indian-owned companies, had formalized their selection processes. Final selection decisions were made by a committee in 7 of these 8 U.S. subsidiaries and in 10 of the 17 Indian companies. Of these 10, only 4 had formalized selection process.

Comparing the situation among the Most Sophisticated companies, we found that in 5 of the American subsidiaries and in 3 out of the 5 Indian companies the selection process was formalized; the final selections were made by a committee in all of the 5 Indian MS companies and in 4 out of the 5 U.S. MS subsidiaries.

Two other features which we noticed were: (1) that the selection of blue- and white-collar workers was, in most cases, within the

Table 4-2   Aspects of Managers' Selection and Training in American
Subsidiaries and Indian Companies

	Overall Comparisons		Management Philosophy					
			Most Sophisticated		Somewhat Progressive		Not Progressive	
	U.S.	Indian	U.S.	Indian	U.S.	Indian	U.S.	Indian
	$n=$ 17	$n=$ 17	$n=$ 5	$n=$ 5	$n=$ 11	$n=$ 7	$n=$ 1	$n=$ 5
Selection process								
Formalized*	8	4	5	3	3	1	–	–
Informal only	9	13	–	2	8	6	1	5
Selection made by								
A committee**	7	10	4	5	3	4	–	1
Chief Executive only	1	3	–	–	–	–	1	3
Chief Executive and other managers	3	2	–	–	3	2	–	–
Other managers†	6	2	1	–	5	1	–	1
Nature of training programs								
O-J-T† and In-Company	3	1	3	–	–	1	–	–
O-J-T† and Outside	5	6	2	5	3	–	–	1
O-J-T† only	4	4	–	–	4	1	–	3
Informed, ad hoc	5	6	–	–	4	5	1	1

* Policies and procedures being explicit and formalized, to a great extent.
** Subject to formal approval by the chief executive.
† Formalized management training and development programs.

purview of the authority of the personnel or industrial relations manager, who would collaborate with the functional managers in terms of their needs and specifications; and (2) the existence of the committee form of selection in companies where the selection process was not formalized.

Training Managers and Technicians

The training and development of members in any organization is a necessary function, not only to upgrade the skills and knowledge of these people but also to develop a pool from which future needs can be met. In our study we attempted to discern the nature of training and development programs for blue- and white-collar workers, for technical staff, and for managers at various levels. The information which we obtained suggested that the training programs for production and other workers were comprehensive and similar in most of the companies in our sample, both in the U.S. subsidiaries and in the Indian-owned companies. Thus, we will focus upon the nature of training programs for managers and technical staff members.

We classified the nature of the programs as (1) on-the-job only, (2) on-the-job plus in-company, and (3) on-the-job plus outside program. Data for technical staff members suggested that while no one particular method was dominant, the practices were equally proportional both in the subsidiaries and the Indian companies. That is, there were 5 Indian and 5 U.S. subsidiaries which had O-J-T programs only; the same number with O-J-T plus in-company; and the same number with O-J-T and outside programs.

When comparisons were made on the basis of management philosophy, data showed that in 3 American and 1 Indian (MS) companies there were O-J-T plus in-company programs while in 2 American and 4 Indian (MS) companies there were O-J-T plus outside programs. In the case of Somewhat Progressive (SP) companies, 5 of the 11 U.S. subsidiaries and 2 of the 7 Indian companies had O-J-T programs only, for the technical staff. While the needs of individual organizations differ somewhat in terms of the O-J-T plus programs for technical staff, it was gratifying to observe that there was adequate recognition by the Indian companies of the importance of such programs.

However, the case was different when the question of training and development of managerial personnel came up. As the data in Table 4-2 indicate, 8 of the 17 American and 7 of the Indian companies had the O-J-T plus programs for managers. Also, 5 of the American and 6 of the Indian companies did not have any formal training and development programs. Whatever they had could best be described as informal, ad hoc, and expeditious. Yet, when we examine the picture among the MS companies, we find that all of the 5 American and the 5 Indian companies had O-J-T plus programs for their managerial personnel.

Compensation and Promotion

Many technical points are to be found in the structure of salaries; however, the company's underlying philosophy is an important cornerstone of such a structure. We attempted to discern whether the underlying philosophy was to compensate at, or above, the prevailing levels. Data, as given in Table 4-3, indicated that 6 of the 17 American subsidiaries and 3 of the 17 Indian companies expressed their philosophy as maintaining salaries and fringe benefits, of both the managerial and nonmanagerial workers, above the going levels. The majority of the companies, on the other hand, followed the practice of compensating their workers at the going levels.

Table 4-3   Aspects of Managers' Compensation and Promotion in American Subsidiaries and Indian Companies

	Overall Comparisons		Management Philosophy					
			Most Sophisticated		Somewhat Progressive		Not Progressive	
	U.S.	Indian	U.S.	Indian	U.S.	Indian	U.S.	Indian
	$n=$ 17	$n=$ 17	$n=$ 5	$n=$ 5	$n=$ 11	$n=$ 7	$n=$ 1	$n=$ 5
Pattern of compensating managers: wages/fringes								
Above the going level	6	3	5	2	1	1	–	–
At the going level	10	13	–	3	9	5	1	5
No policy indicated	1	1	–	–	1	1	–	–
Procedures for managerial succession								
Formal*	7	5	5	4	1	1	1	–
Informal	10	12	–	1	10	6	–	5
Promotional decisions made by								
Chief executive	7	7	–	–	6	3	1	4
Special committee	6	8	4	5	2	3	–	–
Chief executive and divisional/ personnel manager	4	2	1	–	3	1	–	1

* Such as job rotation, understudy, and others.

Comparing the Most Sophisticated American and Indian companies, we found that the U.S. subsidiaries maintained salaries and fringes above the going levels for managers, while a similar trend was noticed only among 2 of the 5 MS Indian companies. The opinion of senior managers in the remaining 3 Indian companies could be summed up as "essential to draw good talent, and we *have* to do it" as expressive of the need to profess and practice the notion of maintaining salary and fringe levels for managers above the prevailing standards.

One of the important ingredients in building effective organizations is systematic managerial succession. Data from the companies surveyed (Table 4-3) indicated that in the majority of cases, whether the companies were U.S. subsidiaries or Indian-owned, managerial succession was quite informal and not very systematic—a reflection perhaps of an absence of high-level manpower planning. However, among those which employed formal procedures to ensure managerial succession, 5 out of the 7 U.S. subsidiaries and 4 out of the 5 Indian companies were in the MS category.

Management Philosophy and Personnel Practices

In order to systematically evaluate the relationships between management philosophy and personnel practices, the following factors were analyzed in 15 pairs of the American subsidiaries and local firms in India:

(1) manpower planning
(2) employee selection
(3) compensation and employee benefits
(4) employee appraisal system
(5) training and development for management and supervisory personnel
(6) training and development for blue-collar workers

Spearman's rank correlation coefficient between the management philosophy scores and the personnel practices index was found to be 0.67. Detailed statistical computations on these variables are given in Appendix A, Tables A-3 and A-4.

Delegation

Many studies of management have indicated that a cardinal reason for the failure of managers is their inability to delegate authority. Although there may be other factors, Gaudet's study of 200 company failures, for example, underscored managers' inability to delegate as the main reason.

To what extent there is delegation of decision-making authority in an organization at any one time is very difficult to assess. We were, however, able to obtain some data on the layers of hierarchy, definition of authority relationships, means of authority giving as indicators of delegation in a formal way, and on the opinions of managers as indicators of delegation in reality.

Data presented in Table 4-4 suggest the following when comparisons are made on the basis of company ownership, i.e., American vs. Indian. In the case of 14 out of 17 U.S. subsidiaries, the number of layers of hierarchy is not great. If we interpret the small number of layers as fewer steps or channels in communication and as indicative of greater delegation of authority, the U.S. companies show this trend while the Indian-owned companies do not. In fact, there were 9 companies with 8 to 15 layers of hierarchy and 8 with 5 to 7 layers. This is as one might expect, particularly when one notes that the style of management in the Indian-owned enterprises has been characterized as "highly centralized and personal," a state of affairs which has its "roots in the nature of the managing-agency system." As a recent observer Pelissier put it, "Delegation is not widely practiced [in India]. Nonetheless . . . I was asked to discuss 'delegation of authority' more frequently than any other management topic."[4]

According to Pelissier, there should be a great deal of interest in such a management practice despite the legacy of the management agency system. If we look at Table 4-4, and make comparisons on the basis of management philosophy, the fact that in our small sample of 17 Indian-owned companies there are 5 progressive companies in which the layers of hierarchy are quite similar to those of the 14 U.S. subsidiaries becomes evident. These five companies are

[4] Raymond Pelissier, "Certain Aspects of Management in India," *Michigan Business Review*, Vol. 16, No. 3 (May 1964), p. 7.

Table 4-4   Organization Structure in American and Indian Companies, Overall and According to Management Philosophy

	Overall Compari-sons		Management Philosophy					
			Most Sophisti-cated		Somewhat Progres-sive		Not Progres-sive	
	U.S.	Indian	U.S.	Indian	U.S.	Indian	U.S.	Indian
	n= 17	n= 17	n= 5	n= 5	n= 11	n= 7	n= 1	n= 5
Layers of hierarchy*								
8 to 15 and more	3	9	–	–	2	4	1	5
5 to 7	14	8	5	5	9	3	–	–
Authority definition via charts								
Yes, with aid from staff dept.	8	2	5	2	3	–	–	–
Yes, without aid from staff dept.	3	6	–	3	3	3	–	–
No charts	6	9	–	–	5	4	1	5
Authority given by								
Written means	10	3	5	3	5	–	–	–
Oral means	7	13	–	2	6	7	1	4
No formal means (unknown)	–	1	–	–	–	–	–	1
Forces which brought change								
Economic/social	12	11	5	5	6	6	–	4
Personality	5	5	–	–	5	1	–	1
Random/unknown	–	1	–	–	–	–	1	–

* Interpreted here as "the larger the number of layers, the greater the number of people through whom issues go; and therefore, the lesser the delegation of decision-making authority."

MS type companies. We can therefore suggest that those companies which profess progressive management philosophy tend to put into practice a system of delegated authority. Let us examine the statement of an executive—an Indian national—of a large U.S. subsidiary which was an MS company:

In our company, a man's authority to do things is limited by his own capacity. We are always looking for an opportunity to delegate decision-making power . . . I do not know how else one can run a large firm effectively. Our promotion criteria are also based upon how well a manager delegates and trains his subordinates . . .

Another executive, also an Indian national, of a large Indian-owned company (MS management philosophy) echoes the above concern in the following manner:

. . . Training and giving an employee a chance to exercise his judgment and make decisions are our way of doing things in this company. There is no one boss . . . All employees are decision-makers . . . and unless one demonstrates his willingness to take up this challenge [i.e., delegation] he will be out of this company very soon. . . .

While the above two illustrations are encouraging, such is not the case with all of the other companies. Again, it is not simply among the Indian-owned companies that delegation is not practiced as well as it could be. That he did not have a great deal of confidence in the capabilities of his subordinates is reflected in the following statement made by an American manager in charge of a U.S. subsidiary:

When it comes to decisions . . . we [i.e., top managers] make them. All our executives from the United States are sent for this purpose . . . we cannot always trust the judgment of the Indian managers. They are alright for routine assignments . . . We do not encourage them to aspire for top jobs . . . .

A centralized and personal management style is revealed in the following observation of an Indian manager in an Indian company, which, according to our classification, was one having a non-progressive management philosophy:

Now-a-days we hear a good deal on "delegation." The American professors give big lectures on delegation . . . I don't understand how anybody can run a business which is not his own. My people are happy doing routine jobs but when it comes to deciding something I can take care of that. Of course, the general manager is on my side and some times I reveal a little about what I might do. Unfortunately our firm is not doing very well, so, I have to make even the small decisions.

Management Philosophy and Decentralization

To examine the relationship between the management philosophy variable and decentralization, the following factors were evaluated:

(1) layers of hierarchy—from top executives to the blue-collar worker
(2) locus of decision-making with respect to major policies (e.g., mergers, major expansions, or suspensions)
(3) locus of decision-making with respect to sales policies, product-mix, standard-settings in production, manpower policies, selection of executives, participation in long-range planning, and the degree of information sharing.

In order to arrive at a composite index for decentralization, we devised a three-point ranking scale for each of the factors evaluated. Details of this scaling are presented in Appendix A, Table A-9. Spearman's rank correlation coefficient between the management philosophy variable and the decentralization index was found to be 0.81. Details on this aspect are given in Table A-7.

INTERNATIONAL COMPARISONS

Formalization of broad policies regarding the management of men in the five countries did not follow any pattern. The proportion of the companies in which there was an indication of formal statement and documentation of personnel policies varied from one country to the next.

In India, in 8 of the 17 U.S. subsidiaries and 12 of the 17 Indian-owned enterprises, there was formalization. Similar numbers for the Latin American group were 5 of the 20 subsidiaries and 5 of the 17 national companies. In the Philippines the proportion was much less, i.e., 3 of the 10 subsidiaries and 1 of the 11 local companies. By far, in the majority of the 92 companies studied, there was an air of informality surrounding company policies toward personnel.

Comparing the most sophisticated (MS) companies with the least sophisticated (NP) companies with respect to such policy statement and documentation, we arrive at the following picture. In India, all of the MS companies, both the U.S. subsidiaries and the Indian companies, formally stated and documented their policies. Among the NP companies, the 1 U.S. subsidiary and 2 of the 5 Indian companies have had no policies, either formal or informal, as such. Whatever the underlying features of their practices, they could best be described as expedients.

In the Philippines, 3 of the 4 MS U.S. subsidiaries and 1 of the 4 MS local companies formally stated and documented their policies. The remaining firms did not do so, but gave the impression that their personnel policies were generally known to all of the participants in their organizations.

Selection of managers followed a group decision-making pattern in all of the five countries. This dominant pattern had two variations: (1) in some cases there was a special committee endowed with the responsibility for selecting capable men for managerial positions; (2) in some others, the decision on selection was made by the chief executive of the company, who would collaborate with other managers in arriving at such selection decisions. The formal committee form and the management philosophies of these companies are provided in Table 4-5.

Table 4-5   Joint Selection of Managers: Comparisons

U.S. Subsidiaries	Local Companies	Country
3 out of 6 (3 SP)	2 out of 5 (2 SP)	Argentina
5 out of 8 (5 SP)	1 out of 7 (SP)	Brazil
3 out of 17 (3 SP)	2 out of 17 (2 SP)	India
2 out of 10 (SP)	6 out of 11 (3 MS, 3 SP)	Philippines
2 out of 7 (SP)	1 out of 5 (SP)	Uruguay

Examination of the formalized training and development of the people selected for managerial positions showed a contrast between the Latin American group and India, as well as the Philippines. In Argentina, Brazil, and Uruguay, training and development were on an informal and ad hoc basis among the U.S. subsidiaries as well as among the local companies, without exception. In India and the Philippines, on the other hand, training was on a formal basis in a number of companies as revealed in the following table. It can be inferred that the MS companies, except the two in the Philippines, tend to provide training and development opportunities for their managers above and beyond those that are available on, and needed for, the job. As important as selecting people for managerial positions and providing them with opportunities to grow,

Table 4-6   Formalized Training-Development: India and Philippines

U.S. Subsidiaries		Local Companies	Country
O-J-T and in-company	3 (MS)	1 (MS)	India
	1 (MS)	2 (MS)	Philippines
O-J-T and outside	5 (2 MS, 3 SP)	6 (5 MS, 1 NP)	India
	5 (2 MS, 3 SP)	7 (1 MS, 6 SP)	Philippines
O-J-T only	4 (SP)	4 (1 SP, 3 NP)	India
	1 (MS)	1 (MS)	Philippines

is the philosophy which underlies their compensation. Data with respect to compensation were available only for the companies located in India and the Philippines. They are given in Table 4-7.

As the above data suggest, in some of the companies located in India there was an underlying philosophy of compensating at a level above and beyond the going rate. There were 5 MS American subsidiaries and 2 MS local companies in India which pursued such a compensation policy. These companies were probably better off in terms of attracting able managers. In the Philippines there were 3 SP American subsidiaries and just 1 SP local company which followed similar practices. The remainder of the companies did not seem to recognize the importance of acquiring superior talent in order to build up their organizations. Our attempts to find out if they were doing anything else—such as planning for managerial succession—which would help strengthen the organization, indicated that no genuine positive steps were being taken in this direction.

Table 4-7   Goal in Managerial Compensation

	U.S. Subsidiaries	Local Companies	Country
To maintain salaries *above* going rates	6 (5 MS, 1 SP)	3 (2 MS, 1 SP)	India
	1 (SP)	3 (SP)	Philippines
To maintain salaries at the going rates	10 (9 SP, 1 NP)	13 (3 MS, 5 SP, 5 NP)	India
	5 (4 MS, 1 SP)	3 (MS)	Philippines
No goal, no policy	1 (SP)	1 (SP)	India
	4 (SP)	5 (1 MS, 4 SP)	Philippines

Summary

Our focus in this chapter was on organization building, by which we referred to the policies and practices which the companies followed in obtaining and retaining managerial manpower resources. Analyses of intracountry (India) data suggested that formalization of general policies upon which organization-building activities could be pursued prevailed in companies with progressive management philosophy (MS) regardless of nationality-ownership. In addition, selection of men for managerial positions was in essence a group-decision process among the U.S. subsidiaries and among the Indian-owned enterprises. Formal training and development schemes were not widely prevalent among the 34 companies, but those which were of the MS-type provided excellent opportunities for growth and self-development.

The limited international comparisons suggested that except in the case of India there was not much formalization with respect to policy for organization building, that selection of managers was a group-decision process in all of the five countries, and that training and development was more formalized in India and the Philippines than in Argentina, Brazil, and Uruguay, irrespective of ownership-nationality.

5

POLICY MAKING, LEADERSHIP, AND MOTIVATION

POLICY MAKING

Policies are guides to decision making. They reflect and interpret organizational objectives, channel decisions which contribute to those objectives, and establish the framework of the various functional segments of the business organization. On the one hand, there generally are company-wide policies, i.e., those which are likely to have company-wide, long-term implications and those which are generally formulated by the top management group. On the other hand, there are those which relate to the functional areas. These two sets, however, are interrelated. As Koontz and O'Donnell expressed it, these "Major policies beget derivative policies to guide the decision-making of subordinate managers."[1] In addition, policies also serve as mechanisms for the control of performance. In Ginzberg's words: "The range of actions which management of large organizations can take to control ineffective performance can be viewed in terms of the need to plan, the stability of policies, and the specifics of policies and procedures."[2] The following data and analysis pertain to the question of who, in fact, formulated the company-wide and functional policies in the companies which we surveyed.

[1] Harold Koontz and Cyril O'Donnell, *Principles of Management* (New York: McGraw-Hill Book Company, 1964), p. 158.
[2] Eli Ginzberg, *The Development of Human Resources* (New York: McGraw-Hill Book Company, 1966), p. 206.

Intracountry Comparisons

Information was obtained from the 17 U.S. subsidiaries and the 17 Indian-owned enterprises with regard to (1) whether or not the chief executive of the company formulated the company-wide policy alone, and (2) to what extent functional managers participated in the policy-making process insofar as their functional departments were concerned. Table 5-1 provides these data.

Examining the overall comparisons we found that in more than half of the Indian-owned companies the chief executive formulated company-wide policies by himself. This phenomenon was not altogether absent in the U.S. subsidiary companies; even among them

Table 5-1   Policy Making in American and Indian Companies

| | Overall Comparisons | | Management Philosophy | | | | | |
| | | | Most Sophisticated | | Somewhat Progressive | | Not Progressive | |
	U.S. $n=$ 17	Indian $n=$ 17	U.S. $n=$ 5	Indian $n=$ 5	U.S. $n=$ 11	Indian $n=$ 7	U.S. $n=$ 1	Indian $n=$ 5
Major policy decisions by								
Top executives only	6	13	–	2	5	6	1	5
Top executives and committee*	11	4	5	3	6	1	–	–
Product policy decisions by								
Top executives only	–	5	–	–	–	–	–	5
Top and manufacturing executives	6	3	–	2	5	1	1	–
Committee*	11	9	5	3	6	6	–	–
Marketing policy decisions by								
Top executives only	9	8	–	–	9	3	–	5
Top and marketing executives only	2	7	1	3	–	4	1	–
Committee*	6	2	4	2	2	–	–	–

* The term committee is used in a general sense. It is said to consist of the chief executive, top manager of a functional area, and other key personnel. Our concern has not so much been with who makes up the committee, as the presence or absence of it for policy-making purposes.

there were 6 companies in which major policies were made by the chief executive. In the remainder of the companies—that is, in 11 of the 17 U.S. subsidiaries and in 4 of the 17 Indian-owned enterprises—the committee form of policy formulation was evident.[3]

Comparisons on the basis of management philosophy tend to alter the above picture. We see that all of the 5 MS-type U.S. subsidiaries and 3 of the MS-type Indian companies follow the committee form. At the other extreme, in all of the NP-type companies —1 U.S. and 5 Indian-owned—it was the chief executive who formulated the company-wide policies with little or no consultation with other members of the organization.

The above held true in the area of company-wide policies. However, this does not appear to be the pattern in the functional areas. Our inquiry was restricted to "product" and "marketing" policies. Data on these (Table 5-1) indicate that in none of the two sets of companies, except in the 5 NP-type Indian-owned enterprises, were product policies made by the chief executive only. In both the U.S. subsidiaries and the Indian companies, some form of group decision making, either in the form of a committee or the chief executive in collaboration with the manufacturing manager, was apparent. When comparisons were made on the basis of management philosophy, all of the 5 MS-type American subsidiaries and 3 of the MS-type Indian companies had constituted committees to formulate product policies.

The area of marketing policies is handled somewhat differently; there, top executives making policies on their own were common. On an overall basis, in nearly half the cases (both U.S. subsidiaries and the Indian companies) the chief executive alone had the task of formulating marketing policies. But again, in the case of MS-type companies, there was group action; 4 of the 5 MS American subsidiaries and 2 of the 5 Indian-owned companies had committees.

International Comparisons

Data in Table 5-2 are consolidated so as to reflect the pattern of policy making in the five countries. The underlying question is:

[3] The term committee is used in a general sense to include formal, ad hoc, special, or any form of group thinking.

Were there country or management philosophy differences insofar as the policy-making role of the chief executives could be ascertained? In the Latin American group (Argentina, Brazil, and Uruguay), the chief executive of the U.S. subsidiary companies, as well as those of national companies, tended to retain for himself the prerogative of formulating major company-wide policies. In India, the committee method of arriving at major decisions prevailed over the practice of allowing the chief executive to arrive at the decisions alone. The picture in the Philippines more nearly approximated that

Table 5-2 Major Policy Making: International Comparisons

Country	Overall Comparisons U.S. Local Sub. Cos.		Management Philosophy					
			Most Sophisticated U.S. Local Sub. Cos.		Somewhat Progressive U.S. Local Sub. Cos.		Not Progressive U.S. Local Sub. Cos.	
	$n=$	$n=$	$n=$	$n=$	$n=$	$n=$	$n=$	$n=$
Argentina-Brazil-Uruguay*	18	14	2	1	16	12	0	1
Major policies by								
Chief executive only	13	11	2	–	11	10	–	1
Chief executive and committee	5	3	–	1	5	2	–	–
	$n=$	$n=$	$n=$	$n=$	$n=$	$n=$	$n=$	$n=$
India	17	17	5	5	11	7	1	5
Major policies by								
Chief executive only	6	13	–	2	5	6	1	5
Chief executive and committee	11	4	5	3	6	1		–
	$n=$	$n=$	$n=$	$n=$	$n=$	$n=$	$n=$	$n=$
Philippines**	9*	10*	4	4	6	7**	0	0
Major policies by								
Chief executive only	1	5	0	3	1	5	–	–
Chief executive and committee	6	2	2	1	4	1	–	–

* In the case of two American subsidiaries and three local firms, information was inadequate on major policies and who makes them.

** In the case of one American subsidiary, indications were that major policies emanated from the parent company in the U.S. And in the case of one local company, there was no policy in any formal sense.

of India than that of the Latin American countries. See Table 5-2.

With reference to product and marketing policies, our data indicated that the functional managers were quite active in such policy formulation in the Latin American group. In the Philippines —while in a larger proportion of U.S. subsidiaries the production manager was the policy-maker at the functional level—the same pattern could also be discerned among comparable national companies.

We can therefore suggest that there appeared to be more managerial participation among the U.S. subsidiary companies than among the national companies in the five countries studied. However, there is also some indication that, irrespective of country ownership, progressive companies tend to manifest participation in policy making more than do nonprogressive companies.

A related but important aspect of policy making is for the top managers to assure that the policies are adequately executed at the middle and lower managerial levels. Whether or not there is participation by subordinate managers could be one indication of the policy-making process, or even of the leadership style, in an organization. On the subject of company planning for the future, we tried to ascertain whether the subordinate managers in the 34 companies located in India participated in the planning activity, and whether some information on the future plans of the companies was shared by the top managers. The following data and quotations focus upon participation and information sharing in the case of the 17 U.S. subsidiaries and 17 Indian-owned enterprises.

Participation and Information Sharing

The comparative data presented in the following table refer to participation and information sharing. While it is often emphasized that participation is a prerequisite to the success of plans and programs in the companies, there is also the implication that American firms encourage more participation and share more information with their subordinate managers than do other nationality firms. Thus, we could raise two questions: Is participation (and information sharing) greater in American companies compared to that of Indian-owned companies? Is participation (and information sharing) greater in MS companies than in SP or NP companies? Let us examine the data (Table 5-3).

Table 5-3   Participation and Information Sharing in Company Planning

Management Philosophy	Participation in the Planning Activity		Means of Reporting on Plans		
	Top level managers only	Top and middle managers	Confi-dential memos/ verbal reports	Special reports	General reports on goals and means
Most sophisticated					
U.S. $n = 5$	–	5	–	–	5
Indian $n = 5$	1	4	1	2	2
Somewhat progressive					
U.S. $n = 11$	5	6	2	6	3
Indian $n = 7$	6	1	3	4	–
Not progressive					
U.S. $n = 1$	1	–	1	–	–
Indian $n = 5$	5	–	5	–	–

The answer to the first question is a qualified "yes." In 11 of the 17 U.S. subsidiaries middle management participation in the corporate planning activity was indicated, compared to only 5 such cases among the 17 Indian-owned enterprises. Also, if we could interpret the means of reporting on plans as indicative of information sharing, confidential reporting was practiced in only 3 of the 17 American subsidiaries whereas it was practiced in about half the Indian companies.

The answer to the second question is a more positive one. Data indicate that all of the five MS subsidiaries and 4 of the 5 MS Indian companies allowed participation by middle managers. All of the five MS subsidiaries also prepared general reports on goals and means and circulated them among subordinate managers. In contrast, all of the NP companies (both U.S. and Indian) indicated no participation by subordinate managers, and their means of reporting on planned activities was either through confidential memos or verbally to selected members of the organization.

While it is difficult to offer explanations as to why these differences exist between the more progressive and the less progressive companies, additional light is shed by the following quotations.

An American executive of an MS-type U.S. subsidiary expressed this conviction: "There are no secrets in our company . . . We make every attempt to inform all our people where we want to go and how far we have gone. This is where our strength lies— in creating a well-committed manpower."

In a similar vein, an Indian executive of an MS-type Indian company pointed to the need to share goals, even with the employees: "We know where we are going and so do the employees . . . It would be fatal for us if they did not know . . . After all they are the ones who have to work to reach the goals."

These two managers were top-level managers and the companies in which they worked were MS companies on our management philosophy scale. It would be interesting, and useful, if we had information on how the subordinate managers in these two companies felt, but we do not have such information. The following two quotations provide a clue to the manner in which subordinate managers might express their views if there were either little or no participation or information sharing among the members.

An assistant works manager in an American subsidiary, which incidentally was not an MS company, expressed the atmosphere of secretiveness which surrounds his company plans: "Our company planning is done by the general manager and his staff . . . No one else is expected to know . . . Of course, I came to know about it through my own channels . . . that is the way it works."

An Indian national, an assistant manager of a soft drink manufacturing company, expressed his total lack of knowledge of production-related figures when he said: "What planning figures? You will have to ask our managing director . . . I don't think even his own son [the plant manager in this case] knows what his father has in mind." The company was Indian-owned and was among the SP group.

LEADERSHIP

Given the frameworks for decision and action, a major input in any organization consists of human effort. The economist may focus upon material inputs such as the physical, financial, and technical resources, but managers of organizations—which are not only economic but social systems—must face such organizational realities as attracting people, inducing them to remain within the system, insuring reliable role performance, and, in addition, stimulating actions which will facilitate organizational accomplishments. These are some of the key aspects of the organizational environment. The responsibility to create a conducive organizational environment generally rests with the men at the top and is closely related to the concept of leadership.

Writers and practitioners of management devote considerable attention to this concept. Some tend to equate leadership with management. We tend to think that leadership is an important aspect of management. The substance of leadership lies in influencing others to become followers. McGregor appealed to managers to adopt a philosophy of leadership based on the assumption that individuals want to be self-actualizing and want to participate in harmony with the organizational environment.[4]

The type of approach which a manager adopts in order to influence his subordinates provides one basis for classifying the form of leadership. If the approach is based primarily on fear, threat, and the use of force, the form of leadership can be described as negative. If, on the other hand, it is based upon incentives and rewards, it can be identified as positive leadership. One can also classify leadership as (1) authoritarian, (2) democratic, or (3) laissez-faire.

Another useful typology of leadership is the one suggested by Selznick, who distinguished between "institutional leadership" and "organization management." To him, leadership involves formulating the decisions which are of the greatest long-term importance for the organization as a whole. In contrast, organization management is viewed as concerned more with the efficiency process of controlling the firm and directing it toward known and defined objectives. Thus, leadership, from the Selznick point of view, is found primarily at the top of the organizational hierarchy.[5]

[4] Warren G. Bennis and Edgar Schein, *Leadership and Motivation, Essays of Douglas McGregor* (Cambridge, Mass.: M.I.T. Press, 1966).
[5] Philip A. Selznick, *TVA and the Grass Roots* (Berkeley: University of California Press, 1953).

For purposes of learning about leadership in the U.S. subsidiary organizations and their Indian counterparts, we adopted the Selznick viewpoint and focused upon what he referred to as "institutional leadership." A variety of direct and indirect questions were asked of the respondents in the companies studied; the data on the classification of leadership style, as well as leaders' perception of their subordinates, are subjectively based, but we tend to think that they are useful for comparative purposes despite this limitation.

Intracountry Comparisons

Data on managers' perception of subordinates pertain to India only. Table 5-4 presents data on the basis of nationality-ownership as well as management philosophy classifications.

The picture which emerges from the data in Table 5-4 is one of contrast; two different categories appear, whether the comparisons are made on the basis of ownership or of management philosophy. While most of the managers in the U.S. subsidiaries tend to perceive their subordinates as confident and trustworthy, their counterparts in the Indian companies look upon them as untrustworthy. Among the MS-type organizations, managers in all 5 of the American subsidiaries regarded their subordinates as trustworthy, while the managers of only 2 of the 5 Indian companies thought simi-

Table 5-4 Manager's (Leader's) Perception of Subordinates in the Indian Context

	Overall Comparisons		Management Philosophy					
			Most Sophisticated		Somewhat Progressive		Not Progressive	
	U.S.	Indian	U.S.	Indian	U.S.	Indian	U.S.	Indian
	$n=$ 17	$n=$ 17	$n=$ 5	$n=$ 5	$n=$ 11	$n=$ 7	$n=$ 1	$n=$ 5
Subordinates seen as confident and trustworthy	16	2	5	2	10	–	1	–
Some condescending confidence in subordinates	–	3	–	1	–	2	–	–
Subordinates not seen as confident or trustworthy	1	12	–	2	1	5	–	5

Table 5-5   Leadership Styles: International Comparisons

Country	Overall Comparisons U.S. Sub. Local Cos.		Management Philosophy					
			Most Sophisticated U.S. Sub. Local Cos.		Somewhat Progressive U.S. Sub. Local Cos.		Not Progressive U.S. Sub. Local Cos.	
	U.S. Sub.	Local Cos.	U.S. Sub.	Local Cos.	U.S. Sub.	Local Cos.	U.S. Sub.	Local Cos.
Argentina-Brazil-Uruguay	$n=$ 20	$n=$ 17	$n=$ 2	$n=$ 1	$n=$ 18	$n=$ 15	$n=$ 0	$n=$ 1
Democratic	13	6	2	1	11	5	–	–
Authoritarian	5	8	–	–	5	7	–	1
Bureaucratic	1	1	–	–	1	1	–	–
Not clear-cut	1	2	–	–	1	2	–	–
India	$n=$ 17	$n=$ 17	$n=$ 5	$n=$ 5	$n=$ 11	$n=$ 7	$n=$ 1	$n=$ 5
Democratic	7	3	4	3	3	–	–	–
Authoritarian	4	9	1	–	3	4	–	5
Bureaucratic	6	5	–	2	5	3	1	–
Philippines	$n=$ 10	$n=$ 11	$n=$ 4	$n=$ 4	$n=$ 6	$n=$ 7	$n=$ 0	$n=$ 0
Democratic	3	4	3	2	1	2		
Authoritarian	7	6	1	1	5	5		
Bureaucratic	–	1	–	1	–	–		

larly of their subordinates. Whatever the valid explanations may be, lack of mutual trust could only be a deterrent to building harmonious superior-subordinate relationships in organizations.

The concept of leadership style refers to the manner in which different individuals occupying similar executive positions in similar organizations make use of the power or authority of their office. Leadership style of U.S. presidents would illustrate this concept well. We identified leadership styles on the basis of information obtained from several respondents in each company. In other words, we identified the style of the chief executive of each of the companies either as democratic, authoritarian, or bureaucratic on the basis of secondary sources of information. We employed the terms *democratic* and *authoritarian* in the sense in which these terms are generally employed in the literature on leadership. In addition to these, we added the *bureaucratic* style. The bureaucratic leader was one who attempted to influence his subordinates by emphasizing the maze of bureaucratic rules, regulations, and operational procedures; he was neither democratic nor authoritarian. Data on leadership styles (Table 5-5) pertain to all five countries. Thus, we could make an international comparison of these styles.

International Comparisons

In Argentina, Brazil and Uruguay, among the 20 U.S. subsidiaries, the dominant style of leadership was the democratic. However, the authoritarian style prevailed in about a fourth of these companies. Among the 15 local companies, the authoritarian form was the dominant pattern, with the democratic form prevalent in some companies. The MS-type companies, however, manifested the democratic style of leadership.

In India, all three forms were prevalent, although the democratic form appeared in proportionately more U.S. subsidiaries than Indian companies.

In the case of companies in the Philippines, the dominant style was authoritarian in the local as well as in the U.S. subsidiary companies. However, in 3 out of 4 MS American subsidiaries, and in 2 out of 4 MS Philippine companies, the leadership style tended to be democratic.

Thus, there were indications that the democratic style of leadership was prevalent in a large number of the companies studied. There was also an indication of an association between progressive management philosophy and democratic leadership.

MOTIVATION

Man is a "wanting" animal, and he wants progressively varied inputs rather than merely more of the same. Once he has his basic and self-esteem needs gratified, he seeks self-fulfillment.

Developing an effective motivational system which can conduce such gratification is a difficult task in organizations. Nevertheless, it is essential. Barnard expressed it "as a basic factor in inducing individuals to work for the organization."[6] If the motivational system can be construed as the reward-penalty system, monetary rewards remain important, despite the fact that modern organization theorists have suggested other types of rewards.

There are many ways in which the reward-penalty system can be analyzed. One typology is that of Clark and Wilson,[7] who suggest that rewards and penalties can be classified as: (1) Material—tangible and usually monetary; (2) Solidary—intangible and derived from associating with others in the organization; and (3) Purposive —intangible and derived from identifying with the goals of the organization.

Taking a lead from the Clark-Wilson typology, we endeavor to ascertain (1) how nonmanagerial employees participated in the organization in relation to their jobs; (2) how managers viewed the

Table 5-6   Motivation Programs in American Subsidiary Companies and Indian Companies

Level of Employees at which Programs Aimed	Overall Comparisons		Most Sophisticated		Somewhat Progressive		Not Progressive	
	U.S. $n=$ 17	Indian $n=$ 17	U.S. $n=$ 5	Indian $n=$ 5	U.S. $n=$ 11	Indian $n=$ 7	U.S. $n=$ 1	Indian $n=$ 5
Managers, middle and above								
Primarily monetary	1	3	–	–	1	2	–	1
Monetary and nonmonetary	16	14	5	5	10	5	1	4
White-collar workers								
Primarily monetary	12	13	2	1	9	7	1	5
Monetary and nonmonetary	5	4	3	4	2	–	–	–
Blue-collar workers								
Primarily monetary	13	17	3	5	9	7	1	5
Monetary and nonmonetary	4	–	2	–	2	–	–	–

The column header "Management Philosophy" spans Overall Comparisons, Most Sophisticated, Somewhat Progressive, and Not Progressive.

[6] Chester I. Barnard, The Functions of the Executive (Cambridge, Mass.: Harvard University Press, 1938), pp. 139–160.

[7] Peter B. Clark and James Q. Wilson, "Incentive Systems: A Theory of Organizations," Administrative Science Quarterly, Vol. 6, No. 2 (September 1961), pp. 129–166.

morale or job satisfaction of the nonmanagerial employees; and (3) how the material and solidary (or monetary and nonmonetary) incentives were designed for the blue-collar, white-collar, and managerial workers. Data on these points are presented in Tables 5-6 and 5-7.

As far as employee participation programs were concerned, the data in Table 5-7 do not indicate any significant differences between the U.S. subsidiaries and the Indian-owned enterprises. This holds true for comparisons on ownership as well as on a management philosophy basis.

However, insofar as manager attitude toward worker morale was concerned, while there appeared to be no significant overall differences, there was an indication of an association between sophisticated management philosophy and favorable attitude toward worker morale.

Table 5-7   Employee Participation Programs and Managerial
Attitude Toward Employee Morale

	Overall Comparisons		Management Philosophy					
			Most Sophisticated		Somewhat Progressive		Not Progressive	
	U.S.	Indian	U.S.	Indian	U.S.	Indian	U.S.	Indian
	$n=$ 17	$n=$ 17	$n=$ 5	$n=$ 5	$n=$ 11	$n=$ 7	$n=$ 1	$n=$ 5
Employee participation programs								
Committees* and suggestion system	7	7	3	3	4	2	–	1
Committees only	6	6	2	2	4	3	–	1
Suggestion system only	2	–	–	–	2	1	–	–
No formal program	2	4	–	–	1	1	1	3
*Managerial attitude** toward employee morale*								
Highly favorable	5	5	4	4	1	1	–	–
Somewhat favorable	7	9	1	1	6	6	–	2
Not favorable	5	3	–	–	4	–	1	3

* Works and other committees.
** As expressed in the emphasis, placed in day-to-day practice, on individual development, fulfillment of sociopsychological needs, social activities, and so on.

Summary

In many companies studied, policy making power appeared to to be solely in the hands of chief executives. Significant exceptions were MS-type organizations where sharing was evident. The democratic style of leadership was prevalent in several of the 92 companies; even among these, however, in the local companies senior managers tended to view their subordinates' trustworthiness quite differently from the senior managers in the U.S. subsidiaries. While similarities in motivational programs existed, manager view of employee morale was perceived differently by the managers in the U.S. subsidiary companies than in the national companies in the 5 countries studied.

6

CONTROL MECHANISMS

The term control, as it is employed here, designates the direction and the integration of organizational effort for accomplishing goals at various levels. Control is a critical regulatory mechanism in the management process. As Arrow has suggested, "Control divides itself into two parts: the choice of *operating* rules—instructing the members of the organization how to act; and the choice of *enforcement* rules—to persuade or compel them to act in accordance with the operating rules."[1]

Although one could describe controlling, in a very practical sense, as ". . . checking existing actions against some desired results determined in the planning process,"[2] as Jerome would put it, "It bespeaks a planned rather than a haphazard approach . . . to the employment of both human and material resources."[3] Thus, controlling represents those forces or rules which make it possible for any organized unit, e.g., a business firm, to function purposefully.

The importance of the controlling function stems both from its universality and from its many implications for the manner in which organizations tend to behave. The widespread research interest in

[1] Kenneth Arrow, "Control in Large Organizations," *Management Science*, Vol. 10, No. 3 (April 1964), pp. 397–408.
[2] William T. Jerome, *Executive Control: The Catalyst* (New York: John Wiley & Sons, 1961), p. 31.
[3] *Ibid.*

leadership, for example, reflects substantial interest in the effects of variations in patterns of control.[4]

A manager controls the work of others according to performance standards. In general, objectives, programs, procedures, and budgets serve to guide the work of the members of the organization toward planned goals. In other words, controlling is a managerial process which is facilitated by a control system or mechanism.

In our survey, we attempted to elicit information from the respondents on a limited number of the elements involved in the control mechanism. We sought the answers to these questions: Who actually sets the performance standards in production, in office work, and in the work of middle managers? How extensively are modern management controls such as quality control, cost control, and budgetary controls used as instruments in the controlling mechanism?

The data and analyses presented in this chapter relate to these important questions. Data are analyzed comparatively at the intra-country and international levels. While we recognize that the information gathered on control mechanisms is rather limited, it nevertheless provides some interesting comparisons.

INTRACOUNTRY COMPARISONS

Information was gathered from the managers and supervisors of 17 U.S. subsidiaries and 17 Indian firms on the standard setting and scope of control instruments.

Setting of Standards

At the overall level, there were some differences between the 17 U.S. subsidiaries and the 17 Indian-owned enterprises with respect to standard setting in the realms of production, office, and middle-management work. Data in Table 6-1 indicate that produc-

---

[4] For such implications, see Daniel Katz, *et al., Productivity, Supervision and Morale in an Office Situation,* Part I (Survey Research Center, the University of Michigan, 1950); Nancy C. Morse, *et al.,* "Regulation and Control in Hierarchical Organizations," *Journal of Social Issues,* Vol. 7, No. 3, pp. 41–48; and, Arnold S. Tannenbaum, "The Concept of Organizational Control," *The Journal of Social Issues,* Vol. 12, No. 2, pp. 50–60.

tion standard setting by chief executives was rare among the American subsidiaries, whereas it was fairly common among the Indian-owned companies. There were also fewer top managers in the U.S. subsidiary group setting standards of performance in office work (4 out of 17) compared to the number in the Indian companies (10 out of 17). The same can be said of standard setting with regard to middle-management work.

On the other hand, if comparisons are made on the basis of the management philosophy classification, the data tend to reflect more similarities than the above-mentioned differences might lead one to expect. Close similarities appear in the formulation of production

Table 6-1 Standard Setting in American and Indian Companies

	Overall Comparisons		Management Philosophy					
			Most Sophisticated		Somewhat Progressive		Not Progressive	
	U.S.	Indian	U.S.	Indian	U.S.	Indian	U.S.	Indian
	$n=$ 17	$n=$ 17	$n=$ 5	$n=$ 5	$n=$ 11	$n=$ 7	$n=$ 1	$n=$ 5
In production by								
Top manager only	1	5	–	–	–	2	1	3
Top manager and production manager	13	9	3	3	10	4	–	2
Executive committee including production manager	3	3	2	2	1	1	–	–
In office by								
Top manager only	4	10	–	–	3	5	1	5
Top manager and personnel manager	5	5	–	4	5	1	–	–
Office manager and personnel manager	7	1	4	–	3	1	–	–
Executive committee	1	1	1	1	–	–	–	–
In middle management by								
Top manager only	3	10	–	–	2	5	1	5
Top manager and personnel manager	8	6	1	4	7	2	–	–
Department and other managers	3	–	2	–	1	–	–	–
Executive committee	3	1	2	1	1	–	–	–

standards. Three of the 5 MS American firms and 3 of the 5 MS Indian firms indicated a joint decision by the top manager and his production chief.

In the remaining companies, executive committees (which included the production or the works manager) performed the task of setting standards. While in practice such close similarities were absent from the areas of standard setting for office and middle management work, the data nevertheless reveal that, in the companies (both U.S. and Indian) which professed the Most Sophisticated management philosophy, standard setting as a management task was not exclusively the prerogative of the chief executive; other individuals, such as the functional managers and the members of the executive committee, had some voice and participation.

Among the SP group of companies, in 4 out of the 7 Indian firms and in 10 out of the 11 American subsidiaries, production standards were set jointly by the chief executive and the functional manager. The top managers were also the exclusive standard setters for both office and middle-management work in 5 of the 7 Indian firms.

The sole U.S. subsidiary in the NP category was very much like the NP Indian companies. The chief executive, like those in 3 of the 5 NP Indian companies, unilaterally established the performance standards in the areas of production, office work, and middle-management jobs.

In addition to the question of whether the chief executive set the standards himself, or whether he shared his power with others, we were also interested in finding out if such modern management control instruments as quality, cost, and budgetary controls were actually in use.

Scope of Control Instruments in Use

Information was obtained on three types of control instruments commonly found in business organizations: quality control, cost control, and budgetary control.

Data revealed that quality control was a formalized activity in 32 of the 34 organizations studied. Cost control was not so widely prevalent. Of the 17 U.S. subsidiaries, 14 had instituted cost control on a formal basis. In the majority of the 17 Indian-owned enterprises, cost control had not been instituted on a formalized basis. In a few cases, cost control was exercised on an ad hoc basis. In one company, a top level manager actually looked upon formal cost control systems with a certain degree of indifference.

With respect to budgetary control, comparisons between the U.S. subsidiaries and the Indian firms indicated the existence of a similar pattern. Of the 17 subsidiaries, 16 of them had instituted elaborate means of budgetary control; of the 17 Indian-owned enterprises, however, only 8 of them had done so.

By themselves, these overall comparisons suggest that modern control instruments are more adequately employed in U.S. subsidiary organizations than in Indian-owned enterprises. Some qualification of this finding, however, seems desirable, for if we make comparisons on the basis of the Most Sophisticated versus Not Progressive

Table 6-2 Scope of Controls in American and Indian Companies

	Overall Comparisons		Management Philosophy					
			Most Sophisticated		Somewhat Progressive		Not Progressive	
	U.S.	Indian	U.S.	Indian	U.S.	Indian	U.S.	Indian
	$n=$ 17	$n=$ 17	$n=$ 5	$n=$ 5	$n=$ 11	$n=$ 7	$n=$ 1	$n=$ 5
Quality control								
Separate department	14	11	5	5	9	3	–	3
As part of production	2	5	–	–	2	4	–	1*
No formal**	1	1	–	–	–	–	1	1
Cost control								
For all products	12	7	5	5	7	2	–	–
For main products	2	–	–	–	2	–	–	–
No formal cost controls**	3	10	–	–	2	5	1	5
Budgetary control								
For the entire company by controller and committee	12	5	5	3	7	2	–	–
For the entire company by others	4	3	–	2	4	1	–	–
No formal budgetary control**	1	9	–	–	–	4	1	5

* As a discrete activity.
** Done randomly, on ad hoc basis, or even being indifferent to the instrument.

companies, we shed additional light upon the use of the control measures.

Introducing the management philosophy variable, we found that there was a close similarity in the controlling practices of the MS American and the MS Indian companies. In the case of Somewhat Progressive companies, cost (as well as budgetary) controls were not formalized in Indian companies to the extent that they were in their American counterparts. It should also be noted that in 2 of the SP American companies, there was no formal cost control system. As far as cost and budgetary controls were concerned, there was no difference between the 1 NP American subsidiary and the 5 NP Indian companies.

INTERNATIONAL COMPARISONS

Setting of Standards

In 2 of the 20 American subsidiaries and in 3 of the 17 local companies in Argentina, Brazil, and Uruguay, manufacturing standards were dictated by the chief executive. However, in the majority of cases, production managers were the officers who set the manufacturing standards. In none of these 37 companies was there any indication of a committee set up to formulate manufacturing standards. The committee form, somewhat unique but not widely prevalent, was found in 3 U.S. subsidiaries and 3 national companies located in India. The companies in the Philippines also had committees for the formulation of manufacturing standards.

The setting of performance standards at the middle-management level is more arduous than in the functional areas of either manufacturing or selling simply because the output of these activities is measurable whereas those of the managerial activities are not, at least not directly. Wherever we could obtain the relevant information, we endeavored to learn who had the power to set middle-management standards. Whether or not such standards represented a formalization of management tools and techniques, or whether they pointed to the one-man style versus the shared style, were not things we could readily discern and analyze. For comparative purposes, we merely ascertained whether there were standards of per-

Table 6-3 Standard Setting in Production: International Comparisons

Country	Overall Comparisons		Most Sophisticated		Somewhat Progressive		Not Progressive	
	U.S. Sub.	Local Cos.	U.S. Sub.	Local Cos.	U.S. Sub.	Local Cos.	U.S. Sub.	Local Cos.
Argentina-Brazil-Uruguay	n= 20	n= 17	n= 2	n= 1	n= 18	n= 15	n= 0	n= 1
Top executive only	2	3	–	–	2	3	–	
Production manager only	12	8	1	1	11	6		1
None (no clearcut responsibility)	2	1	–	–	2	1	–	
Data not available	4	5	1	–	3	5	–	
India	n= 17	n= 17	n= 5	n= 5	n= 11	n= 7	n= 1	n= 5
Top executive only	1	5	–	–	–	2	1	3
Top executive and production manager	13	9	3	3	10	4	–	2
A committee	3	3	2	2	1	1	–	–
Philippines	n= 10	n= 11	n= 4	n= 4	n= 6	n= 7	n= 0	n= 0
Top executive only	1	4	–	1	–	4		
Production manager only	9	5	4	3	5	2		
Top executive and production manager	–	1	–	–	1	–		
Not available	–	1	–	–	–	1		

formance for middle managers, and, if there were, who was instrumental in formulating those standards. Data in Table 6-3 provide some clues.

Examining the data on the Argentina-Brazil-Uruguay group, we found that in the majority of companies there were norms of performance for middle managers in both the U.S. subsidiaries and their local counterparts. Exceptions were 3 U.S. subsidiaries and 4 Latin American firms. The chief executive emerged as the only decision maker in the realm of performance standards. Among the U.S. subsidiaries, in 14 of the 20 cases, these standards were set by the top executive only. The corresponding number in the case of local enterprises was 9 out of 17. There was little indication of an association between the management philosophy variable and the middle management standard setting practices in these companies.

In 3 of the 17 local enterprises in India, there were clear indications that the chief executive was the person who set standards of performance for the middle managers. However, in 6 U.S. subsidiaries and in 1 local company, there was a committee charged with the performance of this task.

However, when comparisons were made on the basis of the MS versus NP management philosophies, data indicated that the MS companies (both U.S. and Indian) tended toward joint standard setting, while the NP companies (both U.S. and Indian) tended to-

Table 6-4   Standard Setting in Middle Management Performance: International Comparisons

Country	Overall Comparisons U.S. Local Sub. Cos.		Management Philosophy					
			Most Sophisticated U.S. Local Sub. Cos.		Somewhat Progressive U.S. Local Sub. Cos.		Not Progressive U.S. Local Sub. Cos.	
Argentina-Brazil-Uruguay	$n=$ 20	$n=$ 17*	$n=$ 2	$n=$ 1	$n=$ 18	$n=$ 15*	$n=$ 0	$n=$ 1
Top executive only	14	9	2	1	12	7	–	1
Top executive and personnel manager	–	1	–	–	–	1	–	–
A committee	3	2	–	–	3	2	–	–
None (no clearcut responsibility	3	4	–	–	3	4	–	–
India	$n=$ 17	$n=$ 17	$n=$ 5	$n=$ 5	$n=$ 11	$n=$ 7	$n=$ 1	$n=$ 5
Top executive only	3	10	–	–	2	5	1	5
Top executive and personnel manager	8	6	1	4	7	2	–	–
A committee	6	1	4	1	2	–	–	–
Philippines	10	11	4	4	6	7	0	0
Top executive only	2	9	2	4	–	5		
A committee	2	2	2		–	2		
None (no clearcut responsibility)	6	–	–	–	6	–		

* Information on a Brazilian company was not available.

ward the practice of standard setting by the chief executive only. If the practices of the four MS subsidiaries are any guide to better management methods, even the MS Indian companies are far behind in this particular respect.

The situation among the companies in the Philippines appeared somewhat different, first in that no clear-cut responsibility for standard setting among the middle managers could be discerned in 6 of the 10 U.S. subsidiaries; and second in that, even among the MS companies (2 U.S. subsidiaries and 4 local firms), it was the chief executive alone, and not a committee, who set the standards.

Supporting evidence was thus indicated only in the case of India insofar as an association between progressive management philosophy and shared authority for standards of performance among middle-level managers was concerned.

Scope of Controls

We could not obtain detailed information on the scope of controls in the case of the companies in Argentina, Brazil, the Philippines, and Uruguay. The following are some of our general observations.

As one might surmise, formalized quality control methods and procedures were prevalent in most of the companies studied in the 5 countries. There were, however, exceptions. There was one American subsidiary and one local company in India in which there were no formal quality control programs. The situation was similar in 3 local firms in the Philippines, and 1 local firm and a U.S. subsidiary in the Latin American group. To a certain degree, there was some inspection and some testing, but not a quality control program in the modern sense.

Comprehensive cost control measures were employed by most companies in the Latin American group as well as in the Philippines. In India, however, there were 11 Indian-owned companies and one U.S. subsidiary which had not instituted formal cost control procedures. The one explanation which seems plausible to account for the lack of the cost control measures in these companies is that the output of these firms generated such high profits that the managers simply did not bother to institute cost control measures. In addition, we did not find any evidence of budgetary control practices in these 11 companies.

Summary

We construed the term "controlling" as designating those mechanisms which make it possible for the organization to function purposefully, with minimum deviation from the defined goals.

Intracountry comparisons between the U.S. subsidiaries and the Indian-owned enterprises showed some differences in standard setting procedures and practices. A significant difference was that, in the Indian companies, the chief executive was more directly involved. The scope of control measures was more comprehensive in the U.S. subsidiaries than in the Indian companies.

On the basis of management philosophy, both in the areas of standard setting and comprehensiveness of controls, there were close similarities between the 5 MS American subsidiaries and the 5 MS Indian-owned companies.

International comparisons suggested that, in a large proportion of the companies, the production (works) managers were the standard setters insofar as manufacturing activities were concerned. Insofar as middle-management work and performance standards were concerned, the prerogative remained with the chief executive. This was especially true of the U.S. subsidiaries in the Latin American group and in the case of local companies in India and the Philippines. Alternatively, one could suggest that there was relatively less delegation of authority to subordinate managers in the American subsidiaries located in Argentina, Brazil, and Uruguay than in those located in India and the Philippines.

While quality control methods and procedures were widely practiced by most of the companies in Argentina, Brazil, the Philippines, and Uruguay, conspicuous by their absence were financial control mechanisms, i.e., cost and budgetary controls.

All of these observations, although based upon limited data, tend to suggest that the more progressive the management philosophy of a company, the more comprehensive and objective will be the control mechanisms. The idea of control incorporates, paradoxically, both constraint and opportunity for managerial decisions.[5] The control aspect of management action is both a process and a result.

[5] Dalton E. McFarland, *Personnel Management: Theory and Practice* (New York: The Macmillan Company, 1968), p. 141.

THREE

COMPARATIVE ANALYSES OF MANAGEMENT EFFECTIVENESS

7

MANAGEMENT EFFECTIVENESS AT THE WORKER LEVEL

In the preceding section we analyzed the influence of the management philosophy variable upon the elements of management processes. On an overall basis, the data indicated that companies in the category of Most Sophisticated management philosophy undertook systematic long-range planning and encouraged greater participation in both the planning process and decision-making in general. They also made use of advanced methods and techniques in the operation of their firms. In these MS companies, the democratic style of leadership was prevalent.

In contrast, those companies classified as manifesting Not Progressive management philosophy were relatively centralized. They also appeared to make very little use of modern managerial practices, methods, and techniques in carrying out various managerial tasks. The prevailing leadership style in these companies can best be characterized as autocratic or bureaucratic. Companies which lay between these two extreme positions, those categorized as Somewhat Progressive management philosophy, also were in between in terms of their management practices.

Management Philosophy, Management Processes, and Decentralization

To examine the relationship between management philosophy, management processes, and decentralization, we computed three different indices:

(1) management processes
(2) personnel practices
(3) decentralization

Details on the computation of these indices and the relationships between the management philosophy variable and these indices are given in Appendix A.

In brief, these statistical analyses indicate positive relationships between the management philosophy variable and management processes, personnel practices, and decentralization. Specifically, Spearman's rank correlation coefficient among these variables was as follows:

Variables	Spearman's Rank Correlation Coefficient
Management Philosophy and Management Process Index	0.72
Management Philosophy and Personnel Practices	0.67
Management Philosophy and Decentralization	0.81

Management Effectiveness

In this and the next chapter we will analyze the relationships that may exist between the management philosophy variable and management effectiveness. Before we analyze this relationship it may be desirable to review briefly the concept of management effectiveness.

In the business and related literature, the term management effectiveness has various connotations. Some writers have used this concept synonymously with "enterprise effectiveness," in terms of profit, sales, and so on. Others have suggested such financial criteria as cost per unit, percentage of net earnings to sales, growth in stock value, utilization of plant and equipment, and new investments in capital assets of the firm.[1]

[1] See Jackson Martindell, *The Appraisal of Management* (New York: Harper and Row, 1962).

Only in recent years have some social scientists suggested measurement of management effectiveness in terms of the utilization of human assets. Among others, Argyris,[2] Bennis,[3] Etzioni,[4] Georgopoulos and Tannenbaum,[5] Likert,[6] Georgopoulos, Mahoney and Jones,[7] McGregor,[8] and Selznick[9] have stressed this criterion.

Rensis Likert, commenting upon traditional management effectiveness variable, had this to say:

All end-result measurements give "after-the-fact" data. This is true of measurements of production, scrap, costs, earnings, and all other financial data. As successful business management has demonstrated, these measurements are valuable. Nevertheless, their predictive power is limited. All too often, end-result measurements can be used only to lock the barn door after the horse is stolen.[10]

He has thus strongly argued for the human asset criteria to be employed as a measure of management effectiveness. These include such factors as qualities of the human organization staffing the plant, level of confidence and trust, motivation, loyalty, and the capacity of the organization to communicate fully, to interact effectively, and to arrive at sound decisions.[11] To Likert, these "intervening variables reflect the internal state and health of the organization; e.g., the

[2] Chris Argyris, *Personality and Organization* (New York: Harper and Row, 1957); *Integrating the Individual and the Organization* (New York: John Wiley and Sons, Inc., 1964).

[3] Warren G. Bennis, *Changing Organizations: Essays on the Development and Evaluation of Human Organization* (New York: McGraw-Hill Book Company, 1966).

[4] Amitai Etzioni, "Two Approaches to Organizational Analysis: A Critique and a Suggestion," *Administrative Science Quarterly*, Vol. 5, No. 2 (September 1960), pp. 257–258.

[5] B. S. Georgopoulos and A. S. Tannenbaum, "A Study of Organizational Effectiveness," *American Sociological Review*, Vol. 22, No. 5 (1957), pp. 534–540.

[6] Rensis Likert, *The Human Organization: Its Management and Value* (New York: McGraw-Hill Book Company, 1967).

[7] B. S. Georgopoulos, G. M. Mahoney, and N. W. Jones, "A Path-Goal Approach to Productivity," *Journal of Applied Psychology*, Vol. 41, No. 6 (December 1957), pp. 345–353.

[8] Douglas McGregor, *The Human Side of Enterprise* (New York: McGraw-Hill Book Company, 1960).

[9] Philip Selznick, "Foundations of the Theory of Organization," *American Sociological Review*, Vol. 13, No. 1 (1948), pp. 25–35.

[10] Likert, *op. cit.*, p. 100.

[11] *Ibid.*, p. 29.

loyalties, attitudes, motivation, performances, goals, and perceptions of all members and their collective capacities for effective interaction, communication, and decision-making."[12]

No one can deny that the ultimate survival and growth of a business organization depends upon its financial or economic strength and that such economic data as profits, cost per unit, sales volume, etc., are good indicators of the firm's financial strength. However, these outputs are the results of what the entire organization does (including its technology, resources, etc.), rather than merely the results of managerial action. Hypothetically, managers could overburden an organization, drain off its long-range potentials, and in the short run impel the organization to achieve higher profits and higher sales. Besides, it is erroneous to use these economic indices to measure management effectiveness, especially in underdeveloped countries where seller's market conditions are widely prevalent. Under such circumstances, one needs some other criteria with which to evaluate management effectiveness. Etzioni's systems approach may be more meaningful in evaluating management effectiveness. He defines the systems approach as:

A pattern of inter-relationships among the elements of the system which would make it most effective in the service of a given goal.[13] . . . [An organization] that devotes all its efforts to fulfilling one functional requirement, even if it is that of performing goal activities, will undermine the fulfillment of this very functional requirement because recruitment of means, maintenance of tools, and the social integration of the unit will be neglected.[14]

Georgopoulos, Mahoney and Jones, Georgopoulos and Tannenbaum, and Selznick also have taken this position in evaluating organizational effectiveness in terms of (1) productivity; (2) intra-organizational strain as indicated by the incidence of tension and conflict among organizational subgroups; and (3) organizational flexibility, defined as the ability to adjust to external or internal changes.[15]

[12] *Ibid.*

[13] Etzioni, *loc. cit.*, quoted from Argyris, *Integrating the Individual and the Organization, op. cit.*, p. 125.

[14] *Ibid.*

[15] Georgopoulos and Tannenbaum, *loc. cit.*, quoted from Argyris, *op. cit.*, p. 125.

Likert has suggested the following factors as measures of management effectiveness:

(1) Leadership process used
(2) Character of motivational force
(3) Character of communication process
(4) Character of interaction influence process
(5) Character of decision-making process
(6) Character of goal setting or ordering
(7) Character of control process[16]

To Argyris, the important variables are: (1) interrelationships among different parts of the organization; (2) awareness of patterns in parts of organization; (3) system effectiveness in achieving the firm's objectives; (4) system effectiveness in influencing its own internal core activities, and (5) system effectiveness in adapting to the external environment.[17]

Management Effectiveness Criteria

Realizing the unsuitability and shortcomings of financial data in evaluating management effectiveness, especially in underdeveloped countries where seller's market conditions are often prevalent, we took a lead from the above-mentioned researchers and devised nine behaviorally-oriented measures of management effectiveness. We concentrated on nine factors among those suggested by Argyris, Likert, and others. The selection of these factors is based upon the availability of data from the industrial firms studied. Some of these are referred to in the management literature as "organizational behavior" variables. They are:

(1) Employee morale and satisfaction in work
(2) Interpersonal relationships in organizational settings
(3) Employee turnover rate
(4) Employee absenteeism
(5) Management effectiveness in attracting high-level manpower
(6) Departmental relationships (subsystem relationships)
(7) Achievement of the firm's overall objectives
(8) Utilization of high-level manpower
(9) Organizational effectiveness in adapting to the external environments

[16] Likert, *op. cit.*, pp. 14–24.
[17] Argyris, *op. cit.*, p. 150.

The first 4 of these factors concern blue-collar employees and are analyzed in this chapter. The next chapter will treat the remaining 5 effectiveness criteria.

The following analyses are undertaken at 2 levels: (1) overall comparison between U.S. subsidiaries and local firms, and (2) comparison in respect to each firm's management philosophy. Intracountry comparisons will be discussed first; the international comparisons will follow. As the reader will recall, intracountry comparison relates to the U.S. subsidiaries and local firms in India (34 companies), while international comparison involves a total of 92 companies (47 U.S. subsidiaries and 45 local companies) in 5 underdeveloped countries, i.e., Argentina, Brazil, India, the Philippines, and Uruguay.

EMPLOYEE MORALE AND SATISFACTION

Many researchers have used the concept of morale to reflect the overall attitude of the employee toward his work, group, supervisor, and company. Barnard, for example, has defined morale as the degree to which individual motives are gratified.[18] Such words or concepts as esprit de corps, identification, satisfaction, solidarity, cohesion, and alienation are employed in the discussion of employee morale.[19]

Although one could cite contradictory findings concerning the relationship between employee morale and productivity, there is considerable consensus among researchers about the positive relationship between these two variables.[20]

In management literature, employee turnover and absenteeism rates are often used as measures of morale. These factors are treated separately in this study.

Comparable and reliable data concerning rates of turnover and absenteeism were not available from many companies in Argentina,

[18] Chester I. Barnard, *The Functions of the Executive* (Cambridge, Mass.: Harvard University Press, 1954), pp. 56–61.

[19] See James L. Price, *Organizational Effectiveness: An Inventory of Propositions* (Homewood, Ill.: Richard D. Irwin, Inc., 1968), p. 18.

[20] See Daniel Katz, Nathan Maccoby, and Nancy C. Morse, *Productivity, Supervision and Morale in an Office Situation* (Ann Arbor, Mich.: Survey Research Center, Institute for Social Research, 1950); and M. Argyle, G. Gardner, and F. Coffee, "Supervisory Methods Related to Productivity, Absenteeism and Labor Turnover," *Human Relations*, Vol. 11, No. 1 (1958), pp. 23–40.

Brazil, India, the Philippines, and Uruguay. Wherever such data were available, there was a great deal of fluctuation among the firms belonging to different industrial sectors. Also, as we will see below, the location of the firm had considerable bearing upon turnover and absenteeism. Therefore, in the five underdeveloped countries, we evaluated employee morale and satisfaction in work on the basis of our interviews with some 500 blue-collar workers, skilled laborers, and supervisory personnel. These interviews, mostly nondirective in nature, nevertheless sought specific information concerning employees' attitudes toward work, working conditions, supervisors, managers, and the company as a whole.

Intracountry Comparison

Data presented in Table 7-1 indicate that slightly less than one-third of the companies in India were able to attain high employee morale. A large majority of the companies (21) were successful in maintaining average morale among their employees, while only 3 Indian companies have had a poor record in this aspect. There were no significant differences between U.S. subsidiaries and their local counterparts. A detailed analysis suggests the existence of a positive correlation between the firm's management philosophy and employee morale. Specifically, companies with Most Sophisticated management philosophy were successful in achieving high employee morale, while the companies with a Not Progressive philosophy had poor employee morale. The companies with Somewhat Progressive management philosophy attained average morale among their employees. The impact of differential management philosophies upon employee morale is revealed in the following expressions of workers in India:

I am happy with my present job. I get paid much more than I used to when I was working for . . . I work harder here, but enjoy doing so. My boss and everybody at the top are nice people. . . . These people are more humane than some of my relatives. . . . I think this is the best company in India to work for . . . [A worker in an American subsidiary, categorized as Most Sophisticated management philosophy.]
. . . Oh . . . who cares for the waste . . . this is the only way we can demonstrate our frustration and disappointment with the management and the monster supervisor. [A worker in an American subsidiary, categorized as Not Progressive management philosophy.]

I would like to run away to my village as soon as possible . . . The big shethias [industrialists] in Bombay are worse than slave-drivers. They do not care for anybody . . . So why should I sweat and tear for them. [A worker in an Indian company, classified as Not Progressive management philosophy.]

International Comparison

A similar picture emerges when one compares the data from other underdeveloped countries, i.e., Argentina, Brazil, the Philippines, and Uruguay. The data reveal that, in a large majority of companies in the 5 countries studied, employees were at least moderately satisfied in their work. In only 10 companies out of 92 did employees show poor morale.

Thus, the overall employee morale in the 5 underdeveloped countries can hardly be described as poor. Still, this may be less than desirable when one considers that the most urgent need of the underdeveloped areas today is to increase their productivity. Industrial productivity is a function of technical and managerial resources, as well as of the attitudes and morale of the workers. Thus, given certain technical and managerial resources, industrial productivity depends largely upon the worker attitude and morale. Those interested in the economic development process have recognized that in order to improve the substandard of living of a large and growing population, underdeveloped countries must increase the productivity contributions of their manpower. How strongly do social factors affect productivity via morale?

In studies of employee morale and commitment to industrial life in underdeveloped countries, much attention is paid to the influence of sociocultural variables. Ornati, for example, in his study of *Jobs and Workers in India*, observed:

Indian workers are not interested in factory work; they resist adjustment to the type of life which goes with industrial employment. In the value scheme of the majority of Indians, factory labor does not offer any avenue for the expression of their individual personalities; wage increase and promotions do not operate as stimulants to greater exertion, nor does greater exertion lead to changes in status.[21]

21 Oscar A. Ornati, *Jobs and Workers in India* (Ithaca, N.Y.: The Institute of International Industrial Relations, Cornell University, 1955), p. 46.

Table 7-1 Employee Morale and Satisfaction

Country	Overall Comparisons U.S.	Local	Most Sophisticated U.S.	Local	Somewhat Progressive U.S.	Local	Not Progressive U.S.	Local
					Management Philosophy			
Argentina	$n=$ 6	$n=$ 5	$n=$ 1	$n=$ 1	$n=$ 5	$n=$ 4	$n=$ 0	$n=$ 0
Highly satisfied	1	2	–	–	1	2	–	–
Somewhat satisfied	3	2	1	–	2	2	–	–
Highly dissatisfied	2	1	–	1	2	–	–	–
Brazil	$n=$ 8	$n=$ 7	$n=$ 1	$n=$ 0	$n=$ 7	$n=$ 6	$n=$ 0	$n=$ 1
Highly satisfied	3	2	1	–	2	2	–	–
Somewhat satisfied	5	2	–	–	5	1	–	1
Highly dissatisfied	–	1	–	–	–	1	–	–
Not available	–	2	–	–	–	2	–	–
India	$n=$ 17	$n=$ 17	$n=$ 5	$n=$ 5	$n=$ 11	$n=$ 7	$n=$ 1	$n=$ 5
Highly satisfied	6	4	5	4	1	–	–	–
Somewhat satisfied	11	10	–	1	10	7	1	2
Highly dissatisfied	–	3	–	–	–	–	–	3
Philippines	$n=$ 10	$n=$ 11	$n=$ 4	$n=$ 4	$n=$ 6	$n=$ 7	$n=$ 0	$n=$ 0
Highly satisfied	1	–	1	–	–	–	–	–
Somewhat satisfied	9	10	3	3	6	7	–	–
Highly dissatisfied	–	1	–	1	–	–	–	–
Uruguay	$n=$ 6	$n=$ 5	$n=$ 0	$n=$ 0	$n=$ 6	$n=$ 5	$n=$ 0	$n=$ 0
Highly satisfied	–	–	–	–	–	–	–	–
Somewhat satisfied	5	4	–	–	5	4	–	–
Highly dissatisfied	1	1	–	–	1	1	–	–

Commenting upon the labor commitment in underdeveloped countries, Kerr and his co-researchers had this to say:

Cultural factors (such as religious and ethical valuations, the family system, class and race) all have a bearing on commitment . . . The greater the strength of extended family, the slower the commitment of workers to industrial life.[22]

Farmer and Richman, following the works of McClelland and others, arrived at this conclusion:

The importance of a country's view of achievement and work as a vital determinant of managerial performance and productivity efficiency must not be understated. . . . Prevailing religious beliefs and cultural values, in connection with parental behavior, child-rearing practices . . . traditional Hinduism, Buddhism, Islam and even Catholicism are not generally conducive to a high achievement drive in their orthodox followers.[23]

Myrdal's monumental study of South Asia also reveals the impact of tradition, custom, value system, and attitudes on labor efficiency in these countries. Myrdal has argued that ". . . in absence of simultaneous changes in institutions and attitudes, the effect on labor utilization and productivity throughout the economy may still be less consequential."[24]

Some scholars, however, expressed doubts on the validity of such generalizations. Morris, for example, has pointed out that:

Much of the literature tends to base interpretation on hypothetical, psychological, and sociological propositions which themselves are highly suspect. The argument typically rests on scattered fragments of evidence taken indiscriminately . . . It is impossible to generate a satisfactory analysis from this sort of mélange.[25]

Our interviews revealed that a firm's management philosophy, and such mediating variables as higher relative wages, working conditions, and opportunity for advancement and self-growth were somewhat effective in augmenting employee morale and increasing employee satisfaction in work. To this extent, we tend to agree with Ganguli, Morris, McMillan, and Fillol. Ganguli, in his study of worker incentives in India, found that:

[22] Clark Kerr, *et al.*, *Industrialism and Industrial Man* (Cambridge, Mass.: Harvard University Press, 1960), p. 97.

[23] Richard N. Farmer and Barry M. Richman, *Comparative Management and Economic Progress* (Homewood, Ill.: Richard D. Irwin, 1965), pp. 154–159.

[24] Gunnar Myrdal, *Asian Drama: An Inquiry into the Poverty of Nations* (New York: The Twentieth Century Fund, 1968), p. 1150.

[25] Morris David Morris, *The Emergence of an Industrial Labor Force in India: A Study of the Bombay Cotton Mills, 1859–1947*. (Berkeley, Calif.: University of California Press, 1965), p. 4.

The four most important things that the workers want are sufficient and adequate income, a sense of security, an opportunity for promotion and advancement, and finally, opportunity to learn a more interesting trade.
. . . In these and also in their aspirations and expectations, there does not seem to be any fundamental difference between this group and other groups of factory employees in other countries.[26]

Morris, in his historical study of the labor force in India, observed that:

It seems safe to conclude that the labor problems with which the industry had to contend did not flow primarily from the psychology of the work force or from the rigid traditions and structure of the rural order. Such instability and indiscipline as did exist stemmed from the character of employer policies. . . .[27]

Morris goes on to say that:

The evidence from Bombay and Jamshedpur suggests that the creation of [a] disciplined industrial labor force in a newly developing society is not particularly difficult . . . The difference in worker stability cannot be accounted for by any substantial differences in the psychology of the raw labor recruited. Nor can it be attributed to dissimilarities in the traditional environment from which the workers came. If there were differences in work-force behavior, these flowed from employer policy.[28]

McMillan's research in Brazil revealed that:

Americans are under less compulsion to probe the attitude of their workers than they are in the United States . . . Enlisting the allegiance of workers is easier, and motivating employees, most Americans appear to agree, is not difficult.[29]

In his study of *Social Factors in Economic Development in Argentina*, Fillol observed that:

There is no reason to believe that Argentina workers have basically different attitudes toward their jobs from workers anywhere else in industrialized Western countries.[30] . . . Industrialists in general do not seem

[26] H. C. Ganguli, "An Enquiry into Incentives for Workers in an Engineering Factory," *Indian Journal of Social Work*, June 1954, p. 10.

[27] Morris, *op. cit.*, p. 202.

[28] *Ibid.*, p. 210.

[29] Claude McMillan, Jr., "The American Businessman in Brazil," *Business Topics*, Spring 1965, reprinted in *International Dimensions in Business* (East Lansing, Mich.: Graduate School of Business Administration, Michigan State University, 1966), p. 103.

[30] Thomas Roberto Fillol, *Social Factors in Economic Development: The Argentine Case* (Cambridge, Mass.: The M.I.T. Press, 1963), p. 76.

to have given any thought to the fact that the productivity, motivation, and cooperation of labor are primarily determined by the management which employs it and not by the more or less enlightened social and economic policies of government.[31]

Environmental factors affecting employee morale mentioned by the interviewees in our study were as follows:
(1) Government attitudes toward the industrial worker and the business world
(2) Management-union relationships
(3) Climatic and working conditions
(4) Health and well-being of workers
(5) Political situation

Let us examine the influence of some of these factors in more detail.

Industrial entrepreneurs in underdeveloped countries seem to have exploited the oversupply which characterizes the labor situation. In other words, as Fillol has observed with respect to Argentina, "Labor tends still to be considered as just another commodity whose services are to be bought as cheaply as possible."[32]

In recent years, governments in underdeveloped areas have remedied such situations by supporting the industrial worker through legislative processes, that is, by modifying the existing labor legislation and enacting more clearly defined laws. In addition, they have actively supported trade union activities, and, so doing, they have greatly increased the expectations and aspirations of the industrial worker. However, actual realization of benefits has lagged behind considerably.[33] Chronic inflation, especially in the Latin American countries, has increased the gap between the worker's gains in wages and his expectation of improving his standard of living.[34]

Caught between the rising cost of living and the fall in purchasing power, the industrial worker in underdeveloped countries has responded to any and every outside force promising him a better deal. In his plight, he has been exploited by political parties, governments, and politically oriented labor unions alike.

On the other hand, industrialists or entrepreneurs are con-

---

[31] Ibid., p. 75.
[32] Ibid., p. 73.
[33] For the case of India, see Charles A. Myers, op. cit., especially Chapter 8; for the Argentine case see Fillol, op. cit., Chapter 4.
[34] Fillol, op. cit., Chapter 4.

vinced that the lack of economic progress in a country is due to unproductive labor. As Fillol so aptly remarked, "all blame for the nation's political, economic, and social troubles is put on labor and, indirectly, on government for fomenting the workers' natural faults and indolence."[35]

At this point, something should be said about the health and well-being of workers, and the climatic conditions, in India and the Philippines. As Myrdal's research on South Asia indicates:

The sultry and oppressive climate that much of South Asia experiences all or most of the time tends to make people disinclined to work. Manual laborers, for example, habitually wield their tools with a feebler stroke and take more frequent and longer rest pauses than workers in cooler climates.[36]

Data presented in Table 7-1 support the contention that a firm's management philosophy and such mediating variables as higher relative wages, better working conditions, and opportunities for advancement and growth serve to augment employee morale and productivity.

INTERPERSONAL RELATIONSHIPS

This measure of management effectiveness reflects the attitudes or feelings of workers toward each other and their respective supervisors. This variable and the previous factor, employee morale and satisfaction in work, are closely related. In a sense, the nature of the interpersonal relationships between the supervisor and the worker is a causal variable, while employee morale is a dependent variable. As Likert has observed:

The more often the supervisor's behavior is ego-building rather than ego-deflating, the better will be the effects of his behavior on organizational performance.[37] . . . The leadership and other processes of the organization must be such as to ensure a maximum probability that in all interactions and in all relationships with organization, each member, in the light of his background, values, desires, and expectations will view the

---

[35] *Ibid.*, p. 74.
[36] Myrdal, *op. cit.*, p. 2136. Also see for economic consequences of climate and malnutrition in Southeast Asia, Chapter 14, pp. 673–705 and Appendix 10, pp. 2121–2138.
[37] Likert, *op. cit.*, p. 47.

experiences as supportive and one which builds and maintains his sense of personal worth and importance.[38]

Studies by Katz and Kahn,[39] Bowers,[40] Bowers and Seashore,[41] and others support Likert's contention.

Intracountry Comparison

From Table 7-2 it can be seen that companies in India, by and large, have failed to create desirable supportive relationships among their employees. In our study of 17 companies, there were only 2 Indian firms whose employees showed great cooperativeness towards each other and towards their respective supervisors. In a large majority of American companies (15 out of 17), we found somewhat cooperative and supportive attitudes among employees; in the 2 remaining companies these attitudes were what Likert calls "ego-deflating" rather than "ego-building."[42]

As compared to the American companies, the Indian counterparts were still worse off in terms of fostering cohesiveness among employees and supervisors. With the exception of 2 companies, which maintained very favorable and cooperative attitudes among their employees, a large majority (15 out of 17) of these companies had failed to create such favorable attitudes. Only 7 of these were able to maintain somewhat favorable and supportive relationships.

As we will see shortly, many factors contributed to this rather unhealthy state of affairs in the Indian industrial enterprise. Although American companies have done better in this respect, ownership by itself is not sufficient to explain the differences in this management effectiveness variable between the two sets of companies. Management philosophy, as an independent variable, is somewhat useful in explaining the nature of the differences among the com-

---

[38] *Ibid.*

[39] D. Katz and R. L. Kahn, "Some Recent Findings in Human Relations Research," in E. Swanson, T. Newcomb, and E. Hartley, eds., *Readings in Social Psychology* (New York: Holt, 1952), pp. 650–655.

[40] D. G. Bowers, "Organizational Control in an Insurance Company," *Sociometry*, Vol. 27, No. 2 (1964), pp. 230–244.

[41] D. G. Bowers and S. E. Seashore, "Predicting Organizational Effectiveness with a Four-factor Theory of Leadership," *Administrative Science Quarterly*, Vol. 2, No. 2 (1966), pp. 238–263.

[42] Likert, *op. cit.*, p. 47.

panies studied. As the data of Table 7-2 show, the majority of the companies which were able to create at least somewhat cooperative attitudes among their employees pursued either a Most Sophisticated management philosophy or a Somewhat Progressive management philosophy. Contrary to our expectations, all the companies with Most Sophisticated management philosophy did not develop utmost cooperative and supportive employee relationships. As mentioned earlier, only two Indian firms were successful in doing so. However, as one would expect in companies with Not Progressive management philosophy, a large degree of mistrust, discontent, and hostility prevailed among the employees.

International Comparison

Our findings in India closely correspond with findings in other underdeveloped countries. A glance at Table 7-2 reveals that, in the large majority of companies studied, employees manifested hostile attitudes toward each other and toward their respective supervisors. Neither the ownership status (American versus local), nor the firm's management philosophy signaled any significant difference in worker attitudes in Argentina, Brazil, the Philippines, and Uruguay. Only one quarter of 92 companies were able to maintain somewhat cooperative attitudes among their employees.

On the basis of such sociocultural traits as the agrarian outlook, strong family ties, low levels of education and standard of living, and high degree of need dependency, one would expect a higher level of cooperativeness among employees and supervisors. However, the data suggest quite the contrary. Which environmental factors affect interpersonal relationships?

Governmental attitudes toward the industrial work force and the business enterprises, the political nature of trade-unionism, chronic underemployment and unemployment, the differences in educational levels and aspirations of younger and older employees, the differential social status of the supervisor and the blue-collar worker, and inflation have all affected the nature of interpersonal relationships in the industrial enterprises of underdeveloped countries. The impact of these factors is briefly examined below.

As we saw in an earlier section, the business communities in

Table 7-2   Interpersonal Relationships in the Five Underdeveloped Countries

	Overall Comparisons		Management Philosophy					
			Most Sophisticated		Somewhat Progressive		Not Progressive	
Country	U.S.	Local	U.S.	Local	U.S.	Local	U.S.	Local
Argentina	$n=$ 6	$n=$ 5	$n=$ 1	$n=$ 1	$n=$ 5	$n=$ 4	$n=$ 0	$n=$ 0
Very cooperative	–	–	–	–	–	–	–	–
Somewhat cooperative	–	–	–	–	–	–	–	–
Hostile	6	5	1	1	5	4	–	–
Brazil	$n=$ 8	$n=$ 7	$n=$ 1	$n=$ 0	$n=$ 7	$n=$ 6	$n=$ 0	$n=$ 1
Very cooperative	–	–	–	–	–	–	–	–
Somewhat cooperative	–	1	–	–	–	–	–	1
Hostile	8	6	1	–	7	6	–	–
India	$n=$ 17	$n=$ 17	$n=$ 5	$n=$ 5	$n=$ 11	$n=$ 7	$n=$ 1	$n=$ 5
Very cooperative	–	2	–	2	–	–	–	–
Somewhat cooperative	15	7	5	3	10	4	–	–
Hostile	2	8	–	–	1	3	1	5
Philippines	$n=$ 10	$n=$ 11	$n=$ 4	$n=$ 4	$n=$ 6	$n=$ 7	$n=$ 0	$n=$ 0
Very cooperative	–	–	–	–	–	–	–	–
Somewhat cooperative	–	–	–	–	–	–	–	–
Hostile	10	11	4	4	6	7	–	–
Uruguay	$n=$ 6	$n=$ 5	$n=$ 0	$n=$ 0	$n=$ 6	$n=$ 5	$n=$ 0	$n=$ 0
Very cooperative	–	–	–	–	–	–	–	–
Somewhat cooperative	2	1	–	–	2	1	–	–
Hostile	4	4	–	–	4	4	–	–

underdeveloped countries have had their faults in that they have exploited both the consumer and the employee. In order to protect employees from exploitation, the national governments (perhaps justifiably) activated labor organizations and enacted legislation. These actions did improve wages and working conditions. However, as the student of underdeveloped economies is well aware, both the governments and the labor unions, in turn, exploited the industrial workers in order to pursue their own political objectives.[43] As a result, although the worker still leans toward the government and the union for higher wages and better working conditions, he has lost faith in both of them.

In underdeveloped countries, many governments and labor unions manifested very hostile attitudes toward the business community. As a leading businessman in India exclaimed: "Government thinks we are traitors and, if they could, they would hang all of us in public parks . . . while unions think that they own our business and we are their servants." Such feelings are not conducive to developing cooperative attitudes between managers and workers.

Thus, the employee is alienated from all sides. In a real sense, he does not belong to any particular reference group. As Fillol has observed, "all blame the employee for the nation's wrongs." Such a situation is hardly conducive to good morale or to constructive interpersonal relationships in any society, developed or underdeveloped.

Other Factors

In the preceding section, we mentioned the impact of inflation and an unstable political situation upon employee morale. These factors had a similarly negative impact on interpersonal relationship.

Three additional environmental factors were responsible for the uncooperative attitudes of the workers: chronic underemployment and unemployment, the differences in educational attainments of younger and older employees, and the wide differences in status between supervisor and worker.

The chronic unemployment and underemployment situations[44]

---

[43] See for example Myers, *loc. cit.*, and Fillol, *loc. cit.*

[44] Unemployment percentages varied from 10–15 percent in Argentina to 25–35 percent in India. The precise data on underemployment are difficult to obtain; but the general consensus was that in Latin American countries, the rate of underemployment varied from 25–35 percent, while in Far Eastern countries, these were as high as 50–60 percent. For interesting and scholarly observations on "Unemployment" and "Underemployment" in Southeast Asia, see Myrdal, *op. cit.*, Chapter 21, pp. 961–1027, and Appendix 16, pp. 2203–2221.

in developing countries contributed a great deal toward building defensive attitudes among the industrial employees.

As has been noted in recent years, both governmental legislation and the activities of the unions have strengthened the employees' bargaining power; still, the nature of the unemployment situation in India and other underdeveloped countries has kept alive the workers' fears and anxieties of losing their jobs. Such anxieties have made the industrial worker very defensive, as can easily be seen from the following expressions of workers in India and Argentina:

I dare not say anything, lest you may tell to my boss, and I will be back to my village . . . My uncle has taught me a good lesson . . . not to trust anybody in the factory . . . and not to tell my secrets to others . . . Mr. . . . I wish I could trust and cooperate with my friend . . . but I am afraid to do so. [A worker in India.]

Mr. . . . cooperation is for the birds . . . we human beings talk a lot about it, but when it comes to save your skin . . . it evaporates . . . I feel sorry for my friend who believed in these cooperative and sympathetic attitudes toward each other and so forth . . . he is still looking for a job. [A worker in Argentina.]

Indeed, such anxieties were founded on economic realities in the countries studied. Even the management personnel of many companies supported this contention. For example, the personnel manager of an American subsidiary in Brazil asserted:

Our management does not believe in training workers, because, as a policy, we let the workers go after 8 years of service . . . of 196 workers only 5 are our permanent employees.

There is yet another element which seems to have increased the hostility among employees, and that is the differences in both educational attainments and aspirations of younger and older workers.[45] The younger generation was more revolutionary and supported the liberal views of government, unions, and political parties; the older workers were more conservative and pro-management. These different perceptions and aspirations have augmented the existing hostilities and fixations among the workers.

[45] The employees in age group of 19–30 were mostly high school graduates, while the age group of 35–55 were either illiterate or had had barely one or two years of schooling. For somewhat similar observations concerning Japanese workers, see Arthur M. Whitehill, Jr., and Shin-ichi Takezawa, *The Other Worker: A Comparative Study of Industrial Relations in the United States and Japan* (Honolulu: East-West Center Press, 1968), pp. 352–353.

The last, but by no means the least important, factor affecting interpersonal relationships in industrial settings in underdeveloped countries is the wide difference in the status of supervisors and workers.

In industrial countries, particularly the United States, the supervisor or foreman symbolizes high skills in both technical and human relation aspects. He justifies a higher salary on the basis of his knowledge and his ability to make decisions. In underdeveloped areas, the supervisor represents higher class status. He identifies himself with the managerial or entrepreneur class even though, in actuality, he may not belong to this class. Such identification, coupled with a lack of technical and human relation skills, arouses worker antagonism. In other words, employees find a good excuse to demonstrate their anxieties, rancor, rage, and frustrations against management through their supervisors. Such circumstances are certain to create unhealthy interpersonal relationships.

To sum up, the list of factors analyzed above was by no means all-inclusive. We attempted to single out only the most important variables. As the reader will recognize, all these were environmental factors over which management could exercise relatively little control. Only a few firms under study were able to overcome these environmental constraints by pursuing permanent employment policies, offering high relative wages and opportunities for advancement and self-growth, and by training supervisors and workers in technical and human relation skills.

Technological factors were not taken into consideration in our discussion. Studies of Trist and Bamforth,[46] Pugh and his colleagues at the University of Aston,[47] and Woodward[48] have demonstrated the impact of technological variables on both management practices and effectiveness.

Detailed statistical analysis of various management processes and effectiveness variables failed to indicate significant differences among the firms belonging to different industrial sectors. However,

[46] E. L. Trist and K. W. Bamforth, "Some Social and Psychological Consequences of the Longwall Method of Goal-Setting," *Human Relations,* Vol. 4 (1951), pp. 3–38.

[47] See D. S. Pugh, "A Conceptual Scheme for Organizational Analysis," *Administrative Science Quarterly,* Vol. 8, No. 3 (December 1963), pp. 289–315.

[48] J. Woodward, *Management and Technology* (London: Her Majesty's Stationery Office, 1958).

these analyses showed positive relationships among management philosophy, management processes, and management effectiveness variables. Statistical analyses on some of these aspects are given in Appendix A.

Our analysis of the data concerning employee turnover and absenteeism, however, revealed considerable differences among the firms belonging to different industries. The analysis of the variables, therefore, is undertaken with respect to the pharmaceutical industry in India. To hold the size of the firm, as well as the product lines, constant, we paired each of 5 American and 5 Indian pharmaceutical companies on the basis of their size and product lines. The analysis of data concerning employee turnover and absenteeism will be presented at 3 levels:

(1) Overall analysis of the five American and Indian companies where technology is held constant.
(2) Analysis of each pair where, besides technology, the size of the firm and product lines are kept constant.
(3) Analysis of each pair, with management philosophy as an independent or causal variable.

EMPLOYEE TURNOVER

The concept of labor turnover signifies an employee's decision to disengage from an organization's activities. Usually, in the management literature, labor turnover is defined as the number of people hired per unit of time in order to maintain a working force at a given figure. The most frequently used formula to measure labor turnover is: $T = R/F$, where T = turnover rate, R = replacements per unit of time, and F = average working force.[49]

This formula includes all kinds of labor turnover, i.e., workers leaving the organization due to death, sickness, dismissal, and for the purpose of joining other organizations.

In our study, however, we concentrated on the labor turnover

---

[49] See E. E. Nemmers and C. C. Janzen, *Dictionary of Economics and Business* (Patterson: Littlefield Adams and Company, 1959), p. 166. For the detailed analysis of the data see Krishna Shetty, *Comparative Analysis of Manpower Management* (unpublished Ph.D. dissertation, submitted to the Graduate School of Business Administration, University of California at Los Angeles, 1967).

that arises from the worker's decision to leave the firm in order to join another firm. Thus, in collecting data, the labor turnover due to sickness, death, and dismissal were excluded. Our data, termed here voluntary turnover rate, hopefully suggests a better correlation between employee morale and labor turnover.

Of course, voluntary labor turnover is a function of many external as well as internal factors such as: economic conditions and opportunities available; sociocultural make-up of employee; legal framework; and working conditions in the organization, including relative wages, opportunities for advancement, and the satisfaction derived from work. Management might not be able to control the so-called external factors influencing voluntary turnover. However, the internal factors mentioned above are in the realm of managerial influence.

Since we are comparing the labor turnover of firms operating with similar technology in the same or similar socioeconomic, political, legal, and cultural environments, this measure may provide some useful insights into the working of the firms under study.

The data regarding the voluntary turnover rates in 10 pharmaceutical firms are presented in Tables 7-3 and 7-4.

As can be seen from Table 7-3, the voluntary labor turnover in American subsidiaries was much lower than that of comparable Indian companies. The average turnover rates for blue-collar workers were 1.6 percent in the former companies, while in the latter com-

Table 7-3   Voluntary Labor Turnover in American Subsidiaries and Local Pharmaceutical Companies in India

Types of Personnel	U.S. Companies (All Located in Bombay) (Avg. 5) 1964	1965	Indian Companies (All Located Elsewhere) (Avg. 5) 1964	1965	Indian Companies (All Located in Bombay) (Avg. 3) 1964	1965
Operators	1.6	1.6	4.74	4.86	2.67	2.00
Clerical	0.8	0.8	2.68	3.48	1.83	2.67
Managerial	0.5(1)*	0.5(1)*	2.28(4)*	2.15(4)*	1.50(2)*	2.00(2)*

* Figures in parentheses represent the total number of companies.

panies the rates were 4.76 percent in 1964, and 4.86 percent in 1965. Also, for the clerical and managerial personnel in the Indian companies, the rates of quitting were three times those of the American subsidiaries. The relatively high rates in the Indian companies, however, were somewhat influenced by the differing labor market conditions for two of these companies.

These 2 companies (Nos. 2 and 4 in Table 7-4) were located in smaller cities not far from farm areas. As a result, the labor force of these companies consisted of transitory farm workers. In Bombay, where other companies were located, the labor force was drawn from far off villages. Due to a higher degree of unemployment in big cities like Bombay, the workers were reluctant to quit their jobs. An earlier study by Ornati[50] indicated similar patterns in labor turnover rates in different cities of India. Thus, if we would exclude these 2 Indian companies and compare American and Indian companies lo-

Table 7-4   Voluntary Labor Turnover in American and Local Pharmaceutical Companies in India

Pair	Company Identification	Type of Personnel	Location	U.S. Subsidiary 1964	1965	Indian Company 1964	1965	Location
I	1–2 (MSP (SP)	Operators	Bombay	3.5	2.0	7.0	9.0	Elsewhere
		Clerical		0.5	0.5	2.0	2.5	
		Managerial		0.5*	0.5*	2.0	2.0	
II	3–4 (MSP) (MSP)	Operators	Bombay	1.0	1.0	8.7	9.3	Elsewhere
		Clerical		1.0	1.0	5.3	6.9	
		Managerial		nil	nil	4.1	2.6	
III	5–6 (SP) (SP)	Operators	Bombay	2.0	2.0	2.5	2.5	Bombay
		Clerical		1.0*	1.0	1.5	1.0	
		Managerial		n.a.	n.a.	1.0	2.0	
IV	7–8 (SP) (SP)	Operators	Bombay	1.5	2.0	2.0	1.5	Bombay
		Clerical		1.0*	1.0	2.0	2.0	
		Managerial		n.a.	n.a.	1.0	2.0	
V	9–10 (MSP) (NP)	Operators	Bombay	1.0	1.0	3.5	2.0	Bombay
		Clerical		0.5*	0.5*	2.0	5.0	
		Managerial		nil	nil	2.0	2.0	

* = less than
n.a. = not available

[50] Ornati, *loc. cit.*

cated in Bombay, we would find that the voluntary quitting rates are considerably lower in those companies. The average quitting rates for blue-collar workers fell from 4.74 percent and 4.86 percent to 2.67 percent and 2.00 percent in 1964 and 1965, respectively. Similar downward trends also were observable among clerical and managerial personnel.

However, the voluntary turnover rates in the American subsidiaries still were lower than those of the Indian companies. Table 7-4 depicts the voluntary turnover rates in each pair of American and Indian companies. As stated above, these companies were paired on the basis of their similarities in size, technology (hardware), and product lines. The companies numbered 1, 3, 5, 7, and 9 were the American subsidiaries, while 2, 4, 6, 8, and 10 were their counterpart Indian companies. Of these, 1, 3, 4, and 9 were categorized as Most Sophisticated management philosophy; numbers 2, 5, and 6 were of Somewhat Progressive philosophy; and numbers 8 and 10 belonged to the Not Progressive philosophy group.

The data in this table reveal that the most influential factor affecting employee turnover rate was labor-market condition, rather than our causal variable of management philosophy. For example, both companies 3 and 4 were classified as Most Sophisticated management philosophy, yet the differences in quitting rates were quite remarkable. However, if we compare the quitting rates with the firms operating in the same location (Bombay), an inference could be drawn concerning the relationship between the firm's management philosophy and its employee turnover rates. For example, companies 9 and 10, having different management philosophies but located in the same area (Bombay), experienced different quitting rates.

ABSENTEEISM

In simple terms, absenteeism means a reduction in the department's efficiency, a loss for the company, and the loss of a day's pay for the employee. There is a mélange of socioeconomic and cultural factors which affect the rate of absenteeism. For example, one finds a greater rate of absenteeism in times of economic prosperity, rising wages, and low unemployment. Conversely, in an economic depression or recession, when jobs are scarce, absentee report forms gather dust. However, under a given socioeconomic and cultural environment, the differences in the number of absentees among different firms might reflect their effectiveness in providing a good working atmosphere. Research studies of Argyris,[51] Fleishman and Harris,[52] Argyle, Gardner, and Coffee,[53] and Lindquist,[45] indicate a positive relationship between absenteeism, turnover, and leadership styles. To Argyris, absenteeism is one kind of defensive mechanism which the employee uses to let out his frustrations, conflicts, and failures in achieving satisfaction in his work. Fleishman and Harris related turnover, as well as grievance rates, to leadership behavior: "The more the leader structures, directs, and controls, the greater the probability of turnover."[55] Argyle, Gardner, and Coffee related directive leadership to absenteeism, while Lindguist demonstrated a causal relationship between unfavorable job adjustment and absenteeism.

In our study, as Table 7-5 and 7-6 illustrate, absenteeism seems to be more a function of the location of the firm than of management philosophy. Two of the Indian firms located in cities other than Bombay were characterized by consistently lower rates of absenteeism and greater quitting rates compared to those of other Indian as well as American, companies located in Bombay. On an average, the rate of absenteeism among American companies was somewhat lower than that of the Indian companies. Higher wage rates, better working conditions, and fair play promotion policies in American companies might explain the differences in rates of absenteeism among the two sets of companies. Generally, American companies in India (and in most other foreign countries, for that matter) pay double the amount of wages paid in local firms. However, the absenteeism rate in the American companies in India is still much higher, if compared to the absenteeism rates in the United States. The average rate of 12.1 percent in 1965 in these companies

---

[51] Argyris, *loc. cit.*

[52] E. Fleishman and E. Harris, "Patterns of Leadership Behavior Related to Employee Grievances and Turnover," Department of Industrial Administration, Yale University, 1961 (Mimeographed).

[53] Argyle, Gardner, and Coffee, *loc. cit.*

[54] A. Lindquist, "Absenteeism and Job Turnover as Consequences of Unfavorable Job Adjustment," *Acta Social*, Vol. 3, Nos. 2 and 3 (1958), pp. 119–131.

[55] Fleishman and Harris, *loc. cit.*, quoted from Argyris, *op. cit.*, p. 60.

Table 7-5   Absenteeism in American Subsidiaries and Local
Pharmaceutical Companies in India

Type of Personnel	U.S. Companies (All Located in Bombay) (Avg. 5)		Indian Companies (All Located Elsewhere) (Avg. 5)		Indian Companies (All Located in Bombay) (Avg. 3)	
	1964	1965	1964	1965	1964	1965
Operators	11.10	12.10	11.04	11.68	14.17	14.33
Clerical	4.50	5.00	4.88(4)*	3.88(4)*	4.75(2)*	3.50(2)*
Managerial	2.00(3)*	2.00(3)*	2.00(1)*	2.00(1)*	n.a.	n.a.

* Denotes number of companies in the figure.

Table 7-6   Absenteeism in American and Local
Pharmaceutical Companies in India

Pair	Company Identification	Type of Personnel	Location	U.S. Subsidiary 1964	1965	Indian Company 1964	1965	Location
I	1–2 (MSP) (SP)	Operators Clerical Managerial	Bombay	8.0 4.0 n.a.	8.5 5.5 n.a.	7.0 5.0 2.0	9.0 4.5 2.0	Elsewhere
II	3–4 (MSP) (MSP)	Operators Clerical Managerial	Bombay	13.0 5.0 2.0	14.0 4.0 2.0	5.7 5.0 n.a.	6.4 4.0 n.a.	Elsewhere
III	5–6 (SP) (SP)	Operators Clerical Managerial	Bombay	14.5 8.0 2.0	15.0 10.0 2.5	15.0 n.a. n.a.	16.0 n.a. n.a.	Bombay
IV	7–8 (SP) (NP)	Operators Clerical Managerial	Bombay	13.0 3.5 2.0	15.0 3.0 1.5	15.0 4.0 n.a.	14.0 3.5 n.a.	Bombay
V	9–10 (MSP) (NP)	Operators Clerical Managerial	Bombay	7.0 2.0 n.a.	8.0 2.5 n.a.	12.5 5.5 n.a.	13.0 3.5 n.a.	Bombay

The data are provided by the companies. In certain cases, the data are based on an estimate, particularly for clerical and managerial personnel.

compares very unfavorably with the 2.6 percent in the United States.[56]

The relatively higher rates of absenteeism in Indian industrial enterprises can be explained in terms of the low standard of living (which affects the health and well-being of workers), climatic conditions in industrial cities (temperature varies from 85–110° F. with 80–100 percent humidity), working conditions in factories, and permissive labor legislation in India.

Summary

This chapter analyzed four variables concerning management effectiveness with respect to blue-collar employees: employee morale and satisfaction in work, interpersonal relationships in industrial settings, labor turnover, and absenteeism.

The analysis of data from 92 industrial firms in 5 underdeveloped countries revealed that the majority of these companies were able to attain average or moderate employee morale and satisfaction in work. The firm's management philosophy (and such mediating variables as relative wages, opportunity for advancement and self-growth, and working conditions) was important in attaining high employee morale.

In the case of interpersonal relationships, however, most of these companies had failed to foster cooperative attitudes among their employees. The environmental variables affecting interpersonal relationships were: underemployment and unemployment situations, governmental attitudes toward the industrial worker and the business community, politically oriented trade unions, inflation, and the differences in educational attainments and aspirations of the younger and older employees.

Due to the many variations among different industrial sectors, labor turnover and absenteeism rates were investigated in ten pharmaceutical firms in India. The analysis of these data revealed that the firm's management philosophy and other mediating factors were somewhat influential. The environmental variables affecting labor turnover and absenteeism rates were: location of the firm (labor-market conditions), climatic conditions, and the general well-being and health of the workers.

[56] Myers, *op. cit.*, pp. 45–54.

8

MANAGEMENT EFFECTIVENESS AT THE MANAGER LEVEL

It has been increasingly recognized that the growth and viability of business organizations depend not only on their ability to innovate in the market and technological realms, but also on their ability to utilize manpower resources effectively. In the preceding chapter we examined 4 measures of management effectiveness, concentrating on nonmanagerial manpower resources: employee morale and satisfaction in work, interpersonal relationships, turnover, and absenteeism.

In this chapter, we will analyze the data pertaining to high-level managerial resources. The issues dealt with in this chapter are: management effectiveness in attracting and retaining high-level manpower; interdepartmental relationships; the executives' perception of company goal-achievement; utilization of high-level manpower and their preoccupation with, and responsiveness to, changes in environmental conditions.

ATTRACTING HIGH-LEVEL MANAGERIAL MANPOWER

In one sense, management effectiveness in attracting and retaining high-level manpower is synonymous with the effectiveness of a company's human organization, effectiveness which assumes special significance in the developing countries. Likert, for example, has observed that:

All activities of an enterprise are initiated and determined by the persons who make up that institution . . . Every aspect of a firm's activity is determined by the competence, motivation and general effectiveness of its human organization. Of all the tasks of management, managing the human component is the central and most important task because all else depends upon how well it is done.[1]

Underscoring the same notion, particularly as it applies to developing countries, Harbison and Myers have said that:

In the march towards industrialism, capital, technology, and natural resources are but passive agents. The active forces are the human agents who create and control organizations. . . .[2]

That corporation strength lies in effective managers has been noted by many company executives. The president of Oji Paper Company (Japan) typically stressed the importance of high-level manpower when he said that:

To my mind, human resources should be properly shown in figures as assets on the balance sheet just as physical assets are, as an indication of corporate strength . . . cultivation of human resources offers a scope of promise vastly wider than that of physical resources.[3]

The actual experiences of companies in hiring and retaining high-level managerial manpower are discussed here, first by comparing the U.S. subsidiaries with the national companies in India, and then by making international comparisons.

Intracountry Comparisons

Data presented in Table 8-1 indicate that proportionately more U.S. subsidiaries were able to recruit and retain highly-skilled man-

[1] Rensis Likert, *The Human Organization: Its Management and Value* (New York: McGraw-Hill Book Company, 1960), p. 1.

[2] Frederick Harbison and Charles Myers, *Management in the Industrial World* (New York: McGraw-Hill Book Company, 1959), p. 3.

[3] Sadao Kumazawa, "Future Management—Effective Use of Human Resources," *Management Japan*, July-September 1967, p. 5.

agers than were their Indian counterparts. Four American and four Indian companies could procure average-skilled managers. However, it should be noted that those companies classified as MS companies were successful in recruiting and retaining skilled managers. Several factors might have facilitated the attracting of superior managerial talent by these organizations. Key factors included relatively better salaries, greater opportunities for advancement, and progressive company image.

Of the remaining companies, 5 U.S. subsidiaries and 8 Indian-owned companies faced problems in attracting superior talent. Four of the five U.S. subsidiaries were headed by British managers whose personnel management philosophy, so far as we could determine by talking to other members in these companies, was not as progressive as that of the subsidiaries (MS) managed by Americans.

In sum, we found that the management philosophy variable accounted in part for a company's ability or inability to attract and retain superior managers within the same socioeconomic environment. Data from Argentina, Brazil, the Philippines, and Uruguay support this view.

International Comparisons

Data presented in Table 8-1 lend support to the notion that the American subsidiaries in the 5 countries were, as a whole, more successful in attracting high-level managerial and technical personnel than the local companies. For example, of the 28 companies (out of the total of 92) in which there were highly trained managers, 20 were American subsidiaries; a majority of these subsidiaries were MS-type organizations. None of the companies classified as Not Progressive were able to hire and retain trained personnel.

In addition to a progressive management philosophy, a company's ability to recruit and retain high-level management personnel depends upon the availability of such manpower in the country. It is well known that there are acute shortages, insofar as technical and managerial talent are concerned, in India and the other 4 countries in our study.

Table 8-1   Management Effectiveness in Hiring and Retaining Trained
Managerial and Technical Personnel

	Overall Comparisons		Management Philosophy Most Sophisticated		Somewhat Progressive		Not Progressive	
Country	U.S.	Local	U.S.	Local	U.S.	Local	U.S.	Local
Argentina	n= 6	n= 5	n= 1	n= 1	n= 5	n= 4	n= 0	n= 0
Able to hire and retain trained personnel	2	1	–	1	2	–	–	–
Able to hire and retain average skilled personnel	–	2	–	–	–	2	–	–
Not able to hire or retain skilled personnel	4	2	1	–	3	2	–	–
Brazil	n= 8	n= 7	n= 1	n= 0	n= 7	n= 6	n= 0	n= 1
Able to hire and retain trained personnel	4	2	1	–	3	2	–	–
Able to hire and retain average skilled personnel	1	2	–	–	1	2	–	–
Not able to hire or retain skilled personnel	3	3	–	–	3	2	–	1
India	n= 17	n= 17	n= 5	n= 5	n= 11	n= 7	n= 1	n= 5
Able to hire and retain trained personnel	8	5	5	5	3	–	–	–
Able to hire and retain average skilled personnel	4	4	–	–	4	4	–	–
Not able to hire or retain skilled personnel	5	8	–	–	4	3	1	5
Philippines	n= 10	n= 11	n= 4	n= 4	n= 6	n= 7	n= 0	n= 0
Able to hire and retain trained personnel	4	–	3	–	1	–	–	–
Able to hire and retain average skilled personnel	2	4	–	1	2	3	–	–
Not able to hire or retain skilled personnel	4	7	1	3	3	4	–	–

Uruguay	$n=$ 6	$n=$ 5	$n=$ 0	$n=$ 0	$n=$ 6	$n=$ 5	$n=$ 0	$n=$ 0
Able to hire and retain trained personnel	2	–	–	–	2	–	–	–
Able to hire and retain average skilled personnel	3	2	–	–	3	2	–	–
Not able to hire or retain skilled personnel	1	3	–	–	1	3	–	–

PROFESSIONALIZATION OF MANAGERS

In recent years, scholars have paid considerable attention to the problems of manpower resources in underdeveloped countries. We cite, among others, the pioneering studies of Harbison and Myers, and their collaborators.[4] These authors revealed that the lack of proper governmental, as well as business, planning has been responsible for the dearth of educational institutions for the training of managers in these countries. Although the number of U.S.-type business schools is increasing every year, there still remains a wide gap between the actual need for such institutions and what is available.

Another environmental factor impeding the professionalization of managers is the owner-manager situation in these countries. Family ownership of industrial enterprises tends to deter the emergence of the professional manager. There is no "room at the top" for the "outsider," regardless of his training. As the owner-manager of a large company in Uruguay asserted:

I do not believe in anybody having anything to do with management except my own family. There is a clear distinction in my organization. My family is on one side, and the rest of the salaried and hourly personnel on the other side.

Studies of Kamala Chowdhry[5] and Sagar Jain[6] in India, Flores[7]

---

[4] Frederick Harbison and Charles A. Myers, *Education, Manpower and Economic Growth* (New York: McGraw-Hill Book Company, 1964).

[5] Kamala Chowdhry, "Social and Cultural Factors in Management Development in India and the Role of the Expert," *International Labour Review*, Vol. 94, No. 2 (August 1966), pp. 132–147.

[6] Sagar Jain, "Old Style of Management," in S. B. Prasad and A. R. Negandhi, *Management for Economic Development* (The Hague: Martinus Nijhoff, 1968), pp. 9–44.

in the Philippines, Fillol[8] in Argentina, and McMillan[9] and Oberg[10] in Brazil, clearly indicate such situations. For example, McMillan observed:

The Brazilian industrialist of the mid-twentieth century is the family owner-manager . . . he is less a promoter of his business interests and more a defender of his aristocratic class.[11]

In the same vein, Oberg found that in Brazil:

The family idea . . . is strong. You get a young fellow with ability, and he works hard expecting to get ahead, and then comes the 20-year-old son of the owner and he's the boss.[12]

Such researchers as Farmer and Richman,[13] and the studies of UNESCO,[14] seem to indicate that the lack of management professionalization in underdeveloped countries is due to the society's unfavorable views toward the managerial class. Farmer and Richman, for example, have argued:

The place of business managers in the prestige hierarchy of a particular country is quite relevant in determining managerial effectiveness. . . .[15] The more favorably a particular society views industrial managers and management, the less likely it is that the profession will lack capable recruits . . . the closer the society comes to viewing industrial managers as only slightly better than mad dogs or vicious exploiters—justly or unjustly—the more likely the profession and the overall staffing function would suffer greatly.[16]

---

[7] F. C. Flores, Jr., "Applicability of American Management Know-How to Developing Countries: The Case of Philippines" (unpublished Ph.D. dissertation, submitted to the Graduate School of Business Administration, University of California at Los Angeles, 1967).

[8] Tomas Roberto Fillol, *Social Factors in Economic Development: The Argentine Case* (Cambridge, Mass.: The M.I.T. Press, 1963).

[9] Claude McMillan, Jr., "The American Businessman in Brazil," *Business Topics* (Spring 1963), reprinted in *International Dimensions in Business* (East Lansing, Mich.: Graduate School of Business Administration, Michigan State University, 1966).

[10] Winston Oberg, "Cross-Cultural Perspectives on Management Principles," *Academy of Management Journal*, Vol. 6, No. 2 (June 1963), pp. 129–143.

[11] McMillan, *op. cit.*, p. 99.

[12] Oberg, *op. cit.*, p. 133.

[13] R. N. Farmer and B. M. Richman, *Comparative Management and Economic Progress* (Homewood, Ill.: Richard D. Irwin, Inc., 1965).

[14] UNESCO, *Report on the World Situation* (Paris, March 9, 1961).

[15] Farmer and Richman, *op. cit.*, p. 113.

[16] *Ibid.*, p. 115.

A study undertaken by UNESCO reports:

A common psychological obstacle to economic achievement is the fact that much higher status tends to be associated with land ownership or government position or professional or intellectual activity than is enjoyed by the businessman, engineer, mechanic, agronomist, or other person concerned directly with material production.[17]

While there is merit to such observations, we think there are good indications of a change in aspiration among the young and educated people in these countries. The fervor, the enthusiasm of the applicants toward U.S.-type business schools, the number of new joint ventures with foreign companies, and the output of business literature impel us to reevaluate the old hypotheses about how people view business, management, and so forth.

Among many factors affecting the professionalization of management in underdeveloped countries, the following factors were frequently mentioned by our interviewees: (1) owner-manager situation; (2) the nature of competition; (3) the "strength" and the bargaining powers of such external and internal agents such as employees, consumers, distributors, suppliers, the government, and the community.

In the last chapter we speculated on the possible relationships among these factors and the professionalization of management.

In Appendix D, we have elaborated the impact of owner-manager and market situations on the professionalization of managers and management. The following two propositions summarize our observations:

(1) The greater the "bargaining powers" of consumers and employees, the higher the degree of professionalization of managers/management.
(2) The greater the degree of separation of owners and managers, the higher the degree of professionalization of managers and management.

INTERDEPARTMENTAL RELATIONS

This management effectiveness criterion refers to the degree of interdependence of the various departments within organizations.

[17] UNESCO Study, *op. cit.,* p. 79.

We investigated three relationships directed toward the interdependence of departments: (1) contributions by the departments toward the objectives of the organization; (2) performance activities and maintenance of integrity; and (3) contributions by one department to the other.[18]

Intracountry Comparisons

The data concerning inderdepartmental relationships, as presented in Table 8-2, indicate that the overall performance of American companies in this respect was better than that of Indian companies. Specifically, in slightly less than two-thirds of the American companies (11 out of 17), the interdependence of different parts (departments) was clear. Additionally, in 5 of these companies, something of a balance was maintained with respect to the interdependence and independence of parts. In only one American company did a single part (in this case the dominant personality of the general manager) control all other parts and their activities. In this particular company, an immediate assistant general manager was asked about his activities. He described them in these words:

Oh! What I do in this firm . . . I dance to the tunes [shouting] of my general manager . . . and all my men do likewise to my tunes. . . . The General Manager is the God Shiva [referring to the Hindu God of anger] whom we aim to please.

Compared to the American companies, the Indian companies showed somewhat "inferior" effectiveness in maintaining healthy

[18] There is an implicit assumption here that the harmonious relationships among different departments will enhance the organizational effectiveness in achieving its stated objectives. We subscribe to the views of Argyris and others. For example, Argyris, in pinpointing the importance of interdependence of different parts (departments) has argued:

It may be important for the parts to be aware of the whole in that frequently organizations are faced with distributing scarce resources. In order to make effective decisions about the share of the resources allocated to each part, knowledge must be available concerning the actual needs of the parts. Parts may define their needs partially as a function of what they know that they need and believe that they will need. However, they may be able to make more effective estimates if they are aware of the organization's needs. This requires that they become aware of the interdependence among parts.

Chris Argyris, *Integrating the Individual and the Organization* (New York: John Wiley and Sons, Inc., 1964), p. 174.

Table 8-2 Interdepartmental Relations

Country	Overall Comparison U.S. Local	Most Sophisticated U.S. Local	Somewhat Progressive U.S. Local	Not Progressive U.S. Local
Argentina	$n=$ 6 $n=$ 5	$n=$ 1 $n=$ 1	$n=$ 5 $n=$ 4	$n=$ 0 $n=$ 0
Very cooperative	1 1	– –	1 1	– –
Somewhat cooperative	1 1	– –	1 1	– –
Poor cooperation	4 3	1 1	3 2	– –
Brazil	$n=$ 8 $n=$ 7	$n=$ 1 $n=$ 0	$n=$ 7 $n=$ 6	$n=$ 0 $n=$ 1
Very cooperative	1 –	1 –	– –	– –
Somewhat cooperative	1 2	– –	1 2	– –
Poor cooperation	6 5	– –	6 4	– 1
India	$n=$ 17 $n=$ 17	$n=$ 5 $n=$ 5	$n=$ 11 $n=$ 7	$n=$ 1 $n=$ 5
Very cooperative	11 5	5 5	6 –	– –
Somewhat cooperative	5 3	– –	5 3	– –
Poor cooperation	1 9	– –	– 4	1 5
Philippines	$n=$ 10 $n=$ 11	$n=$ 4 $n=$ 4	$n=$ 6 $n=$ 7	$n=$ 0 $n=$ 0
Very cooperative	7 5	4 3	3 2	– –
Somewhat cooperative	3 3	– 1	3 2	– –
Poor cooperation	– 3	– –	– 3	– –
Uruguay	$n=$ 6 $n=$ 5	$n=$ 0 $n=$ 0	$n=$ 6 $n=$ 5	$n=$ 0 $n=$ 0
Very cooperative	3 1	– –	3 1	– –
Somewhat cooperative	– 1	– –	– 1	– –
Poor cooperation	3 3	– –	3 3	– –

interdependence of different parts of the organization. There were only 5 companies in which such interdependence was clearly present. Five more companies were able to maintain moderate interdependence of parts; in slightly more than half of these companies, the single part (or personality) dominated all organizational activities.

It may be recalled that in such related issues as employee morale and interpersonal relationships American companies were not as successful as they were in achieving effective interdepartmental relationships. The apparent success of the American companies in this aspect seems due to: (1) clearly stated objectives, policies, and procedures; and (2) use of better communication techniques in informing member participants about their duties and responsibilities in achieving the stated goals.

In terms of a causal variable affecting this management-effectiveness criterion, management philosophy of the firm has had considerable influence. For example, all of the American and Indian companies categorized as having Most Sophisticated management philosophy were able to achieve effective coordination among different departments, while at the other end of the continuum, firms classified as Not Progressive were managed and dominated by a single top executive (general manager in the case of American firms, and an owner in Indian firms). In these companies we found considerable "unhealthy" rivalry among different departments.

A senior executive in the Indian company, a Ph.D. from M.I.T., expressed the views of many other executives of these latter companies when he said:

> What is most important for me and my department is not what I do or achieve for the company, but whether the Master's [i.e., an owner of the firm] favor is bestowed on me. . . . This I have achieved by saying "yes" to everything the Master says or does . . . to contradict him is to look for another job. . . . I left my freedom of thought in Boston.

International Comparison

Some interesting observations can be drawn from the data on interdepartmental relationships in Latin American countries and Far Eastern countries. Relatively speaking, the companies in the Far East (India and the Philippines) experienced less difficulty in maintaining cooperative relationships among their subunits or departments than the companies in the Latin American region. This was true with American subsidiaries as well as local firms in these countries. Why was this so?

There may be a score of factors affecting interdepartmental

relationships in companies in Latin America. However, in our interviews the following two factors were mentioned most frequently: (1) the inadequate delegation of authority and responsibility by the top executives (owner-manager); (2) adverse feelings against U.S. capital in Latin American countries.

Overcentralization of authority, and reluctance to delegate authority and responsibility on the part of the owner-manager, has resulted in the lack of proper training and development of lower managerial cadre, affecting, in turn, the overall efficiency of the enterprise. As Fillol has observed in Argentina, "When the 'road upward' is blocked by family barriers . . . people may look at their jobs as a mere foothold from which to launch their own [small scale] business careers."[19] Under such circumstances, it is unrealistic to expect participants to have real identification with the purposes and goals of the organization.

The owner-manager situation existed in all 5 underdeveloped countries. However, the degree of owner-manager control varied in these 2 regions. There was also a greater awareness on the part of Indian and Filipino entrepreneurs concerning the training of their employees.

American subsidiaries provided better training and opportunities for advancement to their employees than did their local counterparts in these countries. However, the U.S. subsidiaries in Latin American countries were somewhat more centralized than those in India and the Philippines. United States subsidiaries in the former region were also faced wtih another serious problem, the widespread adverse feeling against American capital. McMillan, Gonzalez, and Erickson, in their intensive study of U.S. business in Brazil, quote a well-known Brazilian economist, Aristoteles Moura, who has accused U.S. private investors in Brazil of exploiting his country. In their evaluation of Moura's contention, McMillan, *et al.* asserted:

One would expect that knowledgeable Brazilians would be quick to recognize that Moura's appraisal smacks of fantasy. And yet, there is, in Moura's analysis, a synthesis of the prevalent Latin American apprehension concerning foreign, and particularly U.S. capital.[20]

[19] Fillol, *op. cit.*, p. 61.
[20] Claude McMillan, Jr., and Richard F. Gonzalez with Leo G. Erickson, *International Enterprise in a Developing Economy* (East Lansing, Mich.: Graduate School of Business Administration, Michigan State University, 1964), p. 221.

Of course, this is not to say that hostile feelings against foreign capital were not prevalent in India and the Philippines. Such feelings were not sufficiently strong, however, to affect all managerial activities in these countries. In Latin American countries, such attitudes seem to have lasting effects on all managerial activities, including maintenance of interdepartmental relationships.

ACHIEVEMENT OF THE FIRM'S OVERALL OBJECTIVES: EXECUTIVE PERCEPTION

This variable deals with the question of how the firm's overall objectives and the achievement of those objectives were perceived by the influential member participants of the organization. The term perception is not used in a strict sense, but connotes, rather, the point of view of executives.

Indeed, this factor is closely related to, but not identical to, our criterion of "interdependence of different parts," discussed above. Whereas the latter dealt with the so-called working relationships between different parts of the organization, the former factor sheds light on how the participants themselves view organizational objectives and their roles in achieving them.

Both of these measures, interdependence of different parts and achievement of the firm's overall objectives, were fashioned after Argyris's "Mix Model" variables. The importance of the criterion of achievement in the firm's overall objectives is explained by Argyris in these terms:

An organization as a whole has, by definition, objectives that it must achieve. To be sure, every part has formal sub-objectives but these take on their meanings by being related to the larger overall objectives. The less an organization is guided by its overall objectives and the more the objectives of each part become paramount and are not relatable to the overall objectives, the less the firm approximates the essential characteristics of organization.[21]

Data concerning this measure was collected by asking top- and middle-level executives of different departments about the objectives of the firm within their departments and within other departments.

[21] Chris Argyris, *op. cit.*, p. 153.

They were also asked how well the firm was able to achieve its overall objectives, and whether the achievement of the overall objectives or the departmental objectives were of paramount concern to them. On the basis of this information, we classified the companies as follows: (1) total optimization was perceived as most important; (2) there was much pull and push for sub-optimization; (3) suboptimization was perceived as the ultimate goal.

Intracountry Comparison

Data presented in Table 8-3 show that total optimization was considered most crucial in a large majority of American subsidiaries in India. Such a situation existed in two-thirds of these companies, while, in the other one-third, considerable push and pull for suboptimization was more evident. As a matter of fact, senior executives in three of these latter companies were only vaguely aware of the roles and functions of other departments. To them, the entire company meant nothing more than their own department.

Compared to American companies, Indian companies were worse off in this regard. Only in 7 of these companies (as compared to the 12 American companies) was total optimization of goals considered more important, while more than one-half of the companies' executives were more concerned about their departmental goals and objectives than achievement of the firm's overall objectives. One can argue here that the use of better communication techniques and clearer definition of objectives by the American companies have contributed considerably to the realization of the firm's objectives.

A detailed analysis of these data also reveals that the management philosophy, as a variable, has had some impact on the firm's ability to create an atmosphere where overall objectives are considered most important and crucial. For example, all the companies (5 American and 5 Indian) classified as Most Sophisticated in philosophy aimed at total optimization of goals. However, the converse was not true. There were 7 American and 2 Indian companies where such an atmosphere was widespread in spite of their somewhat less progressive management philosophies. There were also 3 American and 1 Indian companies categorized as Somewhat Progressive in

Table 8-3   Executives' Perception of the Achievement of Firms' Objectives

Country	Overall Comparison U.S. Local		Management Philosophy Most Sophisticated U.S. Local		Somewhat Progressive U.S. Local		Not Progressive U.S. Local	
Argentina	$n=$ 6	$n=$ 5	$n=$ 1	$n=$ 1	$n=$ 5	$n=$ 4	$n=$ 0	$n=$ 0
Total optimization most important	2	1	–	–	2	1	–	–
Much pull and push for suboptimization	4	2	1	1	3	1	–	–
Suboptimization ultimate goal	–	2	–	–	–	2	–	–
Brazil	$n=$ 8	$n=$ 7	$n=$ 1	$n=$ 0	$n=$ 7	$n=$ 6	$n=$ 0	$n=$ 1
Total optimization most important	1	–	–	–	1	–	–	–
Much pull and push for suboptimization	7	5	1	–	6	4	–	1
Suboptimization ultimate goal	–	2	–	–	–	2	–	–
India	$n=$ 17	$n=$ 17	$n=$ 5	$n=$ 5	$n=$ 11	$n=$ 7	$n=$ 1	$n=$ 5
Total optimization most important	12	7	5	5	7	2	–	–
Much pull and push for suboptimization	2	9	–	–	1	4	1	5
Suboptimization ultimate goal	3	1	–	–	3	1	–	–
Philippines	$n=$ 10	$n=$ 11	$n=$ 4	$n=$ 4	$n=$ 6	$n=$ 7	$n=$ 0	$n=$ 0
Total optimization most important	8	6	4	3	4	3	–	–
Much pull and push for suboptimization	2	5	–	1	2	4	–	–
Suboptimization ultimate goal	–	–	–	–	–	–	–	–

Uruguay	$n=$ 6	$n=$ 5	$n=$ 0	$n=$ 0	$n=$ 6	$n=$ 5	$n=$ 0	$n=$ 0
Total optimization most important	3	1	–	–	3	1	–	–
Much pull and push for suboptimization	3	3	–	–	3	3	–	–
Suboptimization ultimate goal	–	1	–	–	–	1	–	–

management philosophy where achievement of the firm's overall objectives was grossly underemphasized and departmental goals were overemphasized. Thus, in this instance, management philosophy as a variable seems to be a contributory factor, but not the determining variable. Such mediating variables as clearer statements of objectives and goals, use of better communication techniques, etc., have had greater influence upon this criterion.

International Comparison

International data presented in Table 8-3 enable us to make the following observations:

(1) American subsidiaries were better equipped to achieve their overall objectives than their local counterparts;
(2) The correlation between the management philosophy variable and the executive's perceptions of objectives was more conspicuous among local firms than among the American subsidiaries. U.S. companies, in other words, regardless of their management philosophy index, were more effective in communicating the firm's overall objectives among their executives;
(3) Companies in the Far Eastern region (India and the Philippines) were more successful in this respect than the companies in Latin American countries.

Let us examine these observations in detail. Executives in more than one-half of the American subsidiaries (26 out of a total of 47) perceived total optimization as most crucial, compared to less than one-third of the executives in the local firms within these countries. The statements of objectives, policies, procedures, and role definitions were in favor of American companies.

In the case of local firms, the higher the score on management philosophy index, the greater the firm's effectiveness in obtaining desirable perception of the overall objectives. For example, of the 26 American subsidiaries whose executives perceived total optimization as being important, only one-third were categorized as Most Sophisticated in management philosophy. Of the comparable local firms, more than one-half (9 out of 15) were in this management philosophy category. These data indicate that, among local companies, the firm's management philosophy (and such mediating variables as clearer statements of objectives, policies, and procedures, as well as job definitions) were positively correlated. This was not so in the case of American companies.

Lastly, we stated that the companies in Far Eastern countries were more successful in obtaining favorable perceptions of their executives concerning the achievement of the firm's overall objectives. Data reported in Table 8-3 show that 33 out of 55 companies studied in this region were able to do so, compared to merely 8 out of 37 companies in the Latin American region. Thus, our contention that the owner-manager situation, resulting in centralization of authority and lack of opportunities for middle-level executives, was stronger in Latin American countries than in the Far Eastern countries is also supported by these data.

Of course, business as well as government in all these underdeveloped countries is plagued by widespread favoritism and nepotism.[22] The degree of such favoritism and nepotism was less in India and the Philippines, however, than in Argentina, Brazil, and Uruguay.

UTILIZATION OF HIGH-LEVEL MANPOWER

To collect data on this aspect, we gathered information concerning two items: (1) what the executives did; and (2) how zealous they were in their work. So far as these two items were concerned, there were no significant differences between the Far Eastern countries and Latin American countries. Therefore, to avoid repetition, we will only analyze the data pertaining to companies

---

[22] For a critical analysis of the causes of corruption in South Asia, see Gunnar Myrdal, *Asian Drama: An Inquiry into Poverty of Nations* (New York: The Twentieth Century Fund, 1968), pp. 937–958.

operating in India. Our findings in the Indian context were applicable to the other underdeveloped countries studied as well.

The executive's job involves a variety of tasks. The relative importance assigned to these depends upon such factors as the structure of industry, the competition, and the socioeconomic, political, and legal conditions prevailing during a particular time. For example, in a country where governmental controls and bureaucracy are excessive, a top executive may spend his entire time dealing with the government. In another case, where labor problems are most acute, a chief executive may spend all of his time resolving these problems. However, there is some agreement on the relative importance of the executive's functions. For example, *Fortune's* survey indicates that the planning and setting of policies and objectives is considered very important by many executives:

The setting of overall company policies and objectives . . . [were] mentioned more often than they mentioned the making of important decisions . . . and of all the other functions they cited, three repeatedly stood out as typical of executive work: Coordinating, organizing, and delegating.[23]

Our comparative data on this aspect were collected from the companies facing more or less identical socioeconomic, political, and legal conditions in India. These, therefore, provide some insight concerning the degree of effective utilization of high-level manpower in these 2 sets of companies. American companies, of course, by the nature of their foreign origin, were at some disadvantage in dealing with the government. However, as the data reveal, this differential treatment did not appear to have much impact on their effectiveness.

Table 8-4 shows that there was a great deal of emphasis on the managerial functions—policy-making and future planning functions —of top executives in the American companies. More specifically, senior executives of 7 American companies spent their entire day, or at least a major portion of it, on policy matters and future planning; in 4 companies, on coordinating their departmental activities with those of other departments; in 5 of these companies, executives

[23] Perrin Stryker, "Who Are Executives?" in *The Executive Life* (Editors of *Fortune*) (Garden City: Doubleday and Company, 1956), p. 22.

Table 8-4   Utilization of High-Level Manpower Resources in Five Underdeveloped Countries

Country	Overall Comparison U.S.	Local	Management Philosophy Most Sophisticated U.S.	Local	Somewhat Progressive U.S.	Local	Not Progressive U.S.	Local
Argentina	$n=$ 6	$n=$ 5	$n=$ 1	$n=$ 1	$n=$ 5	$n=$ 4	$n=$ 0	$n=$ 0
Function								
Policy making, future planning	2	1	1	1	1	–	–	–
Coordination with other departments	2	1	–	–	2	1	–	–
Routine work	–	1	–	–	–	1	–	–
Finding fault with subordinates and others	2	2	–	–	2	2	–	–
Enthusiasm and drive								
Strong	1	1	–	1	1	–	–	–
Moderate	2	1	1	–	1	1	–	–
Defensive, withdrawing	3	3	–	–	3	3	–	–
Brazil	$n=$ 8	$n=$ 7	$n=$ 1	$n=$ 0	$n=$ 7	$n=$ 6	$n=$ 0	$n=$ 1
Function								
Policy making, future planning	1	1	–	–	1	1	–	–
Coordination with other departments	4	3	–	–	4	2	–	1
Routine work	1	2	–	–	1	2	–	–
Finding fault with subordinates and others	2	1	1	–	1	1	–	–
Enthusiasm and drive								
Strong	3	2	1	–	2	1	–	1
Moderate	2	1	–	–	2	1	–	
Defensive, withdrawing	3	4	–	–	3	4	–	–
India	$n=$ 17	$n=$ 17	$n=$ 5	$n=$ 5	$n=$ 11	$n=$ 7	$n=$ 1	$n=$ 5
Function								
Policy making, future planning	7	3	5	3	2	–	–	–
Coordination with other departments	4	4	–	2	4	2	–	–

Table 8-4 (Cont.)

	Management Philosophy							
	Overall Comparison		Most Sophisticated		Somewhat Progressive		Not Progressive	
Country	U.S.	Local	U.S.	Local	U.S.	Local	U.S.	Local
Routine work	5	6	–	–	5	5	–	1
Finding fault with subordinates and others	1	4	–	–	–	–	1	4
Enthusiasm and drive								
Strong	5	4	5	4	–	–	–	–
Moderate	9	4	–	1	9	3	–	–
Defensive, withdrawing	3	9	–	–	2	4	1	5
Philippines	$n=$ 10	$n=$ 11	$n=$ 4	$n=$ 4	$n=$ 6	$n=$ 7	$n=$ 0	$n=$ 0
Function								
Policy making, future planning	6	3	4	3	2	–	–	–
Coordination with other departments	4	4	–	1	4	3	–	–
Routine work	–	2	–	–	–	2	–	–
Finding fault with subordinates and others	–	2	–	–	–	2	–	–
Enthusiasm and drive								
Strong	2	3	2	3	–	–	–	–
Moderate	6	7	2	1	4	6	–	–
Defensive, withdrawing	2	1	–	–	2	1	–	–
Uruguay	$n=$ 6	$n=$ 5	$n=$ 0	$n=$ 0	$n=$ 6	$n=$ 5	$n=$ 0	$n=$ 0
Function								
Policy making, future planning	–	–	–	–	–	–	–	–
Coordination with other departments	4	3	–	–	4	3	–	–
Routine work	–	–	–	–	–	–	–	–
Finding fault with subordinates and others	2	2	–	–	2	2	–	–
Enthusiasm and drive								
Strong	2	2	–	–	2	2	–	–
Moderate	2	1	–	–	2	1	–	–
Defensive, withdrawing	2	2	–	–	2	2	–	–

137

devoted their entire day to routine nonmanagerial work. Only in one of these companies did the executives spend their time politicking and finding fault with everyone, including their own subordinates.

Executives in Indian companies placed less emphasis upon managerial functions. Only in 3 companies were the executives more concerned with policy matters and future planning. In 3 additional companies, their time was spent coordinating departmental activities; in the remaining 11 companies, such nonmanagerial tasks as performing day-to-day operations, and politicking, were their major preoccupations.

Of course, one cannot belittle day-to-day affairs and say that the policy-making and future planning functions are more important than routine work. However, someone has to undertake such vital functions in order to maintain a company's competitive position and plan for viability and growth. Only in stagnant companies are these tasks perceived as unnecessary. Senior executives are in a better position to initiate and provide leadership for the performance of such functions. To this extent, one can assert that the companies using their senior executives in the above fashion are utilizing their high-level human resources better than the companies in which executive time is consumed by routine nonmanagerial tasks or needless politicking.

SENIOR EXECUTIVES' ENTHUSIASM AND DRIVE

While the preceding measure was helpful in discerning executive preoccupation, it fell short of determining the commitments of executives to their work. To confirm this, we noted the degree of enthusiasm and drive displayed by the executives. For the purpose of analysis, these data were categorized as shown below: (1) executives showing enormous enthusiasm and drive in their work; (2) executives showing moderate enthusiasm and drive in their work; (3) executives who were defensive and withdrawing individuals.

Our analysis revealed that, by and large, Indian companies failed to inspire their managerial and technical personnel. In a little more than one-half of the Indian companies, executives were withdrawing individuals whose defensive activities outnumbered their constructive ones.

This state of affairs also existed in 3 American companies. The executives of these firms were no different in terms of defensive activities and withdrawing attitudes than were those of the nine Indian companies referred to above.

However, in a majority of the American companies (14 out of 17), a somewhat healthy atmosphere prevailed. In these companies, executives displayed at least moderate enthusiasm and spirit in their work. All of them felt they were expected to do something worthwhile in this world besides eke out a decent living. Particularly in 5 of these companies, executives demonstrated the zeal of Barnard's "morale-building leaders."[24] To them, the world was full of opportunities and challenges. The same atmosphere and spirit existed among executives in 4 Indian companies; in an additional 4 companies, executives did their work with at least moderate zeal and eagerness.

Table 8-4 shows that there is a positive relationship between a firm's management philosophy and the spirit and enthusiasm of its executives. Five American and four Indian companies categorized as having Most Sophisticated management philosophy were able to generate the utmost drive and enthusiasm among their executives. Conversely, all 5 Indian and the one American company classified as Not Progressive had withdrawing and defensive executives.

Executives expressed their work philosophies in these words:

My job offers me a great opportunity to do something for India besides sending handsome profits to stockowners back home in the U.S. I can never get tired of this work . . . and the more I work, the more I am convinced that there is much to do in this life . . . without work I would be a dead person . . . and without this opportunity in my firm I would be an empty person . . . [An American executive in India, manifesting "high drive and enthusiasm."]

Work is the delight of my life, and I am a happy person that I have this opportunity in this company. I have everything I need to make worthwhile contributions to my company, my country, and to my people . . . my day is never over . . . and I am glad that it is not. Life is wonderful with work, and I never want to "retire" from it, even if the company stops paying me. [An Indian executive in an American subsidiary: "High drive and enthusiasm."]

[24] Chester I. Barnard, *The Functions of the Executive* (Cambridge, Mass.: Harvard University Press, 1964), especially pp. 250–284.

Work is worship for me, and I never get tired of work . . . I strongly believe that it is the man who makes things move . . . there is no substitute for human beings . . . life without work would be like an ocean without its excitements of tides and ebbs . . . this is Mr. . . . life . . . Nehru died working . . . I would like to do the same. [An Indian executive in an Indian company: "High drive and enthusiasm."]

Oh! I can do several things at work . . . I can help my son solve his engineering problems . . . write articles on anything and everything that will earn money. . . . I have much time here . . . it takes only one hour a day to give orders to my staff for routine production activities . . . besides, I have no work here . . . it is damn easy . . . if the company does not grow, it is the managing director's problem . . . we are only educated peons [servants] even the general manager, who is my boss, spends his time helping out the managing director's children and wife in their school work and shopping . . . this is India . . . McGregor's "Y" theory [executive was a student of late Professor Douglas McGregor both at M.I.T. and the Indian Institute of Management in Calcutta] is good on paper . . . it has no meaning for my boss and the managing director . . . and if they do not care, why should I? [An executive, production manager with Ph.D., chemical engineering, in an Indian company: "withdrawing individual."]

Certainly, such differences in perception are bound to affect each executive in his leadership role and, consequently, the growth of the company. However, there were no black and white situations here. These differential perceptions were neither dependent upon one's national origin nor on the ownership of the firm. If anything, as we saw above, it was a function of the overall philosophy of the firm.

EXECUTIVE RESPONSIVENESS IN ADAPTING TO ENVIRONMENTAL CONDITIONS

This measure pertains to a company's capacity to adapt to such outside environmental factors as socioeconomic, political, and legal conditions prevailing in a given country. To quote Argyris, "This dimension points to the fact that all organizations are open systems in the sense that they are influenced by (and they in turn influence) the environment in which they are embedded. The dimensions also suggest that an organization needs to be able to modify its environmentally oriented activities as the conditions require."[25]

In this measure, we were more concerned about what Eells calls the "temper" of the firm in adapting to various environmental changes.[26]

To collect data, we examined such things as the executive's calmness in work, his response to sudden environmental changes, and finally, his gripes about environmental conditions. On the basis of these observations, we evaluated each of the companies under study and classified it according to the following scheme:

(1) Able to adapt without much difficulty
(2) Able to adapt partially with some difficulty
(3) Much difficulty in adapting to environmental changes

Intracountry Comparison

One would expect American companies in India, due to their foreign origins, to have difficulty adjusting to the diverse environmental conditions of India, and thus to be at some disadvantage compared to Indian companies. However, our data revealed a somewhat different picture. As Table 8-5 indicates, a large majority of the American companies were able to adjust to environmental changes successfully. Some 15 out of 17 companies expressed this contention. Only 8 Indian companies, however, were in a similar position. A much larger number of Indian companies (9 Indian versus 2 American) were found to become nervous and out of balance at the slightest change in environmental conditions. Here also, the management philosophy of the firm exerted substantial influence. For example, the 5 American and 5 Indian companies with Most Sophisticated management philosophy were able to adjust to environmental changes, while 1 American and 5 Indian companies categorized as Not Progressive were unable to do so.

[25] Argyris, *op. cit.*, pp. 153, 154.
[26] Richard Eells, *The Meaning of Modern Business* (New York: Columbia University Press, 1960).

Table 8-5   Executive Responsiveness in Adapting to Environmental Conditions

| | Overall Compari-son | | Management Philosophy | | | | | |
| | | | Most Sophisti-cated | | Somewhat Progres-sive | | Not Progres-sive | |
Country	U.S.	Local	U.S.	Local	U.S.	Local	U.S.	Local
Argentina	$n=$ 6	$n=$ 5	$n=$ 1	$n=$ 1	$n=$ 5	$n=$ 4	$n=$ 0	$n=$ 0
Highly adaptable	2	1	1	–	1	1	–	–
Somewhat adaptable	1	–	–		1	–	–	–
Not very adaptable	3	3	–	1	3	2	–	–
Not available	–	1	–	–	–	1	–	–
Brazil	$n=$ 8	$n=$ 7	$n=$ 1	$n=$ 0	$n=$ 7	$n-$ 6	$n=$ 0	$n=$ 1
Highly adaptable	4	1	–	–	4	1	–	–
Somewhat adaptable	–	–	–	–	–	–	–	–
Not very adaptable	3	4	1	–	2	3	–	1
Not available	1	2	–	–	1	2	–	–
India	$n=$ 17	$n=$ 17	$n=$ 5	$n=$ 5	$n=$ 11	$n=$ 7	$n=$ 1	$n=$ 5
Highly adaptable	8	8	5	5	3	3	–	–
Somewhat adaptable	7	–	–	–	7	–	–	–
Not very adaptable	2	9	–	–	1	4	1	5
Philippines	$n=$ 10	$n=$ 11	$n=$ 4	$n=$ 4	$n=$ 6	$n=$ 7	$n=$ 0	$n=$ 0
Highly adaptable	6	8	4	4	2	4	–	–
Somewhat adaptable	4	1	–	–	4	1	–	–
Not very adaptable	–	2	–	–	–	2	–	–
Uruguay	$n=$ 6	$n=$ 5	$n=$ 0	$n=$ 0	$n=$ 6	$n=$ 5	$n=$ 0	$n=$ 0
Highly adaptable	3	1	–	–	3	1	–	–
Somewhat adaptable	1	1	–	–	1	1	–	–
Not very adaptable	1	3	–	–	1	3	–	–
Not available	1	–	–	–	1	–	–	–

International Comparison

In international business literature, one invariably comes across the argument that foreign firms, particularly U.S. firms, get into a mess when dealing with the native cultures of their host countries. It has been implied that although a large number of companies are highly successful in their overseas operations, they have been naive in their understanding of the natives and the native culture. Thus, business literature abounds with suggestions as to what these companies should do before setting out to take advantage of overseas markets. We do not underemphasize the importance of sociocultural understanding. However, the suggestion that American companies are naive in their understanding of the sociocultural patterns of underdeveloped countries is contradicted by our findings in 5 underdeveloped countries. A large majority of the American executives interviewed were by no means ignorant persons. They were, in fact, quite knowledgeable concerning the prevailing socioeconomic, political, legal, and cultural conditions in these countries. However, in line with the American tradition, they did not feel that all the given conditions were God-given and unalterable. Some of the existing conditions in these countries were dysfunctional in terms of business efficiency, and these conditions they aimed to change. In other words, it was the American managers and not the local managers who were the active agents of change.

Even in terms of adaptation to local conditions, the American subsidiaries matched the performance of the local firms. For example, almost one-half of the American subsidiaries were able to adapt to these conditions without much difficulty, compared with the 19 (out of 45) local companies which were able to do so. When one compares the number of companies which were entirely paralyzed by local conditions, he is astonished to find that there are relatively few American companies in this group. Specifically, there were 8 American subsidiaries, compared to 21 local firms, which were not able to adapt to prevailing environmental conditions.

Regionally, the companies in the Far Eastern countries did better than those in the Latin American countries. More than one-half of the companies (30 out of 55) in the former region responded favorably to environmental conditions, compared to the less than one-third (12 out of 37) of the companies in Latin American countries which can make a similar claim.

As Table 8-5 illustrates, there is a positive correlation between the management philosophy variable and a firm's ability to adapt to external conditions.

Management Philosophy, Organizational Practices, and Management Effectiveness

To examine the overall relationships between the management philosophy and management effectiveness and organizational practices and management effectiveness, two additional indices were computed: the management effectiveness index and the organizational practices index. The former index was computed by ranking the behavioral effectiveness criteria discussed in this and the last chapters. The organizational practices index was derived by adding three indices of management processes, personnel practices, and decentralization. Details on these computations are given in Appendix A. Briefly, positive relationships were found between management philosophy and management effectiveness and organizational practices and management effectiveness. Spearman's rank correlation coefficient between management philosophy and management effectiveness was 0.83 (see Table A-5), and organizational practices and management effectiveness was 0.88 (see Table A-12).

ENTERPRISE EFFECTIVENESS

We have suggested that enterprise effectiveness, as measured in sales, profit, and cost per unit, is a function of a firm's management philosophy and practices, its utilization of manpower resources, and the prevailing environmental conditions. In order to measure enterprise effectiveness, we suggested the following economic yardsticks:

(1) Return on sales and on investment
(2) Growth in market share
(3) Increase in sales

(4) Growth in price of stock and P/E ratios
(5) Unit costs
(6) Utilization of plant facilities
(7) Scrap loss

Unfortunately, comparable and reliable data on these factors were not available from many of the companies studied. The unavailability of data was partly due to the poor record-keeping practices of local firms. American subsidiaries, on the other hand, were unwilling to part with such data. Faced with this situation, we decided to evaluate the company's overall growth, as well as we could,

Table 8-6   Enterprise Effectiveness of American Subsidiaries
and Local Firms in India

	Management Philosophy							
	Overall		*Most Sophisticated*		*Somewhat Progressive*		*Not Progressive*	
	U.S.	India	U.S.	India	U.S.	India	U.S.	India
	n=17	n=17	n=5	n=5	n=11	n=7	n=1	n=5
Growth of the company: overall evaluation								
Phenomenal growth	9	10	5	5	4	5	–	–
Moderate growth	4	5	–	–	4	2	–	3
Stagnant or declining	3	2	–	–	2	–	1	2
Not available	1	–	–	–	1	–	–	–
*Percentage increase in sales**								
Over 30%	–	2	–	–	–	2	–	–
10 to 30%	3	6	3	3	–	2	–	1
Under 10%	–	1	–	–	–	–	–	1
Not available	14	8	2	2	11	3	1	3
*Percentage increase in net profit**								
Over 30%	–	2	–	1	–	1	–	–
10 to 30%	2	4	2	1	–	1	–	2
Under 10%	1	3	1	1	–	2	–	–
Not available	14	8	2	2	11	3	1	3

* Data for increase in sales and profit are average of 3 to 5 years.

on the basis of what was said of a company by its executives and by outsiders.

Data presented in Table 8-6 reveal that there were no appreciable differences between American subsidiaries and local firms in India. For example, almost an equal number of U.S. subsidiaries (nine) and local firms (ten) experienced a phenomenal growth in

Table 8-7 American Subsidiaries and Local Firms in the Philippines—
Comparison of Rates of Return and Growth in Sales, 1961 to 1965

Industry and Firm	Net Income in Profit to Assets (Avg. %)	Net income in Profit to Equity (Avg. %)	Firm's Yearly Increase in Sales (Avg. of 5 yrs)	Firm's* Management Philosophy
Appliance				
Local firm A	4.12	10.00	20.50	MS
Local firm B	0.94	4.02	.88	SP
U.S. firm	13.50	23.00	56.90	MS
Cooking Oil				
Local firm	2.32	7.48	111.44	SP
U.S. firm	6.79	11.58	38.20	MS
Drugs and Pharm.				
Local firm A	7.84	14.93	37.70	MS
Local firm B	5.06	15.91	10.05	SP
U.S. firm A	3.43	14.67	15.95	MS
U.S. firm B	6.36	–	12.00	SP
Grain Mill Prod.				
Local firm	3.92	9.50	3.10	SP
U.S. firm	0.49	(0.47)	15.96	SP
Oil and Gasoline				
Local firm	0.44	1.61	14.01	MS
U.S. firm	3.20	4.38	(1.13)	MS
Agric. Mach.				
Local firm	1.18	4.51	(1.46)	SP
U.S. firm	8.46	14.79	1.52	SP
Rubber Products				
Local firm	1.06	5.19	(6.28)	MS
U.S. firm	9.10	15.12	2.83	MS

This table is reproduced from Filmon C. Flores, Jr., *The Applicability of American Management Know-How to Differing Environments and/or Cultures*, Ph.D. dissertation at the Graduate School of Business Administration, U.C.L.A., Los Angeles, California, 1968.
  * The firm's management philosophy is denoted by MS and SP.

sales. The same was true with companies experiencing moderate growth or declining sales. Also, there were no significant differences between the companies categorized as Most Sophisticated and those categorized as Somewhat Progressive. By and large, the firms classified as Not Progressive were either stagnant, or had declining sales. Available sales and profit data of companies in India and the Philippines support our overall evaluation. These data are presented in Tables 8-6 and 8-7.

It is clear from the data that, although the firm's management philosophy influenced enterprise effectiveness measures, environmental conditions were more influential factors. In other words, the seller's market situation in underdeveloped countries enabled firms to harvest huge profits and to augment sales.

Summary

This chapter analyzed 5 measures of management effectiveness concerning high-level manpower in Argentina, Brazil, India, the Philippines, and Uruguay. The measures were management's ability to hire and retain high-level managerial and technical personnel, interdepartmental relationships, executive perception of the firm's overall objectives, utilization of high-level manpower, and executive responsiveness in adapting to environmental conditions.

As mentioned earlier, the management literature refers to some of these factors as "organizational behavior" factors. Whatever title is used to describe these factors, we, like Argyris, Likert, and others, chose to employ them in order to evaluate the managerial effectiveness of the firm.

The analysis of management effectiveness data revealed the following:

(1) As one would expect, the American subsidiaries whose performance was judged by the above effectiveness criteria proved superior to the local firms. Thus, on the surface, ownership status seems to be an influential factor. However, when one analyzes the data in detail, it becomes clear that the managerial philosophy variable is an important influencing factor. By itself, of course, this variable cannot explain all the differences among the firms studied.

(2) Regionally speaking, the companies in the Far East (both Ameri-

can and local) seem to be more effective than those in Latin American countries. The "inferior" performance of the companies in Argentina, Brazil, and Uruguay, was explained on the basis of both the management philosophy variable and such specific environmental factors as the owner-manager situation, economic and political instability, and the adverse feeling against U.S. capital in those countries.

FOUR
PROSPECTS IN COMPARATIVE MANAGEMENT

9

SUMMARY AND IMPLICATIONS

The analysis is complete on all comparative management data gathered in Argentina, Brazil, India, the Philippines, and Uruguay. In analyzing these data, we have made various statements, from which we have drawn conclusions having various degrees of validity and certainty. It might seem, then, that our report should end here.

As stated in the Preface and in Chapter 1, however, our purpose in undertaking this study was twofold. First, of course, we wanted to document and analyze the nature of management practices and the effectiveness of U.S. subsidiaries and the comparable local firms in these five countries. In addition, we wanted to shed light on the usefulness of such comparative studies to the general discipline of management, especially in such areas as concept refining, hypothesis testing, and theory building.

From a pragmatic point of view, we were interested in exploring the real problems involved in transmitting modern management know-how to underdeveloped countries.

Ours was largely an exploratory study, and we recognize fully the broad and ambitious scope of our objectives. We do not pretend to have found all the answers to the many difficult problems we observed. Many studies of this nature are needed in order fully to explore and evaluate the above-mentioned purposes and objectives. It is our hope, however, that what we have learned from this comparative study will prove useful to other researchers.

With this purpose in mind, we will delineate the implications of this study to the emerging field of comparative management and to the management discipline in general. We will outline the major premises upon which this study was based, and review briefly our findings concerning the management practices and effectiveness of U.S. subsidiaries and comparable local firms in the five underdeveloped countries. Next, we will state what we believe to be the implications of these findings for comparative management and the management discipline. In the following chapter, we will outline the relationships between philosophy variable, management practices and effectiveness, and environmental factors.

MAJOR PREMISES OF THE STUDY

Earlier, in Figure 2-2 (Chapter 2), we postulated that enterprise effectiveness, measured in economic and financial terms, is affected by management philosophy, management practices, management effectiveness, and the environmental factors at play in a given country.

Management philosophy and environmental factors are thus to be thought of as independent variables, management practices as intervening variables, management effectiveness as a dependent variable, and enterprise effectiveness as the end result variable. Neither this list of variables nor their expressed relationships should be regarded as all-inclusive. If anything, we only attempted to separate important variables from the innumerable factors that one encounters when one studies management in cross-cultural settings. The variables investigated in this study are defined as follows.

Management Philosophy is the implied and expressed attitude of the firm toward consumers, employees, stockholders, suppliers, distributors, government, and community. This was inferred from the company's manuals and other documents, and from personal interviews with the top, senior, and middle-level executives of the companies studied. As stated in Chapter 2, we considered several factors in our determination of a firm's management philosophy; these are outlined in Appendix B. In order to evaluate the management philosophy of a firm, we devised a three-point ranking scale. The total score represented the company's overall management philosophy. On the basis of this score, we categorized the companies studied ($n = 92$) as (1) Most Sophisticated in management philosophy (MS); (2) Somewhat Progressive in management philosophy (SP); and (2) Not Progressive in management philosophy (NP).

The variable of management philosophy is of significant importance in this study. We have used this variable as an independent, or causal variable. The rationale and the necessity of doing so were discussed in Chapter 2.

Management Practices were defined in terms of managerial functions. They were defined as the way in which the manager of an industrial firm conceives and carries out his functions of planning, organizing, controlling, staffing, and leading. As the reader will recognize, these are, basically, concepts developed within management's classical (or process) school. However, it should be noted that we have used these as subvariables in our empirical research, rather than as principles.

Management Effectiveness criteria took into account the degree to which a firm was able to develop and maintain the company as a social system. The measures of management effectiveness included employee morale, worker turnover and absenteeism, interpersonal relationships among employees, ability of a firm to attract and retain high-level managerial manpower, utilization of high-level manpower, and organizational ability to adapt to changing external conditions. Management effectiveness variables were considered as dependent variables.

Enterprise Effectiveness was established by considering traditional economic financial criteria such as profit, market-share, earnings-price ratios of stock, and the growth of the company. These variables were considered as end-result variables.

In brief, then, there were 4 groups of variables in this study: independent or causal variables, intervening or mediating variables, dependent variables, and end-result variables.

The independent variables included societal environmental conditions and the firm's management philosophy. The environmental factors were, in a sense, residual variables. As such, the evaluation of the impact of these factors upon management practices and upon management and enterprise effectiveness was based on our interviews and discussions with the managers, supervisors, and workers in 92 companies in 5 underdeveloped countries.

Intervening variables were the various elements of the management practices. Dependent variables were related mainly to management effectiveness expressed in behavioral terms. End-result variables were the enterprise effectiveness criteria expressed in economic or financial terms.

We attempted to explore the possible relationships between management philosophy and management practices on the one hand, and between management philosophy and management effectiveness on the other. Based on our data from 92 companies, we have attempted to show linkages among these variables, in the form of propositions, in our next chapter. Let us first examine the major findings of the study.

SUMMARY OF FINDINGS

Management Practices

In this study, we investigated several elements of management practices. These included the planning orientations, management of manpower resources, controlling systems, leadership roles, and motivational devices used by the companies in 5 underdeveloped countries.

Chapter 3 deals with the comparative analysis of 4 elements of the planning process: nature, scope, time horizon, and resulting plans.

The analyses of data concerning the nature and time orientation of planning, as well as the nature and review of plans among those 92 companies, suggest that the U.S. subsidiaries' plans, compared to those of the local firms in the 5 countries studied, are systematic, of long duration (5 years or more), and comprehensive. For example, of the 47 subsidiaries, 33 undertook comprehensive planning for a period of 5 years or more. Of the 45 local companies, only 12 undertook comprehensive planning, and 14 planned for a period of 5 years or more.

However, when these data were subjected to intensive analysis (with respect to the management philosophy variable), it was found that the local companies categorized as Most Sophisticated in management philosophy were more like U.S. subsidiaries in their planning orientations. For example, 3 out of 5 MS local companies in India, and 3 out of 4 MS local companies in the Philippines, undertook long-range planning. Thus, management philosophy as a variable was quite useful in explaining the differential orientations of companies, especially local ones, in their planning function.[1]

Chapter 4 focused attention on some of the important aspects of managing manpower resources in both the U.S. subsidiaries and the comparable local firms in the countries studied. Specifically, we analyzed data concerning the manpower policies, modes of selection and development, and reward systems used in these 2 sets of companies. Data collected in India were somewhat more specific than those collected in other countries.

Analysis of intracountry data (India) concerning the formalization of manpower policies suggested some differences among the U.S. subsidiaries and local companies. For example, 8 of the 17 U.S. subsidiaries and 12 of the 17 comparable local companies in India have formally stated policies. Although we were unable to assess the quality of individual policies, there were some indications that companies with MS philosophy, regardless of their nationality-ownership status, paid much attention to such policies. This became somewhat clearer when we examined data concerning the locus of such policy making. We found that MS companies (both U.S. subsidiaries and local Indian companies) have had extensive discussions among committee members for the purpose of formalizing manpower management policies.

Formalization of manpower policies in the other 4 countries did not necessarily follow this pattern. In Latin American countries, only 5 out of 20 U.S. subsidiaries and 5 of the 17 local companies seemed to have formalized policies. In the Philippines, the proportion was still less: only 3 of 10 U.S. subsidiaries and 1 of the 11 local companies formalized these policies. Examining these data for the management philosophy variable, we found some correlation between management philosophy and the formalization of manpower policies.

Selection procedures, however, received greater attention among the U.S. subsidiaries. Although the selection of managers was based on group decision making in both the U.S. and the local companies in all the 5 underdeveloped countries, U.S. subsidiaries seemed to be more objective in arriving at such decisions.

---

[1] For comparison of management practices of the U.S. companies in the United States, see P. E. Holden, C. A. Pederson, G. E. Germane, *Top Management* (New York: McGraw-Hill Book Company, 1968).

Formal training and development schemes, particularly for managerial and technical personnel, were not prevalent in many of the companies studied. Only in MS companies were there any formalized training and development facilities.

The available data on compensation and promotion policies indicate that only a few companies pursued a policy of maintaining salaries and wages above the going rate. Most of these companies followed the practice of compensating employees at the going rate.

However, among the MS companies, 5 U.S. subsidiaries and 2 local companies in India maintained salaries and fringe benefits well above the going rate.

As was stated in Chapter 4, one of the important ingredients in building effective organizations is a policy of systematic managerial succession. The available data on this subject supports a very pessimistic outlook. Only a small proportion of the companies in India (11 out of 34) had some formal procedures for managerial succession. Companies in the other 4 countries practiced hit and miss methods.

Delegation of Authority and Decentralization Issues

Modest attempts were made to discern the degree of decentralization in the U.S. subsidiaries and in the local companies. Specific data subjected to analysis included: (1) major policy making on both company-wide and functional policies; (2) the degree of participation and information sharing; (3) delegation of authority and layers of hierarchy.

Data concerning the first 2 items were analyzed in Chapter 5, while data for the third item were discussed in Chapter 4.

Major Policy Making

In order to study this segment, we attempted to find out who was responsible for formulating major policies. Data from India indicate that in more than half of the companies the chief executive alone makes such policies. More specifically, such a situation exists in 13 of the 17 Indian-owned companies, and in 6 of the 17 U.S.

subsidiaries in India. In slightly fewer than one-half of these companies, however, these decisions were made by a committee. We also found that 8 of the 10 MS companies followed the committee form of decision making. At the other end of the management philosophy continuum, we found that in all the companies—i.e., in 1 U.S. subsidiary and 5 Indian-owned companies—the chief executive made such decisions.

In Argentina, Brazil, and Uruguay, the chief executive formulated the company's major policies. Data from the Philippines reveals a trend similar to that which prevails in India.

Our inquiries concerning functional policies were restricted to product and marketing policies. Some form of group decision making on product policies was quite apparent in all 5 countries, while decisions regarding marketing were centralized.

Participation and Information Sharing

Comparative data concerning participation and information sharing in the planning process were also collected. These data, however, were available only in India. Here we found that the large majority of the U.S. subsidiaries (11 of the total 17) encouraged their middle-management personnel to participate in planning activities. In contrast, only 5 Indian-owned companies involved middle management in planning activities. However, when we examined these data with respect to the management philosophy variable, we found that all 5 of the U.S. subsidiaries and 4 of the 5 Indian-owned companies categorized as Most Sophisticated in management philosophy encouraged participation in the planning process, while none of the NP companies (1 U.S. subsidiary and 5 Indian companies) showed such willingness.

Layers of Hierarchy

We fully realize that the number of layers of hierarchy in an organization is only a crude measure of the degree of centralization. However, when these data are used along with the data analyzed above, some additional light is shed on organizational patterns.

Data concerning the number of layers of hierarchy in 34 companies in India indicates that the large majority of the U.S. subsidiaries have between 5 and 7 layers of hierarchy, while only 8 of the 17 Indian companies had so few layers. Once again, however, we find that the management philosophy variable exerted considerable influence. The Indian companies categorized as Most Sophisticated in management philosophy were more like the U.S. subsidiary companies in their decentralization orientation. Spearman's rank correlation coefficient between the management philosophy and the decentralization index was found to be 0.81.

Leadership Style

Management scholars and practitioners have devoted considerable attention to leadership concept and style. In earlier days, attention was focused mainly on identifying the attributes of the natural leader. Since then, however, researchers have endeavored to develop more comprehensive theories of leadership.

Although some researchers tend to equate the leadership concept with that of management, we are inclined to consider leadership merely as one important aspect of management.

Selznick,[2] among others, has provided a useful typology of leadership. He has distinguished between "institutional leadership" and "organization management." According to him, institutional leadership involves the formulation of decisions which are of the greatest long-term importance for the organization as a whole. Organization management, however, is concerned more with the process of controlling the firm for the achievement of stated objectives. Thus, leadership, from the Selznick point of view, is found primarily at the top of the organizational hierarchy.

To collect data concerning leadership style in the 5 underdeveloped countries, we took Selznick's viewpoint, and focused upon institutional leadership. On the basis of interviews with executives, managers, and supervisors, we attempted to classify the most prevalent leadership style in each company into 3 categories: (1) authoritarian (2) democratic (3) bureaucratic.

[2] Philip A. Selznick, *TVA and the Grass Roots* (Berkeley: University of California Press, 1953).

The usual management literature definitions are ascribed to these 3 styles of leadership.[3]

We also attempted to learn something about the perception of subordinates by their superiors. These data were classified into 3 categories: (1) subordinates regarded as trustworthy; (2) subordinates regarded as somewhat trustworthy; and (3) subordinates regarded as not trustworthy.

As one might expect, a larger number of U.S. subsidiaries practiced a democratic form of leadership. Specifically, 23 of the 47 subsidiaries, as compared to 13 of the 45 local companies, used this form of leadership.

Data collected from companies in India concerning the perception of subordinates by their superiors supports the above-mentioned findings. We found that in a large majority of the U.S. subsidiaries, superiors perceive their subordinates as trustworthy, while in a large proportion of the Indian companies, superiors did not feel this way. However, there is some indication of an association between a firm's management philosophy and leadership style, and the superior's perception of his subordinates.

To examine the overall relationships between the management philosophy variable and management practices, three different indices were created: the management process index, the personnel practices index, and the decentralization index. All these indices were positively related to the management philosophy variable. Detailed results on these aspects are shown in Appendix A.

Management Effectiveness

In Chapters 7 and 8, we analyzed the management effectiveness of the 92 companies studied. We differentiated between management effectiveness and enterprise effectiveness, the former denoting a firm's effectiveness in managing its human resources, the latter dealing with the traditional economic and financial measures.

Only in a very competitive economy can such traditional financial

---

[3] Jennings has spelled out in great detail the characteristics of autocratic, democratic, and bureaucratic leadership styles. See Eugene E. Jennings, *The Executive: Autocrat, Bureaucrat, Democrat* (New York: Harper and Row, 1962), especially Chapters 5, 6, and 7.

measures as profits, market-share, sales volume, and P/E ratios provide a realistic picture of management effectiveness. In underdeveloped countries, where seller's market conditions are most prevalent, these criteria are misleading. Under such conditions, all firms, irrespective of their management practices, can make higher profits. In order more realistically to evaluate management effectiveness in these countries, we devised 9 behaviorally oriented measures:

(1) Employee morale and satisfaction in work
(2) Interpersonal relationships
(3) Employee turnover
(4) Absenteeism
(5) Management effectiveness in attracting high-level manpower
(6) Interdepartmental relationships
(7) Executive's perception of the firm's overall objectives
(8) Utilization of high-level manpower
(9) Executive's ability to adapt to environmental conditions

The first 4 of these 9 measures concern the blue-collar employee, while the remaining ones pertain to high-level managerial resources.

Data on employee morale, interpersonal relationships, turnover, and absenteeism reveal the considerable impact of socioeconomic and cultural variables.

Such environmental factors as management-union relationships, governmental attitudes toward the industrial worker and the business world, climatic conditions, health and well-being of workers, political situations, and chronic inflation have had considerable influence upon the morale of industrial workers. Despite these factors, however, more progressive companies were able to augment employee morale and satisfaction in work by offering higher relative wages, better working conditions, and opportunities for advancement and self-growth.[4]

The following environmental and cultural factors seem to have affected the interpersonal relationships between workers and their respective supervisors:

(1) Social status and class system
(2) Employment situation

[4] For a similar viewpoint see Chapter A. Myers, *Labor Problems in Industrialization of India* (Cambridge: Harvard University Press, 1958).

(3) Education and aspirations of younger and older employees
(4) Nature of trade unionism
(5) Inflation
(6) Governmental attitudes toward workers and the business community

The management philosophy variable, we found, exerted no appreciable influence upon this criterion.

Data on employee turnover and absenteeism were not available from all the companies studied. Therefore, an analysis of these data pertains to only 10 pharmaceutical companies in India. Here also, such environmental factors as labor-market conditions (location of the firm), climatic conditions, and the general well-being and health of the workers have exerted considerable influence.

All management effectiveness criteria concerning high-level manpower were within the realm of management control. More progressive firms, through such mediating variables as higher relative wages, better working conditions, opportunities for advancement and self-growth, and clearer statements of objectives, goals, and procedures, were able to hire and retain high-level managerial and technical personnel. They were also able to establish cooperative interdepartmental relationships, utilize high-level manpower effectively, and adapt to changing environmental conditions.

In summary then, our findings show that the U.S. subsidiaries are more progressive in their management practices and are able to achieve higher effectiveness in maintaining organizations as social systems.[5] We also found, however, that some comparable local firms in all 5 of the underdeveloped countries studied were able to match the performance of the U.S. subsidiaries. Particularly noticeable was the fact that there were no appreciable differences in management practices and effectiveness between the U.S. subsidiaries and the local firms categorized as Most Sophisticated in management philosophy. In other words, those companies having favorable attitudes toward consumers, employees, distributors, suppliers, stockowners, government, and community tend to have more progressive management practices and higher effectiveness in handling their manpower

---

[5] Dunning's study on the U.S. subsidiaries in Britain also shows the higher effectiveness of the U.S. subsidiaries as compared to the local British firms. See John R. Dunning, "U.S. Subsidiaries in Britain and their U.K. Competitors," *Business Ratios*, Autumn 1966.

resources. Spearman's rank correlation coefficient between management philosophy variable and management effectiveness was 0.83.

We shall now turn our attention to the implications of these findings.

IMPLICATIONS OF THE STUDY

We stated earlier that the comparative approach to research in management could be useful for concept refining and building, hypothesis testing, and theory formulation. We do not pretend to have found final answers for all these areas. However, what little we have learned from this study may be useful to other researchers in this area. It is in this hope that we offer the following comments.

Since we draw no hard and fast boundary lines between the management discipline and the comparative management area, we believe that our comments are pertinent to both.

It may be necessary, however, to mention that the study of management systems in cross-cultural *cum* cross-national settings has come to be identified as comparative management. By itself, the comparative approach is not a new phenomenon in management research. Among others, Udy,[6] Etzioni,[7] and Pugh,[8] have articulated and utilized this approach in their studies of complex organizations. Studies focusing on cross-cultural comparisons in management systems, however, are of recent vintage. Some of the important studies in this area were outlined in Chapter 1. An excellent analytical review of comparative management studies, delineating the impact of culture, has recently been made by Ajiferuke and Boddewyn.[9]

Judging from these and other recent studies, it would seem that many comparative management researchers have had strong orientations toward the human relations and behavioral schools of manage-

[6] Stanley H. Udy, Jr., "The Comparative Analysis of Organization," in James G. March (ed.), *Handbook of Organizations* (Chicago: Rand McNally and Company, 1965), pp. 678–709.

[7] Amitai Etzioni, *A Comparative Analysis of Complex Organizations* (New York: Free Press, 1961).

[8] D. S. Pugh, *et al.*, "A Conceptual Scheme for Organizational Analysis," *Administrative Science Quarterly*, Vol. 8, No. 3 (December 1963), pp. 289–315.

[9] Musbau Ajiferuke and J. Boddewyn, "Culture and Other Explanatory Variables in Comparative Management Studies," *Academy of Management Journal*, Vol. 13, No. 2 (June 1970), pp. 153–162.

ment. Accordingly, they share the common aspirations, beliefs, and biases of these schools of thought, as becomes quite evident in the following discussion. Our comments center mainly around 2 issues: (1) over-emphasis on environmental and cultural variables in cross-cultural management studies, and (2) a tendency by the adherents of one school of thought to reject entirely the ideas, concepts, and principles put forth by the opposing school.

Overemphasis on Environmental and Cultural Variables

Recent writings in comparative management suggest that environmental and cultural variables are dominant factors, and perhaps determinants, in shaping management practices in a given country. For example, Chowdhry, at a recent international conference on social and cultural factors in management development, observed that "Management subjects like administrative practices . . . are especially culture-bound and require to be understood in relation to the social and economic environment of the country."[10]

In advocating new theories for comparative management, Farmer and Richman have argued:

Most studies of management have taken place within a "black-box" labeled management, without much concern for the external environment in which the firm may operate . . . present theory is inadequate to explain comparative differential in efficiency.[11]

As we stated in Chapter 2, it would be immature to suggest that environmental and cultural factors do not affect management practices and effectiveness. However, the actual causal relationships

[10] Kamala Chowdhry, "Social and Cultural Factors in Management Development in India and the Role of the Expert," *International Labor Review,* Vol. 94, No. 3 (August 1966), p. 132.

[11] R. N. Farmer and B. M. Richman, "A Model for Research in Comparative Management," *California Management Review,* Vol. 7, No. 2 (Winter 1964), p. 56. In fairness to these authors, it may be pointed out that in recent years, they have somewhat shifted their attention from a "macro" approach to a "micro" approach to the study of comparative management. However, their main concern is still for environmental constraints. For this modification, see B. M. Richman, "Empirical Testing of a Comparative and International Management Research Model," *Proceedings of the Academy of Management,* 1967, pp. 34–65.

between the two still remain to be determined, and, thus far, systematic attempts to do this have not been made.

Our findings suggest that a cautious attitude is appropriate. For although this study revealed the considerable impact of environmental and cultural factors on management effectiveness—particularly on employee morale, absenteeism, turnover, and interpersonal relationships—various elements of management practices and effectiveness definitely fell under the purview of managerial control. More specifically, management practices concerning planning, organizing, staffing, and controlling—as well as management effectiveness in handling high-level manpower—were not unduly constrained by environmental and cultural factors. In any given socioeconomic and cultural milieu, there are a number of options open to the manager of an industrial enterprise.

A manager is not necessarily a passive agent.[12] He interacts with his environment and tries to mold it in order to achieve certain desired results. How well he molds the environmental constraints will have considerable bearing upon the firm's effectiveness.

We have not investigated the process through which a manager gains a measure of control over external environmental constraints. We attempted simply to measure his attitude toward some of the important internal and external factors, and to determine the impact of differing attitudes on management practices and effectiveness in industrial firms in these 5 underdeveloped countries. This measurement of managerial attitude was treated as an organizational variable, which we termed the management philosophy of the firm. There may, admittedly, be many more such organizational variables affecting management practices and effectiveness, and we do not presume to have exhausted the list.

Our initial attempts to measure the management philosophy variable do, however, seem to provide some clues to understanding the similarities and differences which exist among firms in underdeveloped countries.

On the other hand, by treating environmental variables as determinants, or explanatory variables, in analyses of management practices and effectiveness in cross-cultural settings, we may un-

[12] See Narendra Sethi, *The Setting of Administrative Management in India* (New York: Business Research Institute, College of Business Administration, St. John's University, 1969).

necessarily limit our understanding of other significant variables. As Boddewyn has aptly remarked, "A real danger exists . . . of letting the environment crowd out the comparative analysis. Comparisons are somewhat precariously balanced between management itself and its environment."[13] One therefore needs to take care, he adds "not to throw out the management baby with environmental bath or smother it in a blanket of social context."[14]

We do not mean to deny the influence of the socioeconomic, legal, and cultural variables upon management practices and effectiveness in underdeveloped countries. Our own experience and research in these countries, however, prove the necessity of establishing some priority in the selection of variables used to establish causal relationships between these factors. In our last chapter, we made some tentative efforts in this direction. In Appendix D we have enumerated a few variables (e.g., market condition and profit orientation of the manager) and examined their impact on managerial behavior in underdeveloped countries. We stress, however, that this is only a tentative and preliminary attempt.

Management Theory Jungle

The student of management is well aware of the various contradictions and controversies surrounding the management discipline. In recent years, many fine efforts have been made to reconcile and integrate the diverse approaches and findings. Much confusion, however, still surrounds this discipline, and a tendency of one school of thought to reject, wholesale, all the ideas, insights, concepts, and theories developed by the other school is much in evidence.[15]

An example is the on-going controversy between the classical school and the human relations or behavioral school. Many concepts, such as authority, responsibility, line and staff, chain of command, and the principles derived from such concepts by the classical school

[13] Jean Boddewyn, "Comparative Concepts in Management, Administration and Organization," (Unpublished manuscript), p. 12. Also see his book *Comparative Management and Marketing: Concepts, Constructs, Methodology, Product and Potential* (Chicago: Scott, Foresman and Company, 1969).

[14] *Ibid.*

[15] See Harold Koontz (ed.), *Toward a Unified Theory of Management* (New York: McGraw-Hill Book Company, 1964).

have become targets for criticism by the opposing schools. It is often argued that many of the concepts and principles of the classical school are only parables, and that they are mechanistic. To some extent this criticism is valid. However, a total rejection of all the ideas, concepts, and principles of the classical school has resulted in an ignorance of the benefits which result when they are used as variables or subvariables in empirical research.

Any theory or theory-testing efforts in the social sciences require empirical evidence. As Myrdal has remarked:

Theory . . . must not only be subjected to immanent criticism for logical consistency but must constantly be measured against reality and adjusted accordingly. . . . This is the crux of all science: It always begins a priori but must constantly strive to find an empirical basis for knowledge and thus to become more adequate to the reality under study. . . . Theory is thus no more than a correlated set of questions to the social reality under study.[16]

Whatever the deficiencies of the classical school, the concepts and principles propounded by this school have become the common language in the business world. As Lawrence and Lorsch have pointed out: "The fact that its [classical school] language persists in business usage . . . is sufficient justification for a fresh look at this [classical] theory."[17]

Based on the managerial functions classification suggested by the neoclassical school, we were able to collect data from companies located in seemingly diverse environmental and cultural settings. That this language was understood by the foreign managers in underdeveloped countries gives further support to the plea for a fresh look at many of the classical school's ideas and concepts. It is our contention that many of these have great relevance to industrial firms in underdeveloped countries, at least at this stage of their economic development. For example, our findings suggest that the firms (both U.S. subsidiaries and local) utilizing such basic concepts as authority definition and statement of objectives and goals were more effective in their operations than those not doing so. We feel,

16 Gunnar Myrdal, *Asian Drama: An Inquiry into the Poverty of Nations* (New York: The Twentieth Century Fund, 1968), pp. 24–25.
17 Paul R. Lawrence and Jay W. Lorsch, *Organization and Environment: Managing Differentiation and Integration* (Boston: Division of Research, Graduate School of Business Administration, Harvard University, 1967), p. 161–62.

in other words, that orderliness, systematization, and routinization of various management functions, as proclaimed by the classical school, have not only provided many insights, but were quite useful in augmenting organizational effectiveness.[18]

A recent study by Lawrence and Lorsch seems to support our contention. They identified two environmental variables: (1) rate of technological change in both products and processes, and (2) market forces. Within this environmental context, they found, in firms operating under stable technological and market forces, a relevance to the classical theory. The postulates of the human relations school were more relevant for firms in dynamic technological and market conditions. Lawrence and Lorsch concluded that:

The classical theory tends to hold in more stable environments, while the human relations theory is more appropriate to dynamic situations. . . . Both were needed to explain behavior in organizations operating in distinctly different environments; one theory could not replace the other.[19]

In order to build a theory in management, we, like Lawrence and Lorsch and others,[20] believe that the key ideas and concepts developed by various schools of management could, and should, be translated into the conceptual framework for empirical research.

[18] *Ibid.*, p. 161.
[19] *Ibid.*, p. 183.
[20] For one such attempt to use classical concepts as subvariables see D. S. Pugh, *et al.*, *op. cit.*

10

CONCLUSIONS: PROPOSITIONS ON MANAGEMENT

One of the important purposes of a theory is to provide a causal explanation between 2 or more phenomena. As Homan has observed:

A theory is nothing—it is not a theory unless it is an explanation. . . . A theory of a phenomenon consists of a series of propositions, each stating a relationship between properties of nature . . . not until one has properties, and propositions stating relations between them and the propositions form a deductive system—not until one has all three—does one have a theory.[1]

Proposition building and testing are useful intermediary steps in theory construction. Propositions relate variates to each other.[2] In other words, propositions specify the determinants of some phenomenon and show the causal linkage between determinants and results.

Although proposition building and testing has advanced considerably in the more advanced social sciences (economics, sociology, psychology), there have been relatively few such attempts in management discipline. Of notable exception are the efforts of March and Simon,[3] and recent work by Price, and Berelson and Steiner.[4]

[1] George C. Homans, "Bringing Men Back In," *American Sociological Review*, Vol. 20 (December 1964), reprinted in A. H. Rubenstein and C. J. Haberstroh (eds.) (Homewood, Ill.: Irwin-Dorsey Series in Behavioral Science in Business, revised edition, 1966), p. 38.
[2] For an excellent discussion of the use of propositions, see Hans L. Zetterberg, *On Theory and Verification in Sociology* (Totowa, N.J.: The Bedminister Press, 1965), especially Chapters 4, 5, and 6.

We recognize that the propositions stated in this chapter are highly tentative. They are no more than working hypotheses. Our sole aim in presenting our findings in this form is to highlight topics in the field of management and comparative management which are susceptible to research. In addition to their tentative nature, these propositions also contain an element of selectivity; the list of determinants is not all-inclusive. The selection of independent and dependent variables does not necessarily represent the total reality, but is simply a convenient way of analyzing the interrelationships among pertinent variables within such complex organizations as the industrial enterprise.

In our conceptual scheme, management philosophy and environmental variables (socioeconomic, political, legal, and cultural factors) were conceived as determinants or independent variables; various elements of management processes or practices as intervening variables; management effectiveness criteria as dependent variables; enterprise effectiveness measures as end-result variables.

Relationships between the management philosophy variable and management practices and effectiveness are of central importance to this study. For this reason, the propositions delineating such relationships are herein mentioned first. The propositions showing relationships between environmental variables and management practices and effectiveness are referred to as corollaries of the main propositions.

As we noted in the last chapter, our evaluation of the environmental variables affecting management practices or effectiveness is based on the interview responses. Since the impact of environmental variables upon a particular aspect of management practice and effectiveness was discussed at some length in other chapters, we will not repeat this discussion here. However, the main propositions which serve to delineate relationships between the management philosophy variable and management practices and effectiveness will be supported by data collected in this study.

A few additional comments are in order. Each proposition as-

---

3 James G. March and Herbert A. Simon, *Organizations* (New York: John Wiley and Sons, Inc., 1963).

4 (a) James L. Price, *Organizational Effectiveness: An Inventory of Propositions* (Homewood, Ill.: Richard D. Irwin, Inc., 1968).

(a) B. Berelson and G. A. Steiner, *Human Behavior: An Inventory of Scientific Findings* (New York: Harcourt, Brace, and World, 1964).

sumes "other things being equal." Expressions such as "higher the firm's score on management philosophy" and "the more progressive the management philosophy" are used interchangeably; both mean that the company is in our category of Most Sophisticated in management philosophy.

MANAGERIAL CONTROL

Planning

Planning practices (planning orientation, participation in planning, information sharing, and so forth) in the industrial organizations studied were analyzed in detail in Chapter 3. There we observed that companies with Most Sophisticated management philosophy, regardless of their ownership status, planned on a long-range basis in a systematic manner, and encouraged greater participation in the planning process. Some of the identifiable environmental variables affecting the planning process were: economic instability, governmental control on prices and the availability of raw materials, political instability, the nature of competition, and governmental attitudes toward the business community. The following propositions indicate the relationships among management philosophy, environmental variables, and the planning practices:

Proposition 1-1. All other factors being the same, the higher a firm's score on the management philosophy index, the greater will be its concern for long-range planning.

Corollary 1-2. The greater the degree of competition, the greater will be the need for long-range planning by the individual firms.

Corollary 1-3. The greater the degree of economic and political instability, the lesser the likelihood that private industrial enterprises will undertake systematic long-range planning.

Corollary 1-4. The greater the degree of governmental control over prices and the availability of raw materials, the lesser the likelihood that the firm will undertake systematic long-range planning.

Corollary 1-5. The greater the governmental hostility toward the business community, the lesser the likelihood that a firm will undertake systematic long-range planning.

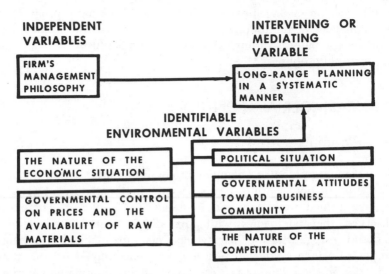

Figure 10-1   Variables Affecting Long-Range Planning

Figure 10-1 depicts the relationships among these variables.

Discussion

Data from Table 3-3 (Chapter 3) have been consolidated in Table 10-1 in order to show the relationship between a management philosophy variable and a firm's orientation toward long-range planning. As this table shows, of the 21 companies categorized as Most Sophisticated in management philosophy (MS), 16 of them (76 percent) undertook long-range plans of 5 to 10 years duration. Of 64 companies categorized as Somewhat Progressive in management philosophy (SP), only 31 (48 percent) engaged in long-range plans; none of the companies categorized as Not Progressive in management philosophy (NP) had long-range plans.

It is interesting to note that among the SP companies undertaking long-range plans, a majority are U.S. subsidiaries. This partly reflects the orientation of the U.S. parent companies, and partly reflects the influence of requirements set by these companies for their subsidiaries abroad.

Table 10-1   Time Orientation of Planning in American Subsidiaries and Local Companies in the Five Underdeveloped Countries

	Management Philosophy		
	Not Progressive	Somewhat Progressive	Most Sophisticated
Long-range plans (5 to 10 yrs.)	– (0)	31 (48)	16 (76)
		23 8	10 6
Short-range plans (1 to 2 yrs.)	3 (43)	21 (33)	4 (19)
	3	8 13	1 3
Nonspecific period	4 (57)	12 (19)	1 (5)
	1 3	4 8	1

U.S. Subsidiaries (n = 47)
Local Companies (n = 45)
Numbers at the top of each pair denote the total number of companies. The numbers in the bottom left of each pair denote U.S. subsidiaries and the numbers in the bottom right denote local companies. Figures in parentheses show the percentage of the total companies in each category.

The data in Table 10-2 provide partial support for the corollary propositions. Environmental factors affecting long-range planning were ranked by the interviewees in the following order:

(1) Nature of competition (lack of competition)
(2) Governmental control over prices and the availability of raw materials
(3) Inflation
(4) Political situation (instability in political conditions)
(5) Governmental attitudes toward business community

There were significant differences, however, in the way these factors were ranked in different countries.

In India, executives were most concerned about governmental control over prices and availability of raw materials and the weak competitive situation; in the Philippines, executives displayed concern over inflation, lack of competition and, to a lesser degree, over governmental control of prices and availability of raw materials. In all 3 Latin American countries (Argentina, Brazil, and Uruguay) chief concern was directed toward inflation and the political situation.

Economic data on these countries, presented in Appendix C, lend support to the views expressed by the executives.

Table 10-2   Impact of Environmental Variables on Long-Range Planning
Practices in the Five Underdeveloped Countries (interview responses*)

	Argentina (n = 65)	Brazil (n = 90)	India (n = 272)	Philip- pines (n = 77)	Uruguay (n = 66)	Total (n = 570)
Nature of competition (seller's vs. buyer's market	30 (46)	47 (52)	180 (66)	38 (49)	35 (53)	330 (58)
Nature of the economic situation (inflation)	45 (69)	75 (83)	90 (33)	48 (62)	40 (67)	298 (52)
Governmental control on prices and the availabil- ity of raw materials	20 (31)	32 (36)	210 (77)	30 (39)	25 (38)	317 (56)
Political situation	40 (62)	50 (56)	32 (12)	10 (13)	30 (45)	162 (28)
Governmental attitude toward business community	22 (34)	35 (39)	45 (17)	20 (25)	26 (39)	148 (26)

* Respondents included the senior and middle-level executives of the companies studied.
Figures in parentheses show the percentage of all respondents. Many respondents mentioned more than one factor, therefore figures are not strictly additive.

Organization

As we stated in our previous Chapter, we made an attempt to evaluate the degree of decentralization and delegation of authority in both the U.S. subsidiaries and the counterpart local firms. The following factors were analyzed: (1) center of decision making on major and functional policies; (2) layers of hierarchy; (3) authority definition; (4) delegation of authority; (5) participation and information sharing in the planning process.

Proposition 2-1. All other factors being the same, the higher a firm's score on the management philosophy index, the clearer the authority definition and the greater the delegation of authority within an organization.

Corollary 2-2. The stronger the owner-manager situation, the less authority is delegated and the less clear the authority definition.

Corollary 2-3. Companies in a relatively weak competitive market are more likely to be centralized than those within a relatively strong competitive market.[5]

Discussion

The data in Tables 4-4, 5-2, 5-3, and 5-4 support proposition 2-1. It can be seen from Table 4-4 that all 10 MS companies in India (5 U.S. subsidiaries and 5 local companies) have few layers of hierarchy, and that the authority granted to the holder of each position is clearly defined via organizational charts. In contrast, the NP companies have more layers of hierarchy and do not seem to have clear definitions of authority for various organizational positions.

The data in Table 5-2 reveal that in 8 out of 10 MS companies in India, major policy decisions are made in a decentralized fashion. That is, such decisions are made by a committee, rather than by the chief executive alone; in all 6 NP companies, these decisions are made by the chief executive himself. Data available from the other 4 countries presented in this table further support this observation.

Proposition 2-1 also receives support from the data pertaining to participation and information sharing in the planning process, and the manager's perception of their subordinates (Tables 5-3 and 5-4). These data show that the MS companies encourage greater participation and information sharing, and that the managers of these companies have a more favorable image of their subordinates.

Corollary propositions 2-2 and 2-3 reflect the nature of owner-manager situations and market conditions in underdeveloped countries. The research findings of McMillan,[6] Fillol,[7] Jain,[8] Chowdhry,[9]

[5] These centralization-decentralization aspects refer only to routine day-to-day decision making. Policy decision making may show almost reverse relationships.

[6] Claude McMillan, "The American Businessman in Brazil," *Business Topics*, Spring 1963, reprinted in *International Dimensions in Business* (East Lansing: Division of Research, Graduate School of Business Administration, Michigan State University, 1966), pp. 97–109.

[7] Thomas R. Fillol, *Social Factors in Economic Development: The Argentine Case* (Cambridge: The M.I.T. Press, 1963).

Oberg,[10] and Flores,[11] as well as our own findings, indicate that a large majority of the firms in underdeveloped countries are owned and managed by a few members of the same family and/or their close relatives. This situation, coupled with the existing seller's market conditions in these countries, creates an over-centralization of authority in the industrial firms. Appendix D illustrates the interrelationships between these factors and their impact on management practices and effectiveness.

Controlling

Proposition 3-1. All other factors being the same, the more progressive the management philosophy, the greater the concern of the firm for quality and cost of products, and the greater the opportunity for group formulation of control activities within the organization.

Corollary 3-2. The weaker the competitive situation, the lesser the concern for quality or cost of products, and the lesser the comprehensive control devices employed by the firm.

Discussion

Proposition 3-1 is supported by the data in Tables 6-1, 6-2, 6-3, and 6-4. Table 6-2 shows that all 10 MS companies in India have formalized quality control activities in a separate department and have utilized cost and budgetary control techniques extensively. In contrast, the 6 NP companies have not instituted any cost and budgetary controls, yet only 3 of them have quality control programs. Also, data from Table 6-1, 6-3, and 6-4 indicate that in the MS com-

---

[8] Sagar Jain, "Old Style of Management," in S. B. Prasad and A. R. Negandhi, *Managerialism for Economic Development* (The Hague: Martinus Nijhoff, 1968), pp. 8–19.

[9] Kamala Chowdhry, "Social and Cultural Factors in Management Development in India and the Role of Expert," *International Labor Review*, Vol. 94, No. 3 (August 1966), pp. 131–147.

[10] Winston Oberg, "Cross-Cultural Perspectives on Management Principles," *Academy of Management Journal*, Vol. 6, No. 2 (June 1963), pp. 129–43.

[11] F. C. Flores, Jr., "Applicability of American Management Know-How to Developing Countries: The Case of the Philippines" (unpublished Ph.D. dissertation, Graduate School of Business Administration, U.C.L.A., 1968).

panies there is a great deal of participation in formulating production and performance standards for middle management and office personnel. The same is not true, however, in the case of NP companies.

Corollary proposition 3-2 suggests once again the existence of a seller's market condition in these countries. Statistical data in Appendix C show how the imbalance between the demand and supply sectors has been created in these countries; Appendix D shows how the impact of seller's market conditions precipitates lack of quality and cost consciousness among industrial managers in those countries.

Leadership

Proposition 4-1. All other factors being the same, the higher a firm's score on the management philosophy index, the more democratic the leadership and the greater the chance of group decision making in various organizational activities.

Corollary 4-2. The stronger the owner-manager situation, the greater the likelihood of autocratic leadership in the industrial firm.

Discussion

In recent years, much has been written on industrial leadership in underdeveloped countries.[12] Briefly, these writings seem to indicate that leadership style is a function of the culture, and that the cultural norms in underdeveloped countries seem appropriate for the autocratic form of leadership.[13] Our research has neither completely validated, nor refuted, this point of view.

Our findings provide only partial support for proposition 4-1. The data on leadership style presented in Table 5-5 show that approximately two-thirds of the MS companies (15 out of 23) practiced the democratic style of leadership, while none of the NP com-

[12] See F. Harbison and C. A. Myers, *Management in the Industrial World* (New York: McGraw Hill Book Company, 1959) especially Chapters 3, 7, 8, 9, 10.

[13] For a comprehensive review on this subject see G. V. Barrett and B. M. Bass, "Comparative Surveys of Managerial Attitudes and Behavior," in Jean Boddewyn (ed.) *Comparative Management Teaching, Training, and Research: Product and Potential* (New York: New York University Press, 1970). For the critical comments on the subject see Anant R. Negandhi's "Comments on Professors Barrett and Bass's Paper," in Boddewyn, op. cit.

panies practiced it. Similar inferences can be drawn from data concerning the managers' perception of their subordinates. These data are provided in Table 5-4.

The corollary proposition merely provides an alternate explanation for the prevailing autocratic leadership in the industrial firms studied. It is our contention that the growth in size and the growing complexities in technological and market environments will loosen the owner-manager stronghold on industrial firms in underdeveloped countries. This should then pave the way for the introduction of a more flexible type of leadership in these countries. We were able to observe such changes in leadership behavior among the heavy chemical and pharmaceutical firms in our sample.

MANAGEMENT EFFECTIVENESS

In Chapters 7 and 8, we analyzed various criteria of management effectiveness. We attempted to ascertain the relationships between the management philosophy variable, environmental factors, and management effectiveness. It was noted that environmental and cultural factors had greater influence upon employee morale, interpersonal relationships, absenteeism, and the turnover rate. All other management effectiveness criteria were under the realm of managerial control. The following propositions are based on the data presented in Chapters 7 and 8:

Employee Morale

Proposition 5-1. All other factors being the same, the more progressive a firm's management philosophy, the higher the employee morale.

Corollary 5-2. All other factors being the same, the greater the pampering of the industrial workers by the government, the greater the degree of hostility between the government and the business, and the poorer the employee morale.

Corollary 5-3. All other factors being the same, the firm with the hostile union is likely to have poorer employee morale than the firm with the cooperative union.

Discussion

The data presented in Table 7-1 have been consolidated in Table 10-3. This table reveals that slightly more than one-half of the 21 MS companies are able to maintain high employee morale; in the additional one-third, employees manifested at least average morale and satisfaction in work. In only 10 percent of these companies was employee morale at a low ebb, and yet in 43 percent of the NP companies the employee morale was poor. An overwhelmingly large majority of the SP companies (79 percent) are able to maintain the average employee morale.

Table 10-3 Employee Morale and Satisfaction in Work in American Subsidiaries and Local Companies in the Five Underdeveloped Countries

	Management Philosophy		
	Not Progressive	Somewhat Progressive*	Most Sophisticated
Highly satisfied	— (0)	8 (13) 4 4	11 (52) 7 4
Somewhat satisfied	4 (57) 1 3	49 (79) 28 21	8 (38) 4 4
Highly dissatisfied	3 (43) 3	5 (8) 3 2	2 (10) 2

U.S. Subsidiaries ($n = 47$)
Local Companies ($n = 43$)
* For two local companies in Brazil such information was difficult to assess.
Numbers at the top of each pair denote the total number of companies. The numbers in the bottom left section of each pair denote U.S. subsidiaries, and the numbers in the bottom right denote local companies. Figures in parentheses show the percentage of the total companies in each category.

As shown in Figure 10-2, a number of environmental and sociocultural factors affect employee morale in industrial firms in underdeveloped countries. Among these, the following factors were mentioned frequently by the interviewees:
(1) Governmental attitudes toward the industrial worker and the business community
(2) Management-union relationships

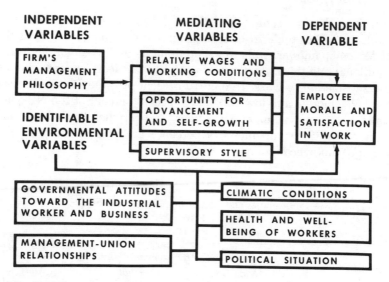

Figure 10-2   Independent and Mediating Variables Concerning Employee
Morale and Satisfaction in Work

(3) Climatic conditions
(4) Health and well-being of workers
(5) Political situation

The influence of these factors upon employee morale is discussed in Chapter 7. Corollary propositions 5-2 and 5-3 simply state
this information in a propositional form, and data presented in Table
10-4 support them.

Interpersonal Relationships

Interpersonal relationships among employees and supervisors
in underdeveloped countries were far from cooperative. Like employee morale, interpersonal relationships were greatly influenced
by environmental and cultural factors in those countries. Here especially, the firm's management philosophy had negligible effect.
Some of the important factors affecting interpersonal relationships

Table 10-4 Impact of Environmental Variables on Employee Morale and Satisfaction in Work in the Five Underdeveloped Countries (interview responses*)

	Argentina (n = 65)	Brazil (n = 90)	India (n = 272)	Philip- pines (n = 77)	Uruguay (n = 66)	Total (n = 570)
Governmental attitudes toward the worker and business community	33 (51)	55 (61)	152 (56)	15 (19)	29 (45)	284 (50)
Management- union rela- tionships	47 (72)	51 (57)	141 (52)	36 (47)	41 (62)	316 (55)
Climatic conditions	_**	_**	166 (61)	19 (25)	_**	185 (32)
Health and well-being of workers	22 (34)	31 (34)	204 (75)	31 (40)	22 (34)	310 (54)
Political situation	39 (60)	37 (41)	27 (10)	15 (19)	37 (54)	155 (27)

* Respondents included the executives, at all levels, supervisors, and the blue-collar workers.
** Less than 1% of the total respondents.
Figures in parentheses show the percentage of all respondents. Many respondents mentioned more than one factor, therefore figures are not strictly additive.

are: the employment situation (chronic unemployment and under-employment situations); the prevailing social status system; the governmental attitude toward the industrial work force and the business community; nature of trade unionism; differences in education and aspirations of younger and older employees; and inflation. Table 10-5 and Figure 10-3 illustrate the relative impact of these factors.

As stated in Chapter 7 (Table 7-2), approximately 25 percent of the firms studied were able to maintain cooperative relationships among their employees and supervisors. Permanent employment policies, higher education of employees, and the democratic supervisory style were contributory factors in attaining cooperative attitudes among employees and supervisors.

The following propositions delineate the relationship between

Table 10-5 Impact of Environmental Variables on Interpersonal Relationships
in Industrial Firms in the Five Underdeveloped Countries
(interview responses*)

	Argentina (n = 65)	Brazil (n = 90)	India (n = 272)	Philippines (n = 77)	Uruguay (n = 66)	Total (n = 570)
Employment situation	39 (60)	30 (33)	144 (53)	42 (54)	30 (46)	285 (50)
Differences in education and aspirations of younger and older employees	45 (69)	56 (62)	122 (45)	35 (45)	41 (62)	299 (52)
Nature of trade unionism	31 (47)	61 (68)	120 (44)	20 (26)	40 (60)	272 (48)
Social status and class system	33 (51)	29 (32)	111 (41)	51 (66)	46 (66)	270 (47)
Governmental attitudes toward worker and the business	53 (81)	51 (57)	92 (34)	32 (42)	32 (48)	260 (46)
Inflation	32 (48)	41 (46)	22 (9)	8 (10)	27 (41)	130 (23)

* Respondents included the executives, at all levels, supervisors, and the blue-collar workers.
Figures in parentheses show the percentage of all respondents. Many respondents mentioned more than one factor, therefore, figures are not strictly additive.

environmental and cultural factors and the nature of interpersonal relationships among employees and the supervisors.

Proposition 6-1. All other factors being the same, the firms pursuing permanent employment policies are likely to have more cooperative attitudes among their employees than the firms pursuing temporary employment policies.

Corollary 6-2. All other factors being the same, the higher the underemployment and unemployment, the greater the degree of mistrust and lack of confidence among workers, and the more severely uncooperative the attitude of the blue-collar employee.

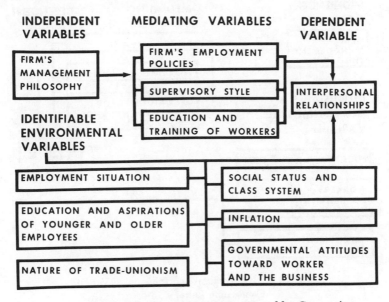

Figure 10-3   Independent and Mediating Variables Concerning
Interpersonal Relationships

Corollary 6-3. The greater the differences in educational attainments of younger and older employees, the greater the hostility and uncooperative attitudes among them.

Corollary 6-4. The greater the differences in social status between supervisors and the blue-collar workers, the lesser the cooperative attitudes among them.

Labor Turnover and Absenteeism

As stated in Chapters 7 and 9, comparable and reliable data concerning employee turnover rates and absenteeism were not available from the companies in Latin America and the Philippines. There was a great deal of fluctuation, even among the firms in India. Therefore, in order to obtain comparable data, we analyzed the employee turnover and absenteeism rates in 10 pharmaceutical firms (5 U.S.

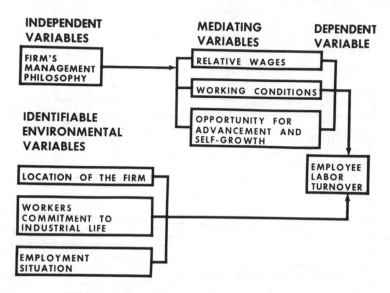

Figure 10-4   Independent and Influencing Variables
Concerning Labor Turnover

and 5 Indian) in India. The analysis of these data indicates that the industrial firm has had relatively less control over these factors. The location of the firm and the employee's commitment to industrial work are variables having greater influence. The firm located in a rural region tends to have a higher turnover rate, but lower employee absenteeism. The reverse is true for the firm located in an industrial location.

The firms located in rural areas tend to draw their work force from the pool of transitory farm workers who apparently quit their jobs during farming seasons. To this extent, they were neither fully committed to industrial life nor dependent upon such work. The firms located in big industrial cities employed workers from these cities. Due to the existence of high unemployment rates, these workers were reluctant to leave their jobs. Their higher absenteeism was due to the general climatic and working conditions, health and well-being of workers, and the permissive labor legislation in India. The relative importance of these variables is shown in Figures 10-4 and 10-5.

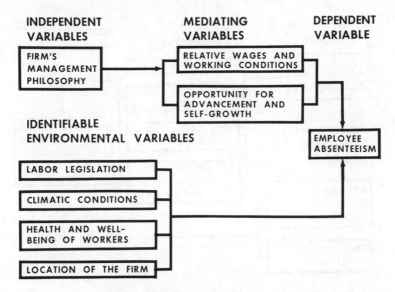

Figure 10-5 Independent and Mediating Variables
Concerning Absenteeism

Management Ability to Recruit High-Level Manpower

The following propositions underscore the nature of relationships among independent, mediating variables and the dependent variable concerning management effectiveness in hiring and retaining high-level manpower in underdeveloped countries:

Proposition 7-1. The higher the score of the firm on the management philosophy index, the higher its relative wages, the greater the opportunities available for individual advancement and growth, the more favorable its public image, and the greater the firm's ability to hire and retain high-level manpower.

Corollary 7-2. All other factors being the same, the higher the relative wages, the greater the firm's effectiveness in hiring and retaining high-level manpower.

Corollary 7-3. All other factors being the same, the higher the

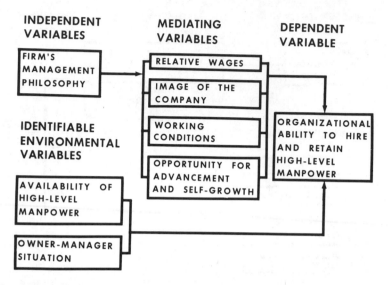

Figure 10-6   Independent and Mediating Variables Concerning Organizational
Ability to Hire and Retain High-Level Manpower

degree of owner-manager situation, the lesser the firm's effectiveness
in hiring and retaining high-level manpower.

Figure 10-6 shows the relationships among these variables.

These propositions indicate the nature of the generalized situation with respect to the firm's ability to hire and retain high-level
manpower in the 5 underdeveloped countries. They also pinpoint the
environmental factors influencing this variable. As we noted in Chapter 8, the third proposition (7-3) draws our attention to the fact that,
in underdeveloped countries, industrial enterprises are owned and
managed by family members. In such a situation, the incentive for a
person to train himself as a professional manager is very low. This,
in turn, has restricted the availability of high-level manpower in
these countries.

Given these conditions, the individual firm still has a fair degree of control over its ability to hire and retain trained personnel.
This control is exercised either by the firm's overall management
philosophy or by its offering higher relative wages and opportunities
for advancement and self-growth. The two are interrelated; that is,

a firm with a progressive management philosophy is also very likely to have a high salary scale. However, the converse is not necessarily true, for a firm can offer high wages and still have a low management philosophy score.

Table 8-1 indicates that management philosophy seems to have helped the U.S. subsidiaries and the local firms in India and the U.S. subsidiaries in the Philippines. The U.S. subsidiaries and local firms in other countries, which were also effective in securing high-level manpower, achieved this by offering higher relative wages and opportunities for advancement and self-growth. In all these countries, the general image of U.S. companies as good paymasters and as fair and honest employers has had considerable impact on their ability to attract trained personnel. At the same time, the owner-manager situation in local firms has had a negative impact on their ability in this aspect.

Interdepartmental Relationships

Independent and mediating variables affecting interdepartmental relationships were: the firm's management philosophy; owner-manager situation; statements of its objectives, policies, and procedures; effectiveness in communicating objectives and policies; role definition and job classification; and education and training of executives.

The relationships among these variables are expressed in the following propositions:

Proposition 8-1. The higher the firm's management philosophy score, the clearer its statements of objectives, policies, and procedures, the more effective its method of communication, the clearer its definitions of the executives' activities, the higher the educational attainment and training of its executives, and the more cooperative its interdepartmental relationships.

These relationships are not necessarily true in their inverse forms. That is, the firm may have clearer statements of its objectives, policies, and procedures, etc., without attaining a higher score on the management philosophy variable. Under such conditions, the following proposition is valid:

Corollary 8-2. The firms with clearer statements of their ob-

Table 10-6   Interdepartmental Relationships in American Subsidiaries
and Local Companies in the Five Underdeveloped Countries

	Management Philosophy					
	Not Progressive		Somewhat Progressive		Most Sophisticated	
Very cooperative	–	(0)	17	(26)	18	(85)
			13	4	10	8
Somewhat cooperative			19	(30)	1	(5)
			10	9		1
Poor cooperation	7	(100)	28	(44)	2	(10)
	1	6	12	16	1	1

U.S. Subsidiaries ($n = 47$)
Local Companies ($n = 45$)
Numbers at the top of each pair denote the total number of companies. The numbers in the bottom left section of each pair denote U.S. subsidiaries, and the numbers in the bottom right denote local companies. Figures in parentheses represent the percentage of the total firms in each category.

jectives, policies, and procedures, role definition and job classification, and higher educational attainments and training of their executives, are more likely to have cooperative interdepartmental
relationships than the firms with fuzzy statements of their objectives,
policies, and procedures, role definition and job classification, and
low levels of education and training of their executives.

The data presented in Table 10-6 (consolidated from Table
8-2) support the first proposition.

Utilization of High-Level Manpower

The following 2 items were investigated in order to ascertain
the degree of high-level manpower utilization in the 5 underdeveloped countries: (1) types of activities undertaken by the executives;
(2) the drive and enthusiasm experienced in their work. Both these
factors were influenced primarily by the firm's management philosophy. Statement of objectives, policies, and procedures, relative
wages, working conditions, opportunity for advancement and self-
growth, education and training of the executives, and the nature of
leadership were the mediating variables. The relative importance of
these factors is shown in Figure 10-7.

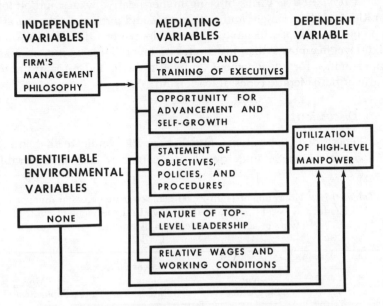

Figure 10-7   Independent and Mediating Variables Concerning
Utilization of High-Level Manpower

Proposition 9-1. The higher the firm's score on management philosophy variable, the higher the educational attainments and training of its executives, the clearer the statements of objectives, policies, and procedures, the higher the relative wages, the more persuasive the leadership, the greater the opportunities for advancement and self-growth of its executives, and the higher the degree of high-level manpower utilization by the firm.

However, the inverse relationships among these variables do not necessarily follow. That is, the high level of education and training of the executives, advancement and self-growth opportunities, etc., are not necessarily a function of the firm's management philosophy. In other words, a company with a low score on management philosophy may still provide higher relative wages, employ the executive with higher educational attainments, and utilize persuasive types of leadership. Under such conditions, the following relationships among mediating variables and the dependent variables of high-level manpower utilization are conceivable:

Corollary 9-2. Firms offering higher relative wages and opportunities for advancement and self-growth, and pursuing a democratic type of leadership, will have a greater degree of utilization of their high-level manpower than firms offering low relative wages, minimal opportunities for advancement and self-growth, and pursuing autocratic or bureaucratic types of leadership.

Discussion

These two propositions, and Figure 10-7, indicate that industrial organizations in underdeveloped countries have considerable

Table 10-7A   Utilization of High-Level Manpower Resources in American Subsidiaries and Local Companies in the Five Underdeveloped Countries (types of activities undertaken by executives)

	Management Philosophy					
	Not Progressive		*Somewhat Progressive*		*Most Sophisticated*	
Policy making and future planning	–	(0)	7 6	(11) 1	17 10	(81) 7
Coordination with other departments	1 1	(14)	29 18	(45) 11	3 3	(14)
Routine work and finding fault with subordinates and others	6 1	(86) 5	28 11	(44) 17	1 1	(5)

U.S. Subsidiaries (*n* = 47)
Local Companies (*n* = 45)
Numbers at the top of each pair denote the total number of companies. The numbers in the bottom left section of each pair denote U.S. subsidiaries, and the numbers in the bottom right denote local companies. Figures in parentheses represent the percentage of the total firms in each category.

control over the utilization of high-level manpower. The firm, either through its overall management philosophy or through such mediating variables as relative wages, working conditions, and leadership style, is capable of achieving desirable results with respect to its high-level manpower utilization. Data consolidated from Table 8-4, and shown in Tables 10-7A and 10-7B, support these propositions.

Table 10-7B Utilization of High-Level Manpower Resources in American Subsidiaries and Local Companies in the Five Underdeveloped Countries (executive's enthusiasm and drive)

	Not Progressive		Management Philosophy Somewhat Progressive*		Most Sophisticated	
Strong enthusiasm and drive	1	1	8 5	(13) 3	16 8	(76) 8
Moderate enthusiasm and drive			30 18	(47) 12	5 3	(24) 2
Defensive, withdrawing	6 1	(100) 5	25 12	(40) 13	–	–

U.S. Subsidiaries ($n = 47$)
Local Companies ($n = 44$)
Numbers at the top of each pair denote the total number of companies. The numbers in the bottom left section of each pair denote U.S. subsidiaries, and the numbers in the bottom right denote local companies. Figures in parentheses represent the percentage of the total firms in each category.
° For one company this information was not available.

Management Effectiveness in Adapting to the External Environmental Conditions

Organizational effectiveness in adapting to external conditions is influenced by the firm's management philosophy, nature of leadership, education and training of the executives, and the nature of the socioeconomic, political, and legal conditions in a given country.

Proposition 10-1. Under given environmental conditions, the higher a firm's score on the management philosophy index, the fewer the difficulties experienced by the firm in adapting to environmental conditions.

Discussion

As we noted in Chapter 8, local (national) firms are not necessarily in a better position to cope with environmental conditions. American subsidiaries, in other words, are not naive in understanding the host country's environmental conditions simply because of

Table 10-8 Management Effectiveness in Adapting to Environmental
Conditions in American Subsidiaries and Local Companies in the
Five Underdeveloped Countries

	Not Progressive		Management Philosophy Somewhat Progressive		Most Sophisticated	
Highly adaptable	—	(0)	23	(36)	19	(90)
			13	10	10	9
Somewhat adaptable			15	(23)	—	(0)
			13	2		
Not very adaptable	7	(100)	26	(41)	2	(10)
	1	6	9	17	1	1

U.S. Subsidiaries ($n = 47$)
Local Companies ($n = 45$)
 Numbers at the top of each pair denote the total number of companies. The numbers in the bottom left section of each pair denote U.S. subsidiaries, and the numbers in the bottom right denote local companies. Figures in parentheses represent the percentage of the total firms in each category.

their foreign origins. Industrial organizations, both U.S. and local, respond well to changing environmental stimuli. The firm's overall management philosophy, education of its executives, and leadership style, are some of the key variables in this aspect. Data presented in Table 10-8 tend to support the above propositions.

Postscript

Adaptive change is a sine qua non in modern business organizations. Generally speaking, the introduction of changes in methods and procedures is a rather slow process in developing nations such as India.

A substantial portion of our original data, upon which the preceding analyses were based, was obtained in 1966–1967 from U.S. subsidiaries operating in India, as well as from comparable Indian-owned enterprises. The question arises whether any significant changes have taken place since 1967.

With this question in mind, we thought it would be appropriate to re-interview at least some of the firms in our Indian sample. One of the authors (Prasad) made a trip to India in February 1969 and held informal discussions with the executives of 2 U.S. subsidiaries and 5 local firms located in Bombay. His general impression was that there have not been any significant changes in these companies, at least insofar as management processes and methods were concerned. Managerial thinking seemed to be basically the same. However, we noted two exceptions.

First, managerial thinking concerning the Indian Government's policies towards industry appeared somewhat critical. An examination of the various actions of the central government on the one hand, and of the economic events in the country on the other, lends a degree of justification of the managers' criticisms of governmental policies.

Second, one of the MS Indian companies has taken a broader, more liberal outlook in terms of its management development; it opened a management training center in 1967. However, the point to be noted here is that it has opened its doors and invited other company personnel to participate. We tend to regard this as very progressive managerial thinking, particularly in light of the fact that even progressive foreign subsidiaries tend to shy away from such an approach.

APPENDIX A

STATISTICAL RELATIONSHIPS AMONG MAJOR VARIABLES

Table A-1 Rank Correlation between the Management Philosophy Score
and Management Process Index

Pair No.	Company	Industry	Manage- ment Philos- ophy Score X	Rank (R_X)	Manage- ment Process Index A	Rank (R_A)	d = | R_X−R_A |	d^2
1	U.S.	Pharmaceutical	100	3	1.0	3	0	0
	Indian	"	95	6	1.5	8.5	2.5	6.25
2	U.S.	Pharmaceutical	100	3	1.8	18.5	15.5	240.25
	Indian	"	59	12	1.8	18.5	6.5	42.25
3	U.S.	Pharmaceutical	71	9	1.6	12.5	3.5	12.25
	Indian	"	42	24	2.3	24.5	.5	.25
4	U.S.	Pharmaceutical	54	14.5	1.6	12.5	2	4
	Indian	"	22	29	2.5	26	3	9
5	U.S.	Consumer non-	59	12	1.3	7	5	25
	Indian	durable goods and soft drinks	46	20.5	2.1	23	2.5	6.25
6	U.S.	Toilet Soaps	100	3	1.0	3	0	0
	Indian	"	100	3	1.0	3	0	0
7	U.S.	Canned Products	49	18	1.6	12.5	5.5	30.25
	Indian	"	22	29	2.8	28.5	.5	.25
8	U.S.	Cosmetics	25	26.5	2.8	28.5	2	4
	Indian	"	22	29	2.9	30	1	1
9	U.S.	Heavy Engineering	51	16.5	1.1	6	10.5	110.25
	Indian	Goods-Metal Ind.	25	26.5	2.6	27	.5	.25
10	U.S.	Elevators	46	20.5	1.8	18.5	2	4
	Indian	"	90	7	1.8	18.5	11.5	132.25
11	U.S.	Heavy Machine	46	20.5	1.6	12.5	8	64
	Indian	and Tools	100	3	1.0	3	0	0
12	U.S.	Typewriters	59	12	1.0	3	9	81
	Indian	"	69	10	1.9	22	12	144
13	U.S.	Auto Tires	43	23	1.8	18.5	4.5	20.25
	Indian	"	54	14.5	1.6	12.5	2	4
14	U.S.	Electric Bulbs	46	20.5	1.8	18.5	2	4
	Indian	"	51	16.5	2.3	24.5	8	64
15	U.S.	Sewing Machines	40	25	1.6	12.5	12.5	156.25
	Indian	"	72	8	1.5	8.5	.5	.25
							Total	1165.50

$$r_s = 1 - \frac{1165.5}{4495} = 1 - .282$$

$r_s = 0.718$ or 0.72
Significant

Table A-2 Ranking Scale for the Factors Evaluated for
Management Process Index

Factors Evaluated	Ranking Scale
1. *Planning Orientation*	
(a) Long-range planning (5 years or more)	1
(b) Medium and short-range (1 year)	2
(c) Ad hoc basis	3
2. *Quality Control*	
(a) Formally and systematically done by qualified personnel	1
(b) Formally done by unqualified personnel	2
(c) Ad hoc basis—no quality control	3
3. *Equipment Maintenance*	
(a) Systematically done by skilled personnel	1
(b) Done by unskilled and semiskilled personnel	2
(c) Done on ad hoc basis	3
4. *Standard Settings in Production*	
(a) Formally and systematically done	1
(b) Partially done	2
(c) Not done—ad hoc basis	3
5. *Standard Settings for White Collar Employees*	
(a) Formally and systematically done	1
(b) Partially done	2
(c) Not done—ad hoc basis	3
6. *Standard Settings for Middle Management Personnel*	
(a) Formally and systematically done	1
(b) Partially done	2
(c) Not done—ad hoc basis	3
7. *Cost Control*	
(a) Qualified personnel—done for all or major products	1
(b) Unqualified personnel—done for major products	2
(c) Not done—ad hoc basis	3
8. *Budgeting and Resources Allocating*	
(a) For entire firm—qualified personnel	1
(b) Partially done for some departments—somewhat qualified personnel	2
(c) Not done—ad hoc basis	3
9. *Leaders' Perception of Subordinates*	
(a) Subordinates confident and trustworthy	1
(b) Subordinates somewhat confident and trustworthy	2
(c) Subordinates not confident and trustworthy	3

Table A-3   Rank Correlation between the Management Philosophy Score
and Personnel Practices Index

Pair No.	Company	Industry	Philos- ophy Score X	Rank (R_X)	Personnel Practices C	Rank (R_C)	d = $\mid R_X - R_C \mid$	d^2
1	U.S.	Pharmaceutical	100	3	1.0	2.5	.5	.25
	Indian	"	95	6	2.0	13	7	49
2	U.S.	Pharmaceutical	100	3	1.0	2.5	.5	.25
	Indian	"	59	12	2.3	20.5	8.5	72.25
3	U.S.	Pharmaceutical	71	9	1.7	8	1	1
	Indian	"	42	24	2.5	24.5	.5	.25
4	U.S.	Pharmaceutical	54	14.5	2.7	28	13.5	182.25
	Indian	"	22	29	2.3	20.5	8.5	72.25
5	U.S.	Consumer non-	59	12	1.7	8	4	16
	Indian	durable goods and soft drinks	46	20.5	2.5	24.5	4	16
6	U.S.	Toilet Soaps	100	3	1.0	2.5	.5	.25
	Indian	"	100	3	1.3	5	2	4
7	U.S.	Canned Products	49	18	2.5	24.5	6.5	42.25
	Indian	"	22	29	2.7	28	1	1
8	U.S.	Cosmetics	25	26.5	2.5	24.5	2	4
	Indian	"	22	29	2.3	20.5	8.5	72.25
9	U.S.	Heavy Engineering	51	16.5	2.8	30	13.5	182.25
	Indian	Goods-Metal Ind.	25	26.5	2.7	28	1.5	2.25
10	U.S.	Elevators	46	20.5	2.3	20.5	0	0
	Indian	"	90	7	2.2	16.5	9.5	90.25
11	U.S.	Heavy Machine	46	20.5	2.0	13	7.5	56.25
	Indian	and Tools	100	3	1.0	2.5	.5	.25
12	U.S.	Typewriters	59	12	2.0	13	1	1
	Indian	"	69	10	2.2	16.5	6.5	42.25
13	U.S.	Auto Tires	43	23	1.7	8	15	225
	Indian	"	54	14.5	2.2	16.5	2	4
14	U.S.	Electric Bulbs	46	20.5	1.8	10.5	10	100
	Indian	"	51	16.5	2.2	16.5	0	0
15	U.S.	Sewing Machines	40	25	1.8	10.5	14.5	210.25
	Indian	"	72	8	1.5	6	2	4

$$r_s = 0.68 \qquad\qquad \text{Total} \quad 1451.00$$

$$r_s = 1 - \frac{1451}{4495} = 1 - .323 = .677$$

Table A-4   Ranking Scales for the Factors Evaluated
for Personnel Practices Index

Factors	Points
1. *Manpower Planning*	
(a) Formalized and rationalized	1
(b) Somewhat formalized and rationalized	2
(c) Ad hoc basis	3
2. *Employee Selection*	
(a) Formalized and rationalized	1
(b) Somewhat formalized and rationalized	2
(c) Ad hoc basis	3
3. *Compensation and Employee Benefits*	
(a) Formalized and rationalized	1
(b) Somewhat formalized and rationalized	2
(c) Ad hoc basis	3
4. *Employee Appraisal*	
(a) Formalized and rationalized	1
(b) Somewhat formalized and rationalized	2
(c) Ad hoc basis	3
5. *Employee Training and Development for Management and Supervisory Personnel*	
(a) Formalized and rationalized	1
(b) Somewhat formalized and rationalized	2
(c) Ad hoc basis	3
6. *Training and Development for Blue Collar Workers*	
(a) Formalized and rationalized	1
(b) Somewhat formalized and rationalized	2
(c) Ad hoc basis	3

Table A-5 Rank Correlation between Management Philosophy Score and Management Effectiveness Index

Pair No.	Company	Industry	Philos-ophy Score X	Rank (R_X)	Management Effective-ness E Index	Rank (R_E)	d = $\mid R_X{-}R_E \mid$	d^2
1	U.S.	Pharmaceutical	100	3	1.0	2.5	.5	.25
	Indian	"	95	6	1.5	8.5	2.5	6.25
2	U.S.	Pharmaceutical	100	3	1.0	2.5	.5	.25
	Indian	"	59	12	2.2	21	9	81
3	U.S.	Pharmaceutical	71	9	1.8	14	5	25
	Indian	"	42	24	2.2	21	3	9
4	U.S.	Pharmaceutical	54	14.5	1.7	11	3.5	12.25
	Indian	"	22	29	2.2	21	8	64
5	U.S.	Consumer non-	59	12	1.8	14	2	4
	Indian	durable goods and soft drinks	46	20.5	2.7	28	7.5	56.25
6	U.S.	Toilet Soaps	100	3	1.0	2.5	.5	.25
	Indian	"	100	3	1.2	5.5	2.5	6.25
7	U.S.	Canned Products	49	18	1.8	14	4	16
	Indian	"	22	29	3.0	30	1	1
8	U.S.	Cosmetics	25	26.5	2.5	26.5	0	0
	Indian	"	22	29	2.8	29	0	0
9	U.S.	Heavy Engineering	51	16.5	1.3	7	9.5	90.25
	Indian	Goods-Metal Ind.	25	26.5	2.5	26.5	0	0
10	U.S.	Elevators	46	20.5	2.3	24.5	4	16
	Indian	"	90	7	1.2	5.5	1.5	2.25
11	U.S.	Heavy Machine	46	20.5	2.3	24.5	4	16
	Indian	and Tools	100	3	1.0	2.5	.5	.25
12	U.S.	Typewriters	59	12	1.5	8.5	3.5	12.25
	Indian	"	69	10	2.2	21	11	121
13	U.S.	Auto Tires	43	23	2.2	21	2	4
	Indian	"	54	14.5	2.0	17	2.5	6.25
14	U.S.	Electric Bulbs	46	20.5	2.0	17	3.5	12.25
	Indian	"	51	16.5	2.0	17	.5	.25
15	U.S.	Sewing Machines	40	25	1.7	11	14	196
	Indian	"	72	8	1.7	11	3	9

$r_S = 0.83$ Total   767.50

x	t	T
100	5	120
59	3	24
54	2	6
51	2	6
46	4	60
22	3	24
25	2	26

Ties not important

$266 << 26,970$

$\Sigma T = 266$

$$\therefore r_S = 1 - \frac{6\Sigma d}{N^3 - N} = 1 - \frac{6(767.5)}{26970}$$

$$= 1 - \frac{767.5}{4495} = 1 - .17$$

$$r_S = 0.83$$

Table A-6   Ranking Scales for the Factors Evaluated for
Management Effectiveness Index

Factors	Points
1. *Management ability to attract and retain high-level manpower*	
(a) Able to attract and retain highly trained personnel	1
(b) Able to attract and retain moderately trained personnel	2
(c) Not able to attract and retain even moderately trained personnel	3
2. *Employee morale and satisfaction in work*	
(a) Excellent morale and highly satisfied	1
(b) Average morale and somewhat satisfied	2
(c) Poor morale and highly dissatisfied	3
3. *Employee turnover and absenteeism*	
(a) 0–5%	1
(b) 6–11%	2
(c) 12% and more	3
4. *Interpersonal relationships in organizational settings*	
(a) Very cooperative	1
(b) Somewhat cooperative	2
(c) Poor cooperation	3
5. *Departmental relationships (Subsystem relationship)*	
(a) Very cooperative	1
(b) Somewhat cooperative	2
(c) Poor cooperation	3
6. *The executive's perception of the firm's overall objectives*	
(a) Total optimization (achievement of the firm's objectives) is perceived as most important	1
(b) Suboptimization (achievement of the departmental objectives) is preferred	2
(c) Achievement of the departmental objectives is ultimate goal	3
7. *Utilization of high-level manpower*	
(a) Policy-making and future planning	1
(b) Coordination with other departments	2
(c) Routine work, day-to-day work and excessive supervision with subordinate's duties	3
8. *Organizational effectiveness in adapting to the external environments*	
(a) Able to adapt without much difficulty	1
(b) Able to adapt partially with some difficulty	2
(c) Not able to adapt	3

Table A-7 Rank Correlation between the Management Philosophy Score
and Decentralization Index

Pair No.	Company	Industry	Manage- ment Philos- ophy Score	Rank (R1)	Decentrali- zation Index	Rank (R2)	d = | R2−R1 |	d²
1	U.S.	Pharmaceutical	100	3	1.2	3	0	0
	Indian	"	95	6	1.6	9	3	9
2	U.S.	Pharmaceutical	100	3	1.2	3	0	0
	Indian	"	59	12	1.8	15	3	9
3	U.S.	Pharmaceutical	71	9	1.9	18	9	81
	Indian	"	42	24	2.0	19.5	4.5	20.25
4	U.S.	Pharmaceutical	54	14.5	1.7	11.5	3	9
	Indian	"	22	29	2.8	27	2	4
5	U.S.	Consumer non-	59	12	1.4	6	6	36
	Indian	durable goods and soft drinks	46	20.5	2.4	25	4.5	20.25
6	U.S.	Toilet soaps	100	3	1.2	3	0	0
	Indian	"	100	3	1.3	5	2	4
7	U.S.	Canned products	49	18	1.8	15	3	9
	Indian	"	22	29	3.0	29.5	.5	.25
8	U.S.	Cosmetics	25	26.5	2.9	28	1.5	6.25
	Indian	"	22	29	3.0	29.5	.5	.25
9	U.S.	Heavy Engineering	51	16.5	1.6	9	7.5	56.25
	Indian	Goods-Metal Ind.	25	26.5	2.5	26	.5	.25
10	U.S.	Elevators	46	20.5	1.8	15	5.5	30.25
	Indian	"	90	7	1.8	15	8.0	64.0
11	U.S.	Heavy Machine	46	20.5	2.2	22.5	2.0	4.0
	Indian	and Tools	100	3	1.1	1	2.0	4.0
12	U.S.	Typewriters	59	12	1.5	7	5.0	25.0
	Indian	"	69	10	2.2	22.5	12.5	156.25
13	U.S.	Auto Tires	43	23	2.3	24	1.0	1.0
	Indian	"	54	14.5	2.0	19.5	5.0	25.0
14	U.S.	Electric Bulbs	46	20.5	2.1	21	.5	.25
	Indian	"	51	16.5	1.6	9	7.5	56.25
15	U.S.	Sewing Machines	40	25	1.7	11.5	13.5	182.25
	Indian	"	72	8	1.8	15	7.0	49.00

$r_s = 0.81$ Total   862.00

$$1 - \frac{862}{4495} = 1 - .191 = 0.81$$

Table A-8   Rank Correlation between Decentralization Index
and Management Effectiveness

Pair No.	Company	Industry	Decentralization Index B	Rank (R_B)	Effectiveness Index E	Rank (R_E)	d = $\lvert R_B - R_E \rvert$	d²
1	U.S.	Pharmaceutical	1.2	3	1.0	2.5	.5	.25
	Indian	"	1.6	9	1.5	8.5	.5	.25
2	U.S.	Pharmaceutical	1.2	3	1.0	2.5	.5	.25
	Indian	"	1.8	15	2.2	21	6	36
3	U.S.	Pharmaceutical	1.9	18	1.8	14	4	16
	Indian	"	2.0	19.5	2.2	21	1.5	2.25
4	U.S.	Pharmaceutical	1.7	11.5	1.7	11	.5	.25
	Indian	"	2.8	27	2.2	21	6	36
5	U.S.	Consumer non-	1.4	6	1.8	14	8	64
	Indian	durable goods and soft drinks	2.4	25	2.7	28	3	9
6	U.S.	Toilet Soaps	1.2	3	1.0	2.5	.5	.25
	Indian	"	1.3	5	1.2	5.5	.5	.25
7	U.S.	Canned Products	1.8	15	1.8	14	1	1
	Indian	"	3.0	29.5	3.0	30	.5	.25
8	U.S.	Cosmetics	2.9	28	2.5	26.5	1.5	2.25
	Indian	"	3.0	29.5	2.8	29	.5	.25
9	U.S.	Heavy Engineering	1.6	9	1.3	7	2	4
	Indian	Goods-Metal Ind. "	2.5	26	2.5	26.5	.5	.25
10	U.S.	Elevators	1.8	15	2.3	24.5	.5	.25
	Indian	"	1.8	15	1.2	5.5	9.5	90.25
11	U.S.	Heavy Machine	2.2	22.5	2.3	24.5	2	4
	Indian	and Tools "	1.1	1	1.0	2.5	1.5	2.25
12	U.S.	Typewriters	1.5	7	1.5	8.5	1.5	2.25
	Indian	"	2.2	22.5	2.2	21	1.5	2.25
13	U.S.	Auto Tires	2.3	24	2.2	21	3	9
	Indian	"	2.0	19.5	2.0	17	2.5	6.25
14	U.S.	Electric Bulbs	2.1	21	2.0	17	4	16
	Indian	"	1.6	9	2.0	17	8	64
15	U.S.	Sewing Machines	1.7	11.5	1.7	11	.5	.25
	Indian	"	1.8	15	1.7	11	4	16

$r_s = 0.91$ Total   385.50

$$r_s = 1 - \frac{6(385.5)}{26970}$$

$$= 1 - \frac{385.5}{4495}$$

$$= 1 - .086$$

$$r_s = 0.914$$

Table A-9   Ranking Scale for the Factors Evaluated
for Decentralization Index

Factors	Points
1. *Layers of hierarchy* (top executive to blue-collar worker)	
(a) 3 to 6 layers	1
(b) 7 to 10 layers	2
(c) 11 and more layers	3
2. *Locus of decision-making* (major policies)	
(a) Broad representation of executives and stockholders	1
(b) Top level executive committee	2
(c) Chief executive or owner only	3
3. *Locus of decision-making* (sales policies)	
(a) Executive committee with representation of all functional areas	1
(b) Chief executive with the help of sales manager	2
(c) Top executive/owner only	3
4. *Locus of decision-making* (product–mix)	
(a) Executive committee with representation of all functional areas	1
(b) Chief executive with the help of production/ marketing manager	2
(c) Chief executive/owner only	3
5. *Locus of decision-making* (standard settings in production)	
(a) Executive committee with representation of all functional areas	1
(b) Chief executive with production manager Production manager only	2
(c) Chief executive only	3
6. *Locus of decision-making* (manpower policies)	
(a) Executive committee with representation of all functional areas	1
(b) Chief executive with personnel manager	2
(c) Chief executive only	3
7. *Locus of decision-making* (selection of executive personnel)	
(a) Executive committee with representation of all functional areas	1
(b) Chief executive with personnel manager	2
(c) Chief executive only	3
8. *The degree of participation in long-range planning*	
(a) All levels of executives–top, middle, and lower	1
(b) Top level with some representation of middle level executives	2
(c) Chief executive/owner only	3
9. *The degree of information-sharing*	
(a) Considerable–general memos on all major aspects of company's operation	1
(b) Fair–special reports on company's affairs distributed to only top level and middle level executives	2
(c) Little–all information kept secret from everybody except few top level executives	3

Table A-10   Rank Correlation between Management Process Index and
                Management Effectiveness Index

Pair No.	Company	Industry	Process Index A	Rank (R_A)	Effectiveness Index E	Rank (R_E)	d = $\mid R_A - R_E \mid$	d²
1	U.S.	Pharmaceutical	1.0	3	1.0	2.5	.5	.25
	Indian	"	1.5	8.5	1.5	8.5	0	0
2	U.S.	Pharmaceutical	1.8	18.5	1.0	2.5	16	256
	Indian	"	1.8	18.5	2.2	21	2.5	6.25
3	U.S.	Pharmaceutical	1.6	12.5	1.8	14	1.5	2.25
	Indian	"	2.3	24.5	2.2	21	3.5	12.25
4	U.S.	Pharmaceutical	1.6	12.5	1.7	11	1.5	2.25
	Indian	"	2.5	26	2.2	21	5	25
5	U.S.	Consumer non-	1.3	7	1.8	14	7	49
	Indian	durable goods and soft drinks	2.1	23	2.7	28	5	25
6	U.S.	Toilet Soaps	1.0	3	1.0	2.5	.5	.25
	Indian	"	1.0	3	1.2	5.5	2.5	6.25
7	U.S.	Canned Products	1.6	12.5	1.8	14	1.5	2.25
	Indian	"	2.8	28.5	3.0	30	1.5	2.25
8	U.S.	Cosmetics	2.8	28.5	2.5	26.5	2	4
	Indian	"	2.9	30	2.8	29	1	1
9	U.S.	Heavy Engineering	1.1	6	1.3	7	1	1
	Indian	Goods-Metal Ind.	2.6	27	2.5	26.5	.5	.25
10	U.S.	Elevators	1.8	18.5	2.3	24.5	6	36
	Indian	"	1.8	18.5	1.2	5.5	13	169
11	U.S.	Heavy Machine	1.6	12.5	2.3	24.5	12	144
	Indian	and Tools	1.0	3	1.0	2.5	.5	.25
12	U.S.	Typewriters	1.0	3	1.5	8.5	5.5	30.25
	Indian	"	1.9	22	2.2	21	1	1
13	U.S.	Auto Tires	1.8	18.5	2.2	21	2.5	6.25
	Indian	"	1.6	12.5	2.0	17	4.5	20.25
14	U.S.	Electric Bulbs	1.8	18.5	2.0	17	1.5	2.25
	Indian	"	2.3	24.5	2.0	17	7.5	56.25
15	U.S.	Sewing Machines	1.6	12.5	1.7	11	1.5	2.25
	Indian	"	1.5	8.5	1.7	11	2.5	6.25

$$r_s = .810 \qquad\qquad\qquad \text{Total} \quad 869.50$$

$$r_s = 1 - \frac{6 \sum d^2}{N^3 - N} = 1 - \frac{6(869.5)}{26,970}$$

$$= 1 - \frac{869.5}{4495} = 1 - .19$$

$$r_s = .81$$

Table A-11   Rank Correlation between Personnel Practices Index and
Management Effectiveness

Pair No.	Company	Industry	Personnel Practices Index C	Rank (R_C)	Effective-ness Index E	Rank (R_E)	d = |R_C−R_E|	d^2
1	U.S.	Pharmaceutical	1.0	2.5	1.0	2.5	0	0
	Indian	"	2.0	13	1.5	8.5	4.5	20.25
2	U.S.	Pharmaceutical	1.0	2.5	1.0	2.5	0	0
	Indian	"	2.3	20.5	2.2	21	.5	.25
3	U.S.	Pharmaceutical	1.7	8	1.8	14	6	36
	Indian	"	2.5	24.5	2.2	21	3.5	12.25
4	U.S.	Pharmaceutical	2.7	28	1.7	11	17	289
	Indian	"	2.3	20.5	2.2	21	.5	.25
5	U.S.	Consumer non-	1.7	8	1.8	14	6	36
	Indian	durable goods and soft drinks	2.5	24.5	2.7	28	3.5	12.25
6	U.S.	Toilet Soaps	1.0	2.5	1.0	2.5	0	0
	Indian	"	1.3	5	1.2	5.5	.5	.25
7	U.S.	Canned Products	2.5	24.5	1.8	14	10.5	110.25
	Indian	"	2.7	28	3.0	30	2	4
8	U.S.	Cosmetics	2.5	24.5	2.5	26.5	2	4
	Indian	"	2.3	20.5	2.8	29	8.5	72.25
9	U.S.	Heavy Engineering	2.8	30	1.3	7	23	529
	Indian	Goods-Metal Ind.	2.7	28	2.5	26.5	1.5	2.25
10	U.S.	Elevators	2.3	20.5	2.3	24.5	4	16
	Indian	"	2.2	16.5	1.2	5.5	11	121
11	U.S.	Heavy Machine	2.0	13	2.3	24.5	11.5	132.25
	Indian	and Tools	1.0	2.5	1.0	2.5	0	0
12	U.S.	Typewriters	2.0	13	1.5	8.5	4.5	20.25
	Indian	"	2.2	16.5	2.2	21	4.5	20.25
13	U.S.	Auto Tires	1.7	8	2.2	21	13	169
	Indian	"	2.2	16.5	2.0	17	.5	.25
14	U.S.	Electric Bulbs	1.8	10.5	2.0	17	6.5	42.25
	Indian	"	2.2	16.5	2.0	17	.5	.25
15	U.S.	Sewing Machines	1.8	10.5	1.7	11	.5	.25
	Indian	"	1.5	6	1.7	11	5	25

$r_s = 0.63$ Total   1675.00

$$r_s = 1 - \frac{1675}{4495} = 1 - .373$$

$$r_s = .627$$

Table A-12   Rank Correlation between Organizational Practices Index[*]
and Management Effectiveness

Pair No.	Company	Industry	Practices Index D	Rank (R_D)	Effective- ness Index E	Rank (R_E)	d = $\lvert R_D - R_E \rvert$	d²
1	U.S.	Pharmaceutical	1.1	2.5	1.0	2.5	0	0
	Indian	"	1.7	10	1.5	8.5	1.5	2.25
2	U.S.	Pharmaceutical	1.3	5	1.0	2.5	2.5	6.25
	Indian	"	2.0	20	2.2	21	1	1
3	U.S.	Pharmaceutical	1.7	10	1.8	14	4	16
	Indian	"	2.3	24.5	2.2	21	3.5	12.25
4	U.S.	Pharmaceutical	2.0	20	1.7	11	9	81
	Indian	"	2.5	26	2.2	21	5	25
5	U.S.	Consumer non-	1.5	6.5	1.8	14	7.5	56.25
	Indian	durable goods and soft drinks	2.3	24.5	2.7	28	3.5	12.25
6	U.S.	Toilet Soaps	1.1	2.5	1.0	2.5	0	0
	Indian	"	1.2	4	1.2	5.5	1.5	2.25
7	U.S.	Canned Products	2.0	20	1.8	14	6	36
	Indian	"	2.8	30	3.0	30	0	0
8	U.S.	Cosmetics	2.7	28.5	2.5	26.5	2	4
	Indian	"	2.7	28.5	2.8	29	.5	.25
9	U.S.	Heavy Engineering	1.8	12	1.3	7	5	25
	Indian	Goods-Metal Ind.	2.6	27	2.5	26.5	.5	.25
10	U.S.	Elevators	2.0	20	2.3	24.5	4.5	20.25
	Indian	"	1.9	15	1.2	5.5	9.5	90.25
11	U.S.	Heavy Machine	1.9	15	2.3	24.5	9.5	90.25
	Indian	and Tools	1.0	1	1.0	2.5	1.5	2.25
12	U.S.	Typewriters	1.5	6.5	1.5	8.5	2	4
	Indian	"	2.1	23	2.2	21	2	4
13	U.S.	Auto Tires	1.9	15	2.2	21	6	36
	Indian	"	1.9	15	2.0	17	2	4
14	U.S.	Electric Bulbs	1.9	15	2.0	17	2	4
	Indian	"	2.0	20	2.0	17	3	9
15	U.S.	Sewing Machines	1.7	10	1.7	11	1	1
	Indian	"	1.6	8	1.7	11	3	9

$r_s = 0.88$ Total   554.00

$$r_s = 1 - \frac{554.0}{4495} = 1 - .123$$

$$r_s = 0.877 = .88$$

[*] Organizational Practices Index was computed by adding all three Indexes of Management Process Index, Decentralization Index, and Personnel Practices Index.

APPENDIX B

ON THE INDEPENDENT VARIABLE, MANAGEMENT PHILOSOPHY— INFERENCE AND MEASUREMENTS

Table B-1 Company's Philosophy toward Employees

Four Factors Evaluated		Company's Attitude
a. Top management's stated policy or philosophy concerning employee development.	to categorize	1. Much concern, or
		2. Moderate concern, or
		3. Little or no concern
b. Employee's perception of the company's concern toward individual development.		
c. Prospective employee's image of the company.		
d. Public image of the company.		

Table B-2 Company's Philosophy toward Consumers

Seven Factors Evaluated		Company's Attitude
a. Company's profit and service objectives—implied, expressed, and implemented.	to categorize	1. Consumer as the King.
		2. Consumers necessary to make profit.
b. Consumer's image of the company and its products.		3. Consumers should take product.
c. Employee's image of the company and its profit objective.		
d. Supplier's image of the company; its products and its profit objectives.		
e. Distributor's image of the company; its products and profit objectives.		
f. Stockholder's image of the company and its profit objective.		
g. Company's pricing policies.		

Table B-3   Company's Philosophy toward Distributors

Four Factors Evaluated		*Company's Attitude*
a. Management policy, statement, and implementation.		1. Honest relationship absolutely necessary
b. Marketing programs and procedures.	to categorize	2. Good relationship helpful
c. Implied and expressed attitude of marketing executives toward the distributors.		3. Relationship is a necessary evil
d. Distributor's attitude toward the company.		

Table B-4   Company's Philosophy toward Suppliers

Five Factors Evaluated		*Company's Attitude*
a. Company's policy statements.		1. Honest relationship absolutely necessary
b. Implementation of policies.		
c. Programs and procedures of purchasing department of the company.	to categorize	2. Good relationship helpful
d. Purchasing agents' or executives' attitudes toward suppliers.		3. Relationship a necessary evil
e. Supplier's evaluation of the company.		

Table C-1 Economic Indicators in Selected Underdeveloped Countries and in the United States

	Argentina	Brazil	Chile	Uruguay	India	Philippines	U.S.
Money supply (in millions of national currency)							
1960	144	692	384	2394	37.0	1659	144.0
1966	787	10275	2594	14734	47.4	2897	178.6
% increase	446.52%	1384.82%	575.52%	515.45%	28.1081%	74.62%	24.02%
International liquidity (in millions of dollars)							
1960	$525	$345	$111	$187	$670	$127	$19,359
1966	216	409	172	196	608	181	14,881
% increase	(58.85%) a	18.55%	54.95%	4.81%	(9.25%)	42.51%	(23.13%)
Foreign exchange (in millions of dollars)							(1961)
1960	$422	$58	$66	$7	$423	$105	$116
1966	132	352	127	50	364	122	132
% increase	(68.72%)	506.89%	92.42%	614.28%	(13.94%)	16.19%	13.79%
Cost of living (1958 = 100)							
1965	771	2050	512	710	143	130	109
Exports (fob) (in millions of U.S. dollars)							
1960	$1079	$1269	$495	$129	$1331	$560	$20584
1965	1493	1595	685	191	1682	767	27400
% increase	38.36%	25.68%	38.38%	48.06%	26.37%	36.96%	33.11%

Table C-1 (Cont.)

	Argentina	Brazil	Chile	Uruguay	India	Philippines	U.S.
Imports (c.f.) (in millions of U.S. dollars)							
1960	$1249	$1462	$526	$218	$2327	$663	$16375
1965	1198	1096	604	151	2906	894	23189
% increase	(4.25%)	(25.03%)	14.82%	30.73%	24.88%	34.84%	41.61%
General government expenditures (in millions of national currency) b					1956–61		
1960	86000	263000	768 1963	3290	36500000 1961–66	.102	93000
1965	330000	290900	2143	6350	63000000	.204	123400
% increase	283.72%	100.61%	179.04%	93.00%	72.60%	100.00%	32.68%
Per capita gross domestic product (at factor cost in thou. $)							
1958	$643	$264	$385	$462	$68	$198	$2370
1965	783	232	579	562	92	237	3210
% increase	21.77%	(12.12%)	50.38%	21.64%	35.29%	16.69%	35.44%
Estimates of midyear population (in thousands)							
1958	19980	65750	7316	2464	410680	25795	174882
1966	22691	83175	8750	2749	495000	33477	196920
% increase	13.56%	36.50%	19.60%	11.56%	20.53%	29.78%	12.60%

Consumer price index (1958 = 100)							
1966	1017	3003	632	389	159	137	112
Index numbers of wholesale prices (1958 = 100) 1966							
Finished goods	912	2534	n.a.	n.a.	143	130	106
Domestic goods	922	n.a.	626	n.a.	n.a.	140	n.a.
Imported goods	869	n.a.	368	n.a.	n.a.	145	n.a.
Estimate of GNP at constant mkt. prices[c]							
1958	945	346	5038 1965	16.7 1965	117 1965	9928 1965	487
1966	1120	510	6583	17.4	146	13670	708
% increase	18.51%	47.39%	30.66%	4.19%	24.78%	37.69%	45.37%

a Figures in parentheses denote percentage decrease.
b U.S.—Millions of Dollars, Uruguay—Millions of Pesos, India—Millions of Rupees, Argentina and Philippines—Millions of Pesos, Chile—Millions of Escudos, Brazil—Millions of Cruzeiros.
c Brazil (1949 = 100), Chile (1961 = 100), Uruguay (1961 = 100), India (1948 = 100), Philippines (1955 = 100), U.S. (1963 = 100), Argentina (1960 = 100).
SOURCE: *Monthly Bulletin of Statistics*, New York: United Nations, Vol. 21 No. 10 (October, 1967), pp. xvii, 1, 134, 160, 180, 190, 196.

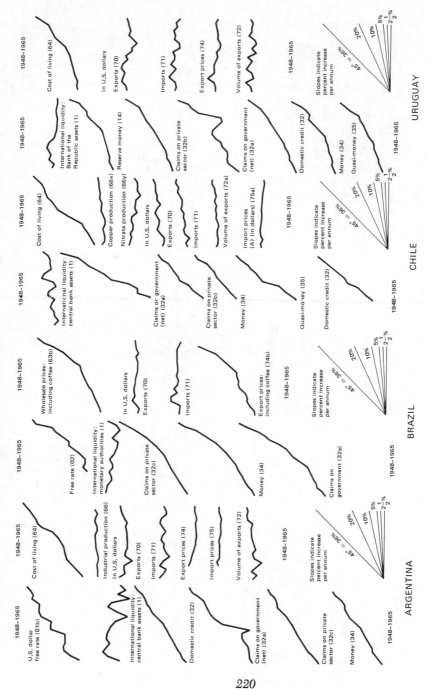

Figure C-1   Economic Indicators in Selected Countries
SOURCE: International Financial Statistics, Special Supplement to 1966–67 issues.

220

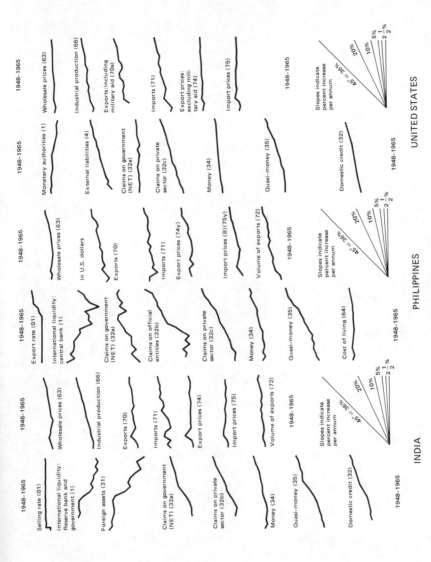

Figure C-2 Economic Indicators in Selected Countries

SOURCE: International Financial Statistics, Special Supplement to 1966–67 issues.

221

Table B-5   Company's Philosophy toward Stockholders

Five Factors Evaluated		*Company's Attitude*
a. Company's policy statement and implementation of the policies.		1. They are owners, masters; best public relation personnel
b. Stockholders' evaluation of the company.	to categorize	
c. Prospective investors' evaluation of the company.		2. They are owners, masters
d. The company's senior executives' viewpoint toward stockholders.		3. They are financiers, profit-eaters
e. Actual programs and procedures of the stock department of the company.		

Table B-6   Company's Philosophy toward Government

Five Factors Evaluated		*Company's Attitude*
a. Top executive's attitude toward government.		1. Good partner
b. Company's participation in governmental policies.	to categorize	2. Necessary evil
c. Senior governmental official's attitude toward the company.		3. Government be damned
d. Program and procedure of the company's public relation department.		
e. Speeches and press statements made by the company's executives on governmental affairs.		

Table B-7   Company's Philosophy toward Community

Six Factors Evaluated		Company's Attitude
a. Programs and procedures of the company's public relation department.	to categorize	1. Very much concern
		2. Some concern
b. Top executive's attitude toward community.		3. Little or no concern
c. Company's participation in community affairs.		
d. Company's contribution toward community chest, hospital facilities, and education.		
e. Attitudes of selected community leaders toward the company.		
f. Attitudes of selected educators (university professors) toward the company.		

APPENDIX C

ECONOMIC INDICATORS IN SELECTED COUNTRIES

APPENDIX D

TRANSMITTING ADVANCED MANAGEMENT KNOW-HOW TO UNDERDEVELOPED COUNTRIES

TRANSMITTING ADVANCED MANAGEMENT KNOW-HOW
TO UNDERDEVELOPED COUNTRIES

Dr. Anant R. Negandhi, Ph. D., Associate Professor, Kent State University, Kent, Ohio,
and Dr. S. Benjamin Prasad, Associate Professor, Ohio State University,
Athens, Ohio, USA.

Management theory and practices as they are known today have evolved largely within a restricted range of countries, and, as industrialization spreads, it is becoming necessary to transfer them into cultural settings far different from those in which they originated.

Transmission of advanced managerial knowledge may be undertaken by a manager from one country going to manage a firm in another, or by people from a developing country coming to study and work in a more industrialized one and returning to take up managerial jobs in their own country; or they may be transferred, as the I. L. O. and certain other bodies such as the eductional institutions from the United States are trying to transfer them, through development and training programs for managers in developing countries. In every case this involves the application of knowledge and practices evolved in one socio-cultural environment in the circumstances of another.

In one sense, economic development is a process entailing the concurrent growth of superior technical and managerial skills. In principle, a people may acquire such skills spontaneously, by internal social processes, or they may acquire them by learning from others or by actually employing others to exercise these skills for them. In practice a people normally does both, the resulting transformation being a complex interaction of internal and external influences.

The problem of transmitting certain knowledge or know-how from one country to another is not a simple or a novel one. For example, focussing on managerial know-how, J. S. Fforde, a decade ago, made an inquiry into the provision of certain British managerial and technical services for the operation of industrial enterprises in underdeveloped countries such as India.[1] Fforde's concern was with the transmission of managerial skills, in a specified manner, from one country to others. He viewed the problem as a particular type of international trade.

The main purpose of this expository paper is to identify the significant managerial variables which act as barriers to the successful adaptation of advanced managerial know-how in underdeveloped countries, and to suggest possible ways and means of demolishing these barriers. The main assumption in this paper is that "management" is one of the most important inputs for industrial development in any nation.

At the outset it is necessary to define what is meant by advanced managerial know-how as employed in this paper. This term is defined as the various managerial practices, principles

---

[1] J. S. Fforde, An International Trade in Managerial Skills (Oxford: Basil Blackwell, 1967).

Reproduced from *Management International Review*, Vol. 7, 1967, No. 6, pp. 75–81.
Permission of the Journal is gratefully acknowledged.

and techniques employed by the manager in the United States and other Western European countries to effectively carry out his five basic functions of planning, organizing, staffing, directing, and controlling.

The Impeding Variables

On the basis of his personal experience in two thoroughly dissimilar developing countries, David Chewning narrates the story of attempts made to transmit advanced managerial know-how into Burma and Puerto Rico.[2]

In the case of Burma where there was an acceptance of technological advancement but a rejection of management improvement in the same projects, Chewning attributes the spotty, ill-defined, poorly supported management improvement programs to the top echelon of the government. The author's message is "Create an environment which accommodates modern management ideas." Evidently the impeding variable in the case of Burma was the weakness in the political management aspect of the government.

In contrast, Puerto Rico, according to Chewning "found a way to import good managers through the device of U.S. capital investment. Thus it did not have to train its own people as managers overnight, though they are absorbing solid management know-how by working with U.S. managers."[3]

There are multifarious variables that one can identify as impeding variables; however, in this paper we are concentrating on what may be referred to as he "managerial variables" per se. What are these "managerial variables"? First, we cite the short run profit maximization philosophy of managers. Second, there is the managerial overemphasis on the production and resource procurement activities of the industrial firms and a lack of emphasis on the frame of mind that regards management as a matter of making things happen, via promotion of organizational efficiency and adaptation of relevant management know-how. While it is true that many a variable will be significant in transmitting advanced managerial know-how, we contend that the two managerial variables cited above appear to us as the most significant impeding variables. Let us examine why they are so, and how they have come about, using the example of India with which the writers have first hand knowledge.

Managerial Philosophy of Short-Run Profit Maximization

In many developing countries industrialization programs carried out in large scale units are predominantly based upon imported technology and know-how. Parallel to the growing use of such technology, a silent but pervasive managerial revolution has also taken place. It is now being increasingly realized that effective management depends more on the coordination of human effort than on the control of operations; that it involves not only directing men and skills but also tapping knowledge, encouraging innovation, and so forth. These attitudes on the part of managers and administrators in the industrialized countries did not evolve overnight. Many forces, an important one of which was keen competition in the market, brought about such an understanding of effective management.

Let us look at the competitive situation in the market in an underdeveloped country such as India. Lack of importation of consumer and durable goods has shielded the Indian

[2] David L. Chewning, "The Transference of Management Techniques," in Karl E. Ettinger (ed.) *International Handbook of Management* New York: McGraw-Hill Book Company, 1965, pp. 70—78.

[3] ibid. p. 73.

economy from competition from abroad. This in itself would not be too [...] there a healthy competition among domestic enterprises. Here again, one [...] of competition due to the insufficient number of entrants into given pr[...] government control apparatus coupled with the low propensity to save and to [...] succeeded in keeping out potential enterprises and thus have shielded the product m[...] from potential competition. The end result in the case of most product markets, except perhaps textiles, is a sort of oligopolistic market situation. This is not typical of the theoretical model of the oligopolistic market in the sense entry is not forbidden to marginal and inefficient enterprises but entry is impossible for reasons of capital funds and capital goods.

In essence, increasing governmental planning expenditures on the one hand, and the lack of supply on the other hand have engendered what is commonly referred to as the "sellers" market in India. The chain reactions of various economic factors resulting in a seller's market position is shown in diagram 1. What is the effect of this market condition upon the managerial philosophy?

It is a well known fact that a large majority of industrial firms in underdeveloped countries such as India are owned and managed by either the family members[4] or small groups of individuals. There are notable exceptions to this situation but they are few in number. In the modal number of cases the separation of ownership and management has not really taken place. The owner, while also playing the role of the manager, makes all decisions, both policy and operational. These decisions in the prevailing sellers' market will be tempered by considerations of maximizing profits in the short run without due regard to the quality of the products, coordination of human effort, encouragement of innovation, or the long run viability considerations for the organization. One might argue that such would be the rational managerial behavior in a seller's market. Perhaps very true. Such a pursuit of a managerial philosophy while it brings increased monetary returns in the short run is neither conducive to introduction of advanced managerial know-how nor to the long run prospects of the organization itself. A nation which is trying to build up an efficient industrial system cannot become complacent if the subsystems, in this case the individual units of production, are weak and ill-structured.

Assuming that there prevails a widespread philosophy of short run profit maximization brought about mainly by the existing sellers' market Situation, one would expect a tendency to overemphasize the production activities of the enterprise. Let us see how this corollary of the managerial philosophy of short run profit maximization is again a hindrance to effective transmission of advanced managerial know-how.

The Emergence of the Technocrat

Where there is overemphasis on the production activities there is likely to be a greater demand for the technically qualified person. A person who knows the art and science of manufacturing is likely to be in greater demand and valued more than a person competent in the managerial arts and science. Under these conditions the technician becomes the revered hero. Situations comparable to this did exist in many industrially advanced Western European countries but the competitive forces generated by the establishment of the European Economic Community have altered greatly this situation. Likewise, in

---

[4] This statement should not be interpreted to imply that family firms per se are inimical to industrial growth. While literature abounds to assert so, empirical evidence appears to lend no support to these assertions. For the interesting case of Lebanon, see Samir Khalef and Emilie Shwayrie, "Family Farms and Industrial Development: The Lebanese Case," *Economic Development and Cultural Change,* October, 1966, pp. 59—69.

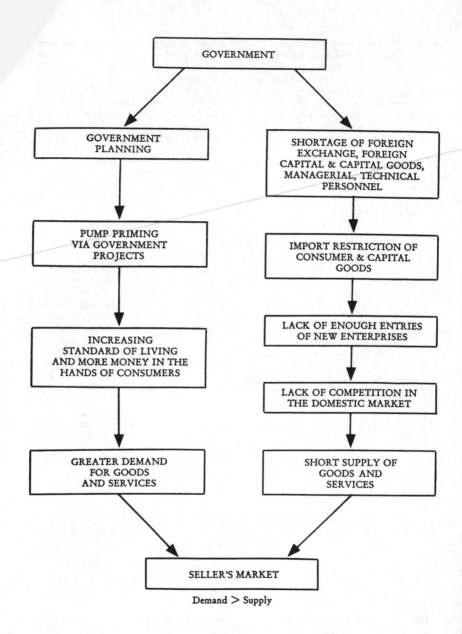

Diagram 1

Emergence of Sellers' Markets in Underdeveloped Countries

many Eastern European country there has been a shift of emphasis from
output orientation to managerial orientation.[5]

Charles A. Myers, as well as Darab Unwalla, two of the astute observ
agerial scene in India, have stated, ". . . family caste and business community
are still important, but some higher managerial positions are being filled by technican,
trained outsiders whose competence is their major admission ticket",[6] and "the industrialists own the concern; the technicians run it. The former are the nominal heads and
the latter effective regents . . ."[7]

The technician, being aware of his indispensability, is likely to demand more in terms
of salaries, recognition and status in industry. To some extent, he can accomplish these
goals by taking up managerial jobs. In other words, he will find the avenues in business
enterprises to become a technocrat occupying middle and higher managerial positions —
for which he may or may not be fully qualified.

When the technician lacks proper management education and training and when he
occupies managerial positions in business enterprises, the discharge of managerial functions
is bound to suffer. For example, in an industrialized country the middle manager is in
charge of such functions as budgeting, cost control, development of performance standards,
performance evaluation, methods improvements and so on. He also contributes to the
development of a future management team by practising delegation of authority and
coaching his subordinates on the job.

In contrast, the technically competent but managerially naive manager in the underdeveloped countries such as India may not play the proper role of the middle manager.
In the advanced countries where free enterprise prevails in one form or another, managerial inefficiency will show up in the competitive weakness of the firm and the cost
structure for its products. However, in an underdeveloped country, any managerial
inefficiency ascribable to the technocrats is likely to go undetected simply because irrespective of quality or cost considerations the business organization will find ready
markets for its products. The sellers' market condition permits the existing business firms
to earn high rates of profits over a period of years, and this in turn is prone to blind the
firms to any existing managerial inefficiency. Thus the system as a whole will comprise
of weak and ill-structured subsystems and such firms are seldom the kind of bricks which
will support an effective industrial foundation so needed in developing countries. Diagram 2 illustrates how the sellers' market has paved the way to the dominance of technocrats.

Still worse is the creation of a web which makes it very difficult to introduce advanced
managerial know-how in countries such as India. Once the technician becomes a technocrat
he is likely to retain and safeguard his own position without regard to the cost structure,
worker morale and productivity, or even organizational efficiency. He is also likely to

[5] For a discussion of the emergence of new managerialism in the U.S.S.R. as well as in Czechoslovakia, see, for example, S. Benjamin Prasad, "New Managerialism in Czechoslovakia and the
Soviet Union," *Academy of Management Journal*, December, 1966, pp. 328—336, and "Prague
goes Pragmatic," Columbia Journal of World Business, March, 1967.

[6] Charles A. Myers, "Management in India," in Harbison and Myers, *Management in the Industrial
World* (New York: McGraw-Hill Book Company, 1959), p. 141.

[7] Darab B. Unwalla, *Textile Technocracy: Human Relations in Factories* (Bombay: Popular Book
Dept, 1958), p. vi.

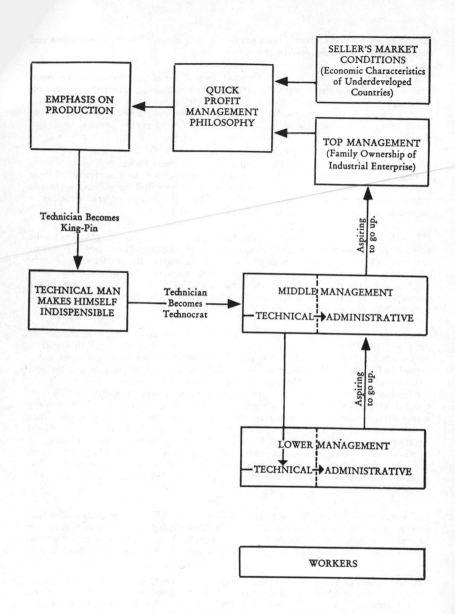

Diagram 2

Emergency of Technocrats

230

build around himself a team of lesser technocrats and build a defense mechanism against those forces, primarily the advanced managerial techniques, which might shake his *status quo.*

Focussing on these two managerial variables, what can be done to improve the situation in underdeveloped countries?

CONCLUSION

We suggested in this paper that it is becoming very important to transfer advanced managerial know-how from industrialized countries to developing countries.[8] While there are many avenues along which such transmission can be undertaken, it has been recognized that there are various social, cultural, and other obstacles which will be in the way. Our concern in this paper has been primarily with what we referred to as the "managerial variables" — the managerial philosophy of short run profit maximization, and that of overemphasis on production activities at the cost of managerial activities.

While these two variables can be regarded as micro-variables, it should be noted that they are brought about by a macro-variable, namely, the sellers' market condition which prevails in India and other developing countries.

One would naturally raise the question, "Well, what is the solution?" We think the solution can be a two-pronged approach. One, to remove excessive controls and restrictions and to create a competitive market situation, and two, to reorientate the managerial philosophy of short run profit maximization.

The first approach is feasible at the governmental level. In the case of India, deliberate attempts to create a healthy competitive market situation will not be contrary to the professed socialist pattern of society.

The second approach of reorientating the managerial philosophy can only be indirect and gradual. While competitive forces will no doubt compel many enterprises to take a close look at their efficiency situation, educational programs might instil into the managers the elements of that frame of mind which seeks to build effective and productive subsystems.

A good many American schools of business administration have been providing management education in various underdeveloped countries, concentrating on the middle level managers. Pessimistic though it may sound, unless there is a perceptible change in the philosophy of the owner-managers and their top salaried managers, the efforts may not yield fruitful results. One may find individuals who are imbued with knowledge of management theory and techniques acquired painstakingly but unable to effectively apply them in a work environment such as it prevails in a large number of industrial enterprises in underdeveloped countries.

---

[8] A. R. Negandhi has provided a scheme to determine the applicability of American management know-how in foreign cultures and environments in the article (with B. D. Estafen) "A Research Model to Determine the Applicability of American Management Know-How in Differing Cultures and/or Environment," *Academy of Management Journal*, December 1965, pp. 309—317.

BIBLIOGRAPHY

Aguilar, Francis, *Scanning the Business Environment* (New York: The Macmillan Company, 1967).

Ajiferuke, Musbau, and J. Boddewyn, "Culture and Other Explanatory Variables in Comparative Management Studies," *Academy of Management Journal,* Vol. 13, No. 2 (June 1970), pp. 153–162.

Argyris, Chris, *Integrating the Individual and the Organization* (New York: John Wiley & Sons, Inc., 1964), pp. 153–164.

Barnard, Chester, *The Functions of the Executive* (Boston: Harvard University Press, 1938).

Barnard, Chester, *Organization and Management* (Boston: Harvard University Press, 1948).

Basu, S. K., *The Managing Agency System* (Calcutta, India: The World Press, 1958).

Bendix, Reinhard, "Concepts and Generalizations in Comparative Sociological Studies," *American Sociological Review,* Vol. 28, No. 4 (August 1962), pp. 529–532.

Bennis, Warren G., and E. Schein, *Leadership and Motivation, Essays of Douglas McGregor* (Cambridge, Mass.: M.I.T. Press, 1966).

Berliner, Joseph, "Managerial Incentives and Decision-Making: A Comparison of the U.S. and the Soviet Union," *Comparisons of the United States and Soviet Union Economics,* Part I (Washington, D.C.: Joint Economic Committee, 1959), pp. 349–376.

Blough, Roy, *International Business: Environment and Adaptation* (New York: McGraw-Hill Book Company, 1966).

Boddewyn, J., "The Comparative Approach to the Study of Business Administration," *Academy of Management Journal,* Vol. 8, No. 4 (December 1965), pp. 261–267.

Chamberlain, Neil, *Enterprise and Environment* (New York: McGraw-Hill Book Company, 1968).

Chewning, David L., "The Transfer of Management Technology," in Karl Ettinger (ed.), *International Handbook of Management* (New York: McGraw-Hill Book Company, 1965).

Chowdhry, Kamala, "Social and Cultural Factors in Management Development in India and the Role of the Expert," *International Labour Review,* Vol. 94, No. 2 (August 1966), pp. 132–147.

Chowdhry, Kamala, and A. K. Pal, "Production Planning and Organization Morale," *Human Organization,* Vol. 15, No. 4 (Summer 1963), pp. 11–16.

Clark, D. G., and T. M. Mosson, "Industrial Managers in Belgium, France, and the United Kingdom," *Management International Review,* 2/3 (1967), pp. 95–100.

Clark, Peter B., and J. Q. Wilson, "Incentive Systems: A Theory of Organizations," *Administrative Science Quarterly,* Vol. 6, No. 2 (September 1961), pp. 129–166.

Clemmer, Donald, *The Prison Community* (Boston: The Christopher Publishing House, 1940).

Davis, Keith, and R. C. Blomstrom, *Business and Its Environment* (New York: McGraw-Hill Book Company, 1966).

Dill, William R., "Environment as an Influence on Managerial Autonomy," *Administrative Science Quarterly,* Vol. 2, No. 4 (March 1958), pp. 409–443.

Drucker, Peter, "Long Range Planning—Challenge to Management Science," *Management Science,* Vol. 5, No. 7 (April 1959), pp. 238–249.

Dunning, John, "U.S. Subsidiaries in Britain and their U.K. Competitors," *Business Ratios* (London), No. 1 (Autumn 1966), pp. 5–18.

England, George W., "Personal Value Systems of American Managers," *Academy of Management Journal,* Vol. 10, No. 1 (March 1967), pp. 67–68.

Evan, William M., "Indices of the Hierarchical Structures of Industrial Organizations," *Management Science,* Vol. 9, No. 3 (April 1963).

Farmer, Richard, and B. Richman, *Comparative Management and Economic Progress* (Homewood, Ill.: Richard D. Irwin, Inc., 1965).

Farmer, Richard, and B. Richman, "A Model for Research in Comparative Management," *California Management Review,* Vol. 7, No. 2 (Winter 1964), pp. 55–68.

Fayerweather, John, *The Executive Overseas* (Syracuse: Syracuse University Press, 1959).

Fforde, J. S., *An International Trade in Managerial Skills* (Oxford, England: Basil Blackwell, Ltd., 1957).

French, John R. P., J. Israel, *et al.,* "An Experiment on Participation in a Norwegian Factory," *Human Relations,* Vol. 13, No. 1, pp. 1–9.

Ginzberg, Eli, *The Development of Human Resources* (New York: McGraw-Hill Book Company, 1966), p. 206.

Granick, David, "Functional Divisions of Company Management: A Reflection of National Styles," *Journal of Industrial Economics*, Vol. 10, No. 2 (March 1962), pp. 100–117.

Haire, Mason, E. Ghiselli, and L. Porter, *Managerial Thinking: An International Study* (New York: John Wiley & Sons, Inc., 1966).

Harbison, Frederick, *et al.*, "Steel Management on Two Continents," *Management Science*, Vol. 2, No. 1 (October 1955), pp. 31–39.

Harbison, Frederick, and E. Burgess, "Modern Management in Western Europe," *American Journal of Sociology*, Vol. 60, No. 1 (July 1954).

Harbison, Frederick, and Charles A. Myers, *Management in the Industrial World* (New York: McGraw-Hill Book Company, 1959).

Heady, Ferrel, *Public Administration: A Comparative Perspective* (Englewood Cliffs, N.J.: Prentice-Hall, Inc., 1966), p. 4.

Holden, P. E., C. A. Pederson, and G. E. Germane, *Top Management* (New York: McGraw-Hill Book Company, 1968).

Homans, George C., *The Human Group* (New York: Harcourt, Brace and World, Inc., 1950).

Humblet, J. E., "A Comparative Study of Management in Three European Countries," *Sociological Review*, Vol. 9, No. 2 (November 1961), pp. 351–360.

Jennings, Eugene E., *The Executive: Autocrat, Bureaucrat, Democrat* (New York: Harper and Row, 1962).

Khalef, Samir, and E. Shwayrie, "Family Firms and Industrial Development: The Lebanese Case," *Economic Development and Cultural Change*, Vol. 15, No. 1 (October 1966).

Koontz, Harold, and C. O'Donnell, *Principles of Management* (New York: McGraw-Hill Book Company, 1964), p. 158.

Koontz, Harold, and C. O'Donnell, *Principles of Management* (New York: McGraw-Hill Book Company, 1968).

Lee, James A., "Developing Managers in Developing Countries," *Harvard Business Review*, Vol. 46, No. 6 (November-December 1968), pp. 55–65.

Lokanathan, P. S., *Industrial Organization in India* (London, England: George Allen Unwin, 1935).

March, James, and H. A. Simon, *Organizations* (New York: John Wiley & Sons, Inc., 1958).

Maule, H. B., "Application of Industrial Psychology in Developing Countries," *International Labour Review*, Vol. 92, No. 4 (October 1965).

Mayo, Elton, *The Social Problems of Industrial Organization* (Boston: Harvard University Press, 1945).

McCann, Eugene, "An Aspect of Management Philosophy in the United States and Latin America," *Academy of Management Journal*, Vol. 7, No. 2 (June 1964), pp. 149–152.

McClelland, David, *The Achieving Society* (New York: D. Van Nostrand Company, 1961).

McClelland, David, "Business Drive and Material Achievement," *Harvard Business Review*, July-August 1962.

McCurdy, John, *The Structure of Morale* (Cambridge: Cambridge University Press, 1943).

McFarland, Dalton, *Personnel Management: Theory and Practice* (New York: The Macmillan Company, 1968), p. 141.

McGuire, Joseph, *Business and Society* (New York: McGraw-Hill Book Company, 1963).

Megginson, Leon, "The Interrelationship between the Cultural Environment and Managerial Effectiveness," *Management International Review*, Vol. 7, No. 6 (1967), p. 69.

Merton, Robert K., *et al.*, *Reader in Bureaucracy* (Glencoe, Ill.: Free Press, 1952).

Metcalf, H. C., and L. Urwick, (eds.), *Dynamic Administration, The Collected Papers of Mary Parker Follet* (New York: Harper and Row, 1941).

Morris, L. W., "Moral Hazards of American Executives," *Harvard Business Review*, Vol. 38, No. 5 (September-October 1960), pp. 72–80.

Miller, Delbert, and W. H. Form, *Industrial Sociology* (New York: Harper and Row, 1951).

Myrdal, Gunnar, *Asian Drama: An Inquiry into the Poverty of Nations* (New York: The Twentieth Century Fund, 1968).

Negandhi, A. R., and B. D. Estafen, "Determining the Applicability of American Management Know-How in Differing Environments and Cultures," *Academy of Management Journal*, Vol. 8, No. 4 (December 1965), pp. 319–323.

Negandhi, A. R., and S. B. Prasad, "Transmitting Advanced Management Know-How to Underdeveloped Countries," *Management International Review*, Vol. 7, No. 6 (1967), pp. 75–81.

Nowotny, Otto, "American Vs. European Management Philosophy," *Harvard Business Review*, Vol. 42, No. 2 (March-April 1964).

Oberg, Winston, "Cross-Cultural Perspective on Management Principles," *Academy of Management Journal*, Vol. 6, No. 2 (June 1963), pp. 141–42.

Pathak, Arvind, "Environmental Constraints and Managerial Problems in a Developing Economy," *Management International Review*, Vol. 8, Nos. 2/3 (1968), pp. 137–141.

Pelissier, Raymond, "Certain Aspects of Management in India," *Michigan Business Review*, Vol. 16, No. 3 (May 1964), p. 7.

Prasad, S. B., "Comparative Managerialism as an Approach to International Economic Growth," *Quarterly Journal of AIESEC International*, Vol. 2 (August 1966), pp. 22–30.

Prasad, S. B., *Directions of Research in Administrative Science* (Athens, Ohio: Division of Research, College of Business Administration, 1968).

Prasad, S. B., and A. R. Negandhi, *Managerialism for Economic Development* (The Hague: Martinus Nijhoff, 1968).

Pugh, Derek, S., *et al.* "A Conceptual Scheme for Organizational Analysis," *Administrative Science Quarterly*, Vol. 8, No. 3 (December 1963), pp. 289–315.

Schneider, Eugene, *Industrial Sociology* (New York: McGraw-Hill Book Company, 1959).

Selekman, Benjamin, *A Moral Philosophy of Management* (New York: McGraw-Hill Book Company, 1959).

Simon, Herbert A., *Administrative Behavior* (New York: The Macmillan Company, 1961), p. 37.

Steiner, George, "Does Planning Pay Off?" *California Management Review*, Vol. 5, No. 2 (Winter 1962), p. 37.

Steiner, George, "The Nature and Significance of Multinational Corporate Planning," in G. A. Steiner and W. M. Cannon (eds.), *Multinational Corporate Planning* (New York: The Macmillan Company, 1966), p. 9.

Stewart, Rosemary, and P. Duncan-Jones, "Educational Background and Career History of British Managers with some American Comparisons," *Explorations in Entrepreneurial History*, December 1965, pp. 61–73.

Sullivan, A. M., "Moral Responsibility of Management," *Advanced Management-Office Executive*, Vol. 2, No 4 (April 1963), pp. 7–10.

Takezawa, Shinichi, "Socio-cultural Aspects of Management in Japan," *International Labour Review*, Vol. 94, No. 2 (August 1966), pp. 147–174.

Thompson, Stewart, *Management Creeds and Philosophies* (New York: American Management Association, Research Study No. 32, 1958).

Udy, Stanley H., "The Comparative Analysis of Organizations," in James G. March (ed.), *Handbook of Organizations* (Chicago: Rand McNally and Co., 1965).

Unwalla, Darab, *Textile Technocracy: Human Relations in Factories* (Bombay, India: Popular Book Depot, 1958).

Waldo, Dwight, *Perspectives of Administration* (University: University of Alabama Press, 1956).

Walton, Scott, *American Business and Its Environment* (New York: The Macmillan Company, 1966).

Warner, W. Lloyd, and O. Low, *The Social Systems of the Modern Factory* (New Haven: Yale University Press, 1947).

Wortman, Max, "A Philosophy of Management," *Advanced Management Journal*, Vol. 26, No. 10 (October 1961), pp. 11–15.

Whyte, William F., "Framework for the Analysis of Industrial Relations: Two Views," *Industrial and Labor Relations Review*, Vol. 3, No. 3 (April 1960).

NAME INDEX

SUBJECT INDEX

241

Date Due